UNDERDEVELOPMENT AND DEVELOPMENT IN BRAZIL

Vol. I: Economic Structure and Change, 1822–1947

Underdevelopment and Development
in Brazil

Vol. I:
Economic Structure and
Change, 1822–1947

NATHANIEL H. LEFF

London
GEORGE ALLEN & UNWIN
Boston   Sydney

George Allen & Unwin (Publishers) Ltd,
40 Museum Street, London WC1A 1LU, UK

George Allen & Unwin (Publishers) Ltd,
Park Lane, Hemel Hempstead, Herts HP2 4TE, UK

Allen & Unwin Inc.,
9 Winchester Terrace, Winchester, Mass 01890, USA

George Allen & Unwin Australia Pty Ltd,
8 Napier Street, North Sydney, NSW 2060, Australia

First published in 1982

British Library Cataloguing in Publication Data

Leff, Nathaniel H.
  Underdevelopment and development in Brazil.
Vol. 1: Economic structure and change, 1822–1947
1. Brazil – Economic conditions – History
I. Title
330.981   HC187
ISBN 0-04-330324-2

Library of Congress Cataloging in Publication Data

Leff, Nathaniel H.
  Underdevelopment and development in Brazil.
Contents: v. 1. Economic structure and change, 1822–1947 – v.2.
Reassessing the obstacles to economic development.
1. Brazil – Economic conditions. 2. Brazil – Economic policy. I. Title.
HC187.L5238   330.981   82-4026
ISBN 0-04-330324-2 (v. 1)   AACR2
ISBN 0-04-330325-0 (v. 2)

Set in 10 on 11 point Times by Bedford Typesetters Ltd,
and printed in Great Britain
by Billing & Sons Ltd, Guildford, London & Worcester

To The Memory
of
Zelda Gross Leff

Para que se conheça na terra teu caminho, e
entre todas as gentes tua salvação
Psalmos, LVII

Contents

List of Tables

Statistical Appendix

Preface

Many years ago, I heard Edmundo Flores pose a classic question: why had the Latin American countries failed to develop economically during the nineteenth century in a manner similar to the United States and the other regions of recent settlement? Many answers have of course been given to this question. However, in the course of research on the economic development of Brazil, I became increasingly aware that some of these standard explanations were not applicable to the case of that country. Also, it appeared that important aspects of Brazil's economic retardation and development had been neglected or misunderstood. Accordingly, in the late 1960s and early 1970s I wrote a number of journal articles on this subject.

At the same time, other researchers were also working on questions pertaining to Brazil's economic history. Their research made available a wealth of new analyses, perspectives, and data, which opened up the opportunity for a much more comprehensive work. My focus throughout is on economic analysis rather than on the history of ideas. For this reason, I have not written a historiographical survey, and have referred to other writers only when the reference is relevant for the substantive picture presented. But this study owes an important debt to the work of other researchers in this field. Indeed, the availability of this complementary research played an important role in my decision to return to the subject of Brazil's economic underdevelopment and development with a full-length study.

The additional scope of the present work has resulted in some significant advantages. Material from my earlier journal articles constitutes less than a third of this study, the growth of which has stemmed from a number of causes. The availability of new analyses and data has enabled me to extend and deepen the discussion of many key issues. (In some cases, new material enriched and corroborated my earlier interpretations; in others, new information and criticism led to changed perspectives.) In addition, the book analyses many topics which had earlier been slighted or omitted. Finally, the format of the book forces a coherence of perspective and a tying-together of loose ends which can easily be avoided in a series of individual papers.

In addition to the friends who gave helpful suggestions and were thanked in my earlier papers, I want to express gratitude to the people who aided in preparation of this study. In particular, Herbert Klein gave valuable advice and suggestions; Lincoln Gordon made an important suggestion at an early stage of the study; Stephen De Canio, Peter Eisenberg, Richard Graham, Thomas Holloway, Martin Katzman, and Gene Kroch commented with insight on some penultimate drafts; and Claudio Haddad provided important statistical estimates and discussion on related issues. However, I owe a special debt to Stanley Engerman, David Felix, and Kazuo Sato. These thoughtful scholars went out of their way to provide comments which were particularly comprehensive. Without in any way implicating them for the final product, I wish to express my deep thanks to all of these people.

I am also glad for the opportunity to thank the other people and institutions that helped make this study possible. I am grateful to my father, Mr Louis Leff, for his constant encouragement. The Faculty Research Program of Columbia University's Graduate School of Business, the Tinker Foundation, and the Social Science Research Council were generous in their financial support. Columbia University provided an ideal research setting for this study. The intellectual stimulus of the Columbia Graduate School of Business, the Columbia University Seminar in Economic History, and the Columbia University Latin American Institute was very helpful. Haydee Piedracueva, Bibliographer of Columbia's Latin American Library Collections, gave top-level professional assistance. I am also grateful to research assistants Bruce Phillips, Michael Sterling, Shing Fung, and the late John Millar, whose efforts went far beyond the call of duty. Some chapters in this volume draw on material which appeared in earlier form in *The Journal of Economic History* (1969); *The Economic History Review* (1972); *The Review of Income and Wealth* (1972); *The Journal of Political Economy* (1973); and *The Journal of Interdisciplinary History* (1974). I thank the editors of those journals for permission to utilize that material.

Finally, I am especially grateful to my wife, Judith. Her advice has been invaluable. And in addition to pursuing her own professional career and joint family responsibilities, she helped make possible the environment within which this book could be written.

NATHANIEL H. LEFF
New York
November 1981

1
Introduction

Purpose of The Study

This study analyzes the economic history of Brazil between 1822 and 1947. These years begin with the country's proclamation of formal political independence, and extend to Brazil's rapid economic expansion of the post-Second World War period.

The book focuses on some of the larger questions of Brazil's economic experiences. One major issue is why, unlike the United States, Australia, and other regions with abundant unimproved land and initially sparse population, nineteenth-century Brazil did not develop as an economy characterized by relatively high wages and income levels. At first glance, this contrast may seem surprising; for Brazil, too, had high land–labor ratios, and might have been expected to follow a similar pattern with respect to labor productivity, the distribution of income, and economic development.[1] Many possible explanations for Brazil's poor economic experience during the nineteenth century come to mind. But as we shall see, not all of these interpretations are in accordance with historical fact.

Brazil's failure to develop more rapidly during the nineteenth century also raises some general analytical questions. The economy's initial conditions appear to contrast with models of underdevelopment whose chief feature is surplus labor. The Brazilian case also does not fit some other standard explanations of economic backwardness of the less-developed countries. During most of the century, the country was relatively free from both far-reaching imperialist domination and the substantial political instability which afflicted most other Latin American countries following independence. Also, as we shall see, the absence of generalized development in nineteenth-century Brazil cannot be attributed to some of the intrinsic deficiencies of export-led growth which have been discussed in the theoretical literature on international trade and economic development. Finally, there are serious problems with citing psychological 'values' or sociocultural conditions as factotum explanations of Brazil's underdevelopment

As the preceding discussion suggests, this book may be of interest not only to students of Brazilian history, but also to economists concerned to understand long-term economic backwardness and development. Similarly, historians who are interested in a comparative perspective on slavery, plantation agriculture, and development (or retardation) under trade-oriented expansion may also find the book useful. The day has passed when 'economic history' was the study largely of the United States and Europe, while analysis of the experience of other areas was referred to as 'regional studies'.

The sequel to Brazil's slow economic development during the nineteenth century was a quickening in the pace of economic progress toward the end of the century. This shift to a higher rate of development raises some obvious questions. What were the conditions which led to the onset of more rapid development in Brazil? Why had they not operated earlier? What were the major consequences of the accelerated economic growth and structural changes which took place in Brazil during the first half of the twentieth century?

As this discussion indicates, the book addresses some major questions in Brazil's economic history. In attempting to answer these questions, the study necessarily provides an overall framework for interpreting Brazil's economic experience between 1822 and 1947. Such an integrative study may be especially appropriate in the present state of Brazilian economic historiography. The past three decades have seen a great increase in research on the country's economic history.[2] Although existing material still cannot be compared with what is available for the more developed countries, researchers now have much more information about Brazil's economic history than could be called upon in the late 1940s. For this reason, it may be helpful to assemble the pieces which are presently available in a broad interpretive work. This is not to say that wholesale revisionism is in order. On the contrary, on many points the new material has corroborated the insights of earlier writers. It would be surprising, however, if such confirmation occurred in all cases. And indeed on some questions, the analytical and empirical materials which have become available suggest new interpretations. Constructing an overall interpretation which makes use of the valuable studies and data compilations that have appeared in the past decades is itself a worthwhile task. And such an overall perspective may also help future research by providing a context within which to formulate and interpret new historical studies.

Clarifications

This book is subject to some limitations which must be recognized at the outset. These constrain any study of Brazil's economic history during this period, and are too important to be ignored or glossed over. Despite the flowering of research in recent decades, primary and secondary material on the economic history of nineteenth-century Brazil is still much less plentiful than it is, for example, for the United

States. Because of the paucity of available material, the analysis and hypotheses advanced below can only be considered preliminary and tentative. For the same reason, some important topics are omitted or discussed only briefly.

The discussion here also presupposes a basic familiarity with the main features of Brazilian history.[3] Further, the book is primarily interpretive. I have presented new conclusions concerning some basic economic variables, for example, the pace of per capita income growth and the rate of inflation in nineteenth-century Brazil. But I have not done archival research, and have drawn instead on the primary data collected by professional historians. Thus most of the study is devoted to analyzing, with presently available data, the structure and dynamics of this economy.

I have attempted to write the book in a manner comprehensible to historians as well as to economists. Scholars from these two disciplines sometimes have different approaches, however, and for this reason some comments on methodology are in order. Implicitly or explicitly, all historiography utilizes theory in order to construe its observations and reach its conclusions. Hence, there is nothing novel in the use of analytical ideas to understand economic processes in history. The analytical framework that is developed here does involve a relatively high degree of abstraction. This perspective follows from the broad scope of the study and of the phenomena which it seeks to clarify. Consequently, the discussion proceeds at a high level of aggregation, both over time and across space. In addition, the book's focus abstracts from much of the nuance and texture of history. This approach stems from my concern to provide an analysis rather than a detailed reconstruction of Brazil's economic history during this period. Also, the level of abstraction is by no means exceptional. In a world in which it is sometimes necessary to think at even higher levels of generalization – for example, 'Latin America', the 'Third World', 'the modern period' – license may perhaps be given to a discussion of Brazil's economic history from 1822 to 1947. Finally, the methodology does not insist on the importance of economic conditions, exclusively, in shaping Brazil's economic history. On the contrary, geography and politics also appear to have been of crucial importance.

In the course of the study I have sometimes utilized econometric techniques. Some clarification is necessary on the use of such methods, and particularly on their application to Brazilian data. Most of the statistical data used in the study were compiled by the Brazilian Ministry of Finance and published in the 1939 Statistical Yearbook (*Anuário Estatístico*) of the Brazilian Institute of Geography and Statistics. This is the source for data not otherwise cited. The principal time series which I have used are presented in the Statistical Appendix of this book. Despite the semi-official status of these data, questions arise concerning the validity of drawing useable conclusions from numbers whose accuracy is questionable. Similar questions arise in connection with the other data sets utilized in this study. In fact, however, the problem of data quality is not as serious as might at first appear. Econometric theory indicates that meaningful conclusions can be derived from data which are not absolutely accurate.[4] What is important in such a context is not whether errors in measurement exist, but whether such errors are systematically distributed, and if so, in what manner.

The single most important use to which I have put these data is the computation of rates of growth over time. These rates of growth were estimated by regressing the logarithm of the relevant time series against a time trend. Such logarithmic trends are not distorted if the series' observations are under- or overstated by a constant proportion. Also, if errors of measurement in the dependent variable are not systematically correlated with the independent variable – and I am unaware of reasons to indicate that they are – the parameter estimate for the trend term is unbiased. Errors of measurement do increase the variance of the trend term and may bias the t-statistics toward zero. In other words, our tests of statistical significance are relatively conservative, since they are biased in the direction of rejecting numerical relationships which are in fact valid. Further, the parameter estimates for most of the trends reported below were significant at levels well above the 95 percent confidence limit. Hence it is unlikely that false relationships will inadvertently be accepted as valid.

Similar considerations related to the systematic or random nature of the errors in measurement apply to other regression equations in which these data have been used. One standard use, for example, has been the estimation of elasticities.[5] Again, the presence of errors in the data does not *ipso facto* invalidate the results. Thus in the common case where both the dependent and the independent variables contain errors, but these are not correlated, the magnitude of the estimated elasticity will to some degree be understated. However, in most instances, the estimates computed (taken together with a knowledge of the direction of bias) are sufficient for the purposes of our study: to discern likely relationships and to establish orders of magnitude. Two other cases can also be distinguished. In one, the variance of the measurement error in the independent variables is not large relative to the variance of the error in the dependent variable. In such a situation, bias in the estimators will be of negligible magnitude. In the other case, high correlation between the error process and the independent variable is present (e.g. serial correlation). This would bias parameter estimates. Fortunately, econometric theory has developed techniques to deal with such problems. Transformations of the data are applied, which free the regression equation of statistical inconsistency. I have utilized these techniques in the contexts where the discussion requires relatively accurate measurement of the relevant parameters.

Further, in assessing the application of statistical analysis to the Brazilian data, one must also consider the use to which the econometric materials are put. Professional convention dictates that the regression results be reported to the third decimal place, and I have followed that practice in the pages which follow. But the reader will notice that the study uses such results mainly to establish orders of magnitude concerning basic parameters and variables in the Brazilian economy. The focus throughout this work is not on precise quantitative measurement, with its potential pitfall of spurious accuracy. Rather, the econometric results in this study are utilized to provide the basis for inferences concerning the *qualitative* nature (e.g. positive vs negative, large vs small) of key relationships in Brazil's economic past.

It is also pertinent to note that, whether overtly or not, people inevitably make numerical judgments and qualitative statements. Historians must necessarily reach similar conclusions if they are to perform their descriptive and analytical task. And such qualitative judgments are no less numerous in historiography which draws its inferences from informed impressions rather than from statistical analysis. Indeed, it may be preferable that the source of the underlying data and the way in which they were analyzed be stated overtly. As this discussion suggests, before rejecting formal econometric methods scholars must consider the practical alternatives to the use of such techniques. Implicitly or explicitly, numerical description and qualitative analysis are a normal part of the historian's fare. The inferences presented in this book can hardly be considered less reliable because they have been derived on the basis of formal statistical analysis. If we avoid the delusion of quantitative precision, the use of such techniques may even permit some progress in elucidating Brazil's economic history during these years.

Some Advantages

This study considers a time span which encompassed distinct economic contrasts for Brazil. During most of the nineteenth century, the pace of economic development and per capita income growth in Brazil seem to have been relatively slow. However, toward the end of the century, the tempo of development rose sharply; and thereafter, Brazil embarked on a path of sustained economic expansion and structural change. Thus this study deals with the causes of both economic retardation *and* rapid economic development in Brazil. Understanding either of these states is of course a matter of prime concern for students of development. The chance to consider both states (as well as the transition from one to the other) within the same historical context lends special analytical interest to the Brazilian experience in these years.

Clarifying Brazil's industrialization and economic development in the first half of the twentieth century is a task of obvious importance. I will devote two long chapters to some of the issues which that period raises. But the period to which this study gives most attention is the nineteenth century. This was in many ways a critical one for the Brazilian economy. One central aspect of the century was Brazil's failure to keep pace with the United States and the industrializing economies of Western Europe. Another feature was the establishment within Brazil of structural traits that were to dominate the country's economic and social evolution in the future. Brazil's economic experience during the first eight decades that followed its political independence is also of special interest from the viewpoint of today's independent countries in Asia and Africa.

Despite the importance of the nineteenth century and despite the pioneering work of scholars working in this area, Brazil's economic history during this period is still something of a *terra incognita*. Much of the research on Brazilian economic history has focused on the (pre-1822) colonial period. For example, Roberto Simonsen's basic work, which has provided much of the empirical material for subsequent interpretation, stopped at 1820.[6] A similar emphasis on the colonial period has also characterized many other works on Brazil's economic history. Because of this research focus, important information on the nineteenth-century Brazilian economy is sometimes lacking. For this reason, an attempt to analyze the Brazilian economy during this period sometimes resembles an effort to put together a jigsaw puzzle in which some pieces are missing.

The preceding discussion suggests two conclusions. First, a new study of Brazil's economic backwardness and incipient development may yield important substantive and analytic returns. Second, because of present informational limitations, definitive results concerning Brazil's economic history during this period are not now feasible. Any macro study of nineteenth-century Brazil's economic history which failed to stress these constraints would be less than candid with its readers.

Notwithstanding these limitations, I believe that a number of considerations justify the present work. First are the special gains to be realised from integrating the rich flow of new research which has been generated over the past decades. The need for such a synthesis and overall view, both for specialists and for non-specialists, has become increasingly clear. Also, I believe that the broad outlines of the picture presented in the chapters that follow are more accurate – in the sense of being more logically consistent and closer to the available facts – than are some alternative views of Brazil's economic experience. The absence of some essential primary and secondary materials has not impeded the divulgation of other macro interpretations in this area. But unlike the present work, these efforts have sometimes been advanced without adequate emphasis on their tentative nature and frail underpinnings. Further, economic history is a subject which has often been closely related to economic ideology and other meta-rational considerations.[7] These may sometimes inspire to special insights; but they can also lead to distortions.

There are also gains to be achieved in the context of future research. I have attempted to analyze some of the main features of the Brazilian economy's structure and change between 1822 and 1947. In view of the informational limitations noted, subsequent studies may well modify particulars or major points of the analysis. However, if only for purposes of research consolidation, it is important to see how the major features of the picture now fit together. Moreover, formulation of a coherent overall framework may help stimulate future research on neglected topics. Existing macro perspectives inevitably influence the nature of the primary data which are collected and the direction of the micro and sectoral studies which are undertaken. By focusing on what appear to be the key issues, presentation of an overall view may aid further historical and analytical research on this economy.

A Broader Perspective

We have thus far considered this study largely within the context of Brazilian economic historiography. In that setting, the research should be of interest to both historians and students of Brazilian development. However, this book is also part of a wider literature on the economic history of the underdeveloped countries.[8] In addition to its intrinsic historical interest, that literature offers some special advantages for economists and other social scientists who are concerned with general issues of economic development. I have already mentioned the opportunity to study economic retardation and development within the same historical context. Further, historical studies offer special advantages for gaining a broader perspective on development models and on the less-developed countries (LDCs).

In the early postwar period, explanations of economic under-development often assumed that the LDCs suffered from stagnation. The latter phenomenon, in turn, was attributed to the LDCs' supposed inability to overcome various obstacles to economic development. The post-Second World War experience did not substantiate these fears concerning generalized stagnation. Most LDCs demonstrated impressive rates of growth, both in manufacturing and in aggregate output.[9] These rates of output growth were clearly insufficient in terms of the need to end world poverty, and numerous problems obviously remain.

But the postwar experience has indicated that the picture of the LDCs as locked in economic stagnation was not accurate. Consequently, efforts at explaining the low income levels of these countries have shifted from putative current obstacles to refocus instead on what Simon Kuznets called 'the past failure to modernize and grow'.[10] That is, the causes of current underdevelopment are essentially historical, for economic history provides the initial conditions which constrain subsequent changes. In some instances (e.g. income distribution), such initial conditions may exert a powerful lingering effect. Accordingly, a better understanding of economic history can improve our understanding of economic development.

Another question is also involved – the general attitude with which people view countries like Brazil. Because of their current, relatively low levels of economic development, LDCs have sometimes been considered to be especially prone to economic failure. And following this approach, less-developed countries have often been regarded with condescension.[11] Such attitudes of condescension may either be of a patronizing or of a contemptuous variety; in neither case do they facilitate relations of mutual respect. Moreover, apart from their other negative features, such attitudes concerning proneness to economic failure may have no objective basis. As we will see below, Brazil has demonstrated sustained economic development since approximately the beginning of the twentieth century. The country's low level of economic development in the post-Second World War period stem from Brazil's poor economic experience during the nineteenth century. These results of historical research have an important corollary. For a country like Brazil, the causes of present underdevelopment are a matter of distant economic history, and do not reflect recent rates of economic achievement. There is no basis for regarding such an economy as more 'failure prone' than any other country.

Further, research on economic history may also affect current levels of well-being in the less-developed countries. First, perceptions of the past often provide subjective utility (or disutility) to later generations.[12] This latter phenomenon (unhappiness) seems to be especially common among some intellectuals from LDCs. History has not left their countries in an enviable position. Accordingly, the story of how they reached their present state is not always a happy one, and if this unhappiness is based on false perceptions of history, the need for accurate economic historiography is all the more desirable. Furthermore, interpretations of earlier experience often influence current policy-making in developing countries. Specific policy orientations are sometimes rooted implicitly in a reading of the country's economic history. Conversely, in some cases the absence of explicit economic historiography may lead to what Albert Hirschman has termed 'amnesia' within the policy-making process – the inability to benefit from past experience in dealing with chronic problems.[13] Finally, the development strategies chosen and the options which are subjectively available in a country often depend on interpretations of its economic past. As noted earlier, economic history and economic ideology are sometimes closely related. And perceptions concerning earlier economic experience may help provide the assumptions and climate of opinion that underly a country's general development strategy. For all of these reasons, it is important that impressions concerning a country's economic history be analytically accurate. Otherwise, the energy mobilized to change the status quo may be misspent in policies which are counterproductive from the viewpoint of the policy-makers' own goals.

There are also some general analytical advantages to be gained from studying the economic history of the less-developed countries. The understanding of economic development can benefit from a range of experience which goes beyond the 'standard cases' of Europe and the United States. As many observers have noted, the values of key economic parameters in those instances may have been so unique as to render them special cases. Hence the economic history of those regions does not provide an adequate basis for generalizations concerning economic development. Further, including experiences of economic retardation in the development literature may also be helpful for analytical progress. We can learn from studying abortive as well as successful efforts at economic development.[14]

Historical research can also be useful to assess the empirical relevance of theoretical models of long-term development. History is hardly a testing ground for theory; and deductive models may be formulated for purely theoretical reasons. Nevertheless, it is also interesting to examine the explanatory power of *a priori* theory. For example, a considerable theoretical literature exists on the possible intrinsic deficiencies of a development process which is led by the growth of exports. That discussion has focused on imperialism, the division of the gains from trade, cyclical instability, and conditions which might make for immiserizing export growth. As Harry Johnson noted, the usefulness of these models for interpreting the historical experience is basically an empirical question.[15] But unfortunately, relatively few studies of trade and development are available for individual LDCs from the first decades of the nineteenth century. Thus, the empirical relevance of many theoretical models of trade and development is not always evident.

Studies of the economic history of the underdeveloped countries can also be useful in providing parameters for long-term development models. That is, historical research can provide an indication of the likely numerical range of key parameters, and thus facilitate quantitative assessment of the model's results. For example, a model of the onset of economic development in a pre-industrial economy may yield very different long-term results if the annual rate of population growth is 1.8 percent, as in nineteenth-century Brazil, rather than the much lower values frequently assumed for the underdeveloped countries in the nineteenth century. The usefulness of realistic parameter values is clear. But in the absence of research on the economic history of the underdeveloped countries, parameter values may be based on *a priori* notions or casual empiricism.

A final methodological implication is the progression from economic history to theoretical model building. Economists have long been familiar with the potential dangers which are involved in implicit theorizing. Similar pitfalls exist with respect to what might be termed implicit historiography. Stylized facts are often basic inputs to models of long-run development. These standard assumptions are often derived from casual impressions concerning economic history. But the models built may be analytically more useful to the extent that the assumptions on which they are built are closer to historical reality. The possibility that, in the absence of empirical studies, 'ignorance turns into hunch, hunch into belief, and ultimately, belief into knowledge' has been recognized with respect to current economic magnitudes.[16] Because of the role that perceptions of history or stylized facts play in providing the framework for models of long-term development, it is all the more important that these assumptions be grounded in fact rather than in casual impressions.

Two Final Notes

This study of Brazil's economic experience in the nineteenth century takes place in two stages. It would be tempting to proceed at once in search of the underlying (or 'ultimate') causes of Brazil's economic backwardness during the nineteenth century, and the subsequent acceleration to sustained economic development in the twentieth century. But before we can seek ultimate causes, we need a clear idea of the historical picture which the ultimate causes are to explain. Establishing the proximate empirical and analytical conditions of Brazil's economic history during this period is no trivial task. Indeed, it occupies the whole of the present volume.

The underlying causes of Brazil's economic experience is too exciting a subject to be long deferred, however. Because of space restraints, that discussion could not be included in this volume. Consequently, our consideration of the underlying causes of Brazil's economic retardation and subsequent accelerated development is being published as a companion volume, under the title, *Reassessing the Obstacles to Economic Development*. The present volume draws on that analysis at some points; these are cited in the notes below. But by the same token, the present volume cannot answer all of the questions posed at the beginning of this chapter.

Finally, before we begin, one last introductory note is necessary. This study of long-term underdevelopment and development in Brazil is addressed to a varied readership. Students of history, Latin American studies, and economic development may all be interested in some of the topics discussed. But not all readers will find equally useful the equations and econometric techniques which are sometimes employed to pursue the analysis. However, this is after all a study in long-term economics. And the analytical approach used to answer questions cannot always be separated from discussion of the answers provided. Consequently, the technical material which is central to the overall discussion is not relegated to appendices. Nevertheless, non-economists need not be deterred or distracted by the technical material. Those readers can, if they wish, proceed directly to the results that the techniques yield, which are presented in non-technical terms. With this introduction, we turn to consider economic structure and change in Brazil during the nineteenth century.

Notes

1 Alternatively, a different route may lead to the same question. The idea that nineteenth-century Brazil could have developed along the lines of the United States, Australia, and the other regions of recent settlement may strike some readers as far-fetched. In that case, the question is *why*, despite some apparent similarities, it nevertheless seems incorrect to consider Brazil a 'region of recent settlement'. That line of reasoning leads to the same research agenda as the one posed in the text.

2 The monographs, articles, and dissertations on which the present work has drawn are cited in the chapters which follow. An important bibliographical study is Nícia Villela Luz's essay on Brazil in Roberto Cortes Conde and Stanley J. Stein (eds), *Latin America: A Guide to Economic History, 1830–1930* (Berkeley: University of California Press, 1977). Both because of its substantive findings and because of its empirical-analytical method, the work of Stanley Stein has played a central role in launching the outpouring of high quality research on Brazil's economic history during this period. See, in particular, his *Vassouras: A Brazilian Coffee County, 1850–1890* (Cambridge, Mass.: Harvard University Press, 1957); and *The Brazilian Cotton Textile Manufacture: Textile Enterprise in an Underdeveloped Area, 1850–1950* (Cambridge, Mass.: Harvard University Press, 1957).

3 For English language readers, see, for example, Rollie E. Poppino, *Brazil: The Land and People* (New York: Oxford University Press, 1973).

4 The discussion which follows here draws on material presented in J. Johnston, *Econometric Methods*, 2nd edn (New York: McGraw-Hill, 1972), pp. 281–91; and P. Rao and L. Miller, *Applied Econometrics* (Belmont, California: Wadsworth, 1972), pp. 179–84.

5 An 'elasticity' measures the degree to which a percentage change in one variable is associated with a percentage change in another variable. For example, if the elasticity of prices with respect to changes in the money supply is estimated at 0.8, it means that a 10 percent change in the money supply is associated with an 8 percent

change in the price level. Such elasticities are often estimated by the use of regression equations in which both variables are expressed in logarithmic form.

6 Roberto C. Simonsen, *História Econômica do Brasil (1500–1820)*, 4th edn (São Paulo: Companhia Editora Nacional, 1962).

7 Compare a somewhat extreme comment by Daniel Cósio Villegas in a paper entitled 'History and the Social Sciences in Latin America'. 'The fact which I find most striking is that the Latin American by far prefers inventing history to studying it. . . .'. He goes on to cite with approval another writer's statement that 'In Latin America, in addition to its "scholarly" function, history serves a great variety of purposes, all of which, or almost all, are respectable: patriotic purposes, partisan purposes, literary purposes'. See pp. 131 ff. in Manuel Diégues Jr and Bryce Wood (eds), *Social Science in Latin America* (New York: Columbia University Press, 1967). Of course people other than Latin Americans (or historians) have also been known to 'invent' history.

8 See, for example, Carlos F. Diaz-Alejandro, *Essays on The Economic History of the Argentine Republic* (New Haven: Yale University Press, 1970); William McGreevy, *An Economic History of Colombia, 1845–1939* (Cambridge University Press, 1971). Charles Issawi, *The Economic History of Iran, 1800–1914* (Chicago: University of Chicago Press, 1971).

9 See, for example, World Bank, *World Development Report* (New York: Oxford University Press, 1979).

10 Simon Kuznets, *Modern Economic Growth: Rate, Structure, and Spread* (New Haven: Yale University Press, 1966), p. 46.

11 For a discussion of some of the conditions involved in this context, see O. Manoni, *Prospero and Caliban: The Psychology of Colonialism*, trans. P. Rowsland (New York: Praeger, 1964).

12 Charles Wolf, Jr. has analyzed this phenomenon in his paper, 'The Present Value of the Past,' *Journal of Political Economy,* vol. 78 (July 1970).

13 Albert O. Hirschman, *Journeys Toward Progress* (New York: Doubleday, 1965), p. 320.

14 Albert O. Hirschman, *The Strategy of Economic Development* (New Haven: Yale University Press, 1958), p. 134, n.

15 Johnson's comment is presented in H. M. Southworth and B. F. Johnston (eds), *Agricultural Development and Economic Growth* (Ithaca, NY: Cornell University Press, 1967), p. 451.

16 The quotation is from Arnold C. Harberger, 'Some Evidence on the International Price Mechanism,' *Journal of Political Economy*, vol. 65 (December 1951), p. 508.

Part 1

The Nineteenth Century

2

An Overview

Before beginning a detailed discussion of economic structure and change in Brazil during the nineteenth century, it will be helpful to note some of the economy's principal features. Because nineteenth-century Brazil was largely an agrarian economy, our discussion focuses initially on conditions that influenced productivity in agriculture. We then consider briefly some other key features, which are the subject of the subsequent chapters.

Population and Land

In 1822, the year in which Brazil declared political independence from Portugal, Brazil's population numbered some 4.7 million people. During the nineteenth century, population grew rapidly, at an annual geometric rate of approximately 1.6 percent from 1822 to 1849; and at an annual rate of some 1.8 percent from 1850 to 1900. This growth was the result mainly of natural increase and the importation of slaves. For reasons that will be discussed later, Brazil did not attract much free immigration until the 1870s. In the last decades of the century, however, Brazil experienced a relatively large inflow of European immigrants. In 1913, the country's population was approximately 23.7 million.[1]

Despite an abundant supply of land *in natura* and a high ratio of land to labor, nineteenth-century Brazil did not develop as an economy that was characterized by high labor productivity. In part, low output per worker reflected the country's low technological levels.[2] Even in the more advanced, export agricultural activities, the technology used seems to have been extremely primitive.[3] Some of the techniques utilized, such as slash-and-burn agriculture, may be explicable as a rational response to the factor proportions prevailing in a land-rich economy.[4] It has also been suggested that special features of Brazil's terrain made the hoe or the digging stick economically more efficient implements than the plough. What is most striking, however, is the failure to develop and diffuse high-productivity techniques which were suited to the indigenous conditions, as was the case in countries like Japan and Australia.[5]

Productivity growth was also hindered by the economy's high

transportation costs. These limited the access of many agricultural producers to markets beyond their immediate locale. As a result, the volume of intraregional, inter-regional, and international trade was curtailed. Because of the high ratio of land to labor, cultivation was land-extensive, and distances to the markets large. Low-cost transportation facilities were therefore crucial for developing a high-productivity agriculture. Brazil's geography and topographical conditions, however, made for relatively high transport costs from the production areas to the market centers.[6]

Rivers and coastal shipping were used for transportation. But some of the country's rivers (e.g. the Amazon) were poorly located from the viewpoint of promoting economic development; others flowed in a direction that was not advantageous from the perspective of production and markets. There was also another serious deficiency which hampered low-cost shipments of bulky commodities from deep in the interior. Unlike the United States with its Mississippi and Great Lake systems, Brazil did not have an extensive *network* of internal waterways that were navigable and interconnecting.[7] Further, road conditions in the interior were so poor at the beginning of the period that wheeled vehicles could seldom be used.[8] As a result, transport costs were so high that they absorbed a third of the value of coffee shipments in Brazil's Southeast during the pre-railroad era. Similar transportation conditions prevailed in the Northeast. For example, the cost of shipping cotton from the São Francisco Valley to Bahia in the 1850s amounted to some 50 percent of the prices received.[9] In these conditions of high-cost transportation and low levels of technology, abundant land was not associated with a high value of output per worker in agriculture.

The highest productivity sectors in agriculture were in the export activities. This was indicated by the ability of producers in the major export products, coffee and sugar, to bid away scarce factors from other activities in their respective regional economies. Access to production in the country's major export activities was limited however, because of relatively large minimum scale, high capital intensity, and imperfections in the capital and land markets. The principal export commodities required substantial capital, both for production and for processing (which, for technological-economic reasons, was usually done by the same enterprise). Because of capital-market imperfections, large and medium-size plantations dominated the major export activities, and there was little participation of peasants and family farms.

The effects of capital-market imperfections on allocational inefficiency were compounded by government land policy. The situation here contrasted notably with that of the United States. There, following the Revolution, a more equal distribution of power and a more egalitarian political ethos dictated a liberal land policy. In Brazil, however, the government did not make available public lands in relatively small lots and on favorable credit terms for small farmers. When Brazil achieved independence, most of the country's land of economic importance was already in the hands of large landholders. Squatting by poor families was a common practice. However, as land values rose with the construction of infrastructure facilities and the growth of export production, the large landholders used their economic and political power to expropriate squatters. These effects on the initial social structure were maintained with the country's first land legislation, in 1850 and 1854. One of the main consequences of this legislation was to facilitate appropriation of land by large landholders.[10]

Finally, agricultural productivity was also lowered because of other factor-market imperfections. The large landowners within each area were oligopsonists in local labor markets as well as oligopolists in local land markets. They used their market power to deny freeholders secure tenure of land in the plantation areas, in order to reduce the cost of the free labor which they employed, for example, in risky or infrequently recurring activities.[11] These imperfectly competitive conditions were also not conducive to achieving economic efficiency in the various forms of share-tenancy that prevailed.[12] Thus institutional distortions, as well as the technology and transportation conditions mentioned earlier, affected productivity and income levels in Brazil at the beginning of the nineteenth century. In addition, there were serious constraints on the economy's capacity to expand output more than the growth of population, and thus to permit a rapid increase in per capita income.

Social Overhead Capital

Efforts at modifying geographical conditions and lowering transportation costs by construction of a man-made infrastructure were slow to materialize in nineteenth-century Brazil. There was virtually no canal construction. Similarly, the country's rivers remained without improvements.[13] Consequently, the boats used for internal transportation were small and entailed high unit costs. The country's first railroad legislation was promulgated in 1835. Actual railway construction, however, was late in coming to Brazil. The country's earliest railway, extending some 15 kilometers, was built in 1854. Ten years later, approximately 424 kilometers of track were in operation; but as late as 1890, the country had only 9,973 kilometers of operating trackage. This did not amount to much in terms of Brazil's overall expanse of some 8.1 million square kilometers.[14] Similarly, the country's road network was also extremely limited. As late as 1923, São Paulo state,

Table 2.1   *The Ratio of All Students to the Total Population in Selected Countries, 1850, and the Ratio of Primary School Enrollments to Total Population in Brazil, 1857*

Country	Percent	Country	Percent
Brazil	1	Great Britain	14
United States (excluding		France	10
slaves)	22	The Netherlands	7
Prussia	16	Russia	2

Note: Although the ratios for the other countries are expressed in terms of the total number of students, Brazilian enrollments in secondary and higher education were so small that they would hardly change the overall picture.

Source: Data for all countries but Brazil are from D. C. North, *Growth and Welfare in The American Past* (Englewood Cliffs, N.J.: Prentice-Hall, 1966), p. 85. The figure for Brazil is from Table 2.2 below.

one of the largest and most developed in Brazil, had only 1,025 kilometers of highways (of which 55 were macadamized) suitable for automobile use. And in 1930, *after* a presidential administration that was noted for its road-building activity, Brazil's total road network amounted to only 121,800 kilometers. Of this total, some 900 kilometers were paved.[15]

The growth of productivity was also impeded by Brazil's small stock of human capital. For the population at large, attendance at primary schools may be considered a necessary condition for achieving literacy. However, in 1857 only 1 percent of Brazil's population was enrolled in primary schools. And as the data of Table 2.1 indicate, educational enrollments were much lower in Brazil than in some countries that were able to achieve substantial economic development during the nineteenth century.

In the second half of the century, however, primary school enrollments in Brazil seem to have increased notably. Table 2.2 presents information on this phenomenon (see especially columns 2 and 3). Nevertheless, the ratios of enrollments to the country's school-age and total population remained low in absolute terms (see columns 4 and 5). Thus in 1878 approximately 10 percent of the cohort aged 7–11 was enrolled in schools. The enrollment ratio in Brazil presented a sharp contrast with the situation in another country which was in many ways underdeveloped at this time, Japan. There, in 1875, some 34 percent of the population aged 6 to 13 was receiving some formal schooling.[16] As early as 1868, the literacy rate for the male population in Japan exceeded 40 percent.[17]

As a reflection of Brazil's highly skewed income distribution, the enrollment ratios in the country's secondary and university education were much lower than the figures for primary education. Furthermore, despite the rapid growth of primary school enrollments during the

Table 2.2 *Primary School Enrollments in Brazil, 1857–1907*

(1) Year	(2) Total Primary School Enrollment (thousands)	(3) Annual Geometric Growth Rate Since Previous Observation (%)	(4) Primary School Enrollment as a Percentage of Total Population (%)	(5) Primary School Enrollment as a Percentage of Population Aged 7–11 (%)
1857	83	—	1.0	7
1869	106	2.1	1.1	8
1878	176	5.2	1.6	10
1889	259	4.0	1.9	14
1907	638	5.1	3.1	20

Source: Computed from data in Robert Havighurst and J. Roberto Moreira, *Society and Education in Brazil* (Pittsburgh, 1965), p. 85.

second half of the century, the consequences of the country's low educational allocations in the earlier period were to be felt in Brazil for a long time. In 1890, approximately 85 percent of the country's population was still illiterate;[18] illiteracy rates earlier in the century – before the surge of enrollment – must have been even higher. Another point is also relevant. We are concerned in this context mainly with the impact of education on economic development, in particular the effects of education on the economy's rate of technical progress. Education would have been important because of its role in the development and diffusion of new, improved techniques.[19] Such productivity gains would have helped in both Brazil's export activities and the domestic sector, but perhaps more in the latter, where there were fewer opportunities for technological borrowing. Technical innovation and diffusion, however, depended more on the country's stock of human capital than on the flow of newly literate personnel. Consequently, low initial levels of investment in education probably slowed Brazil's economic development long after the rise in enrollment rates.[20]

The reasons for the low level of Brazil's human-capital stock during the nineteenth century are not entirely clear. It cannot be attributed simply to the prevalence of slavery and a reluctance, for social and institutional reasons, to invest in the education of slaves.[21] Indeed, in 1877, only some 21 percent of the *free* population (including immigrants) was literate.[22] Further, at least after 1869, primary school enrollment in Brazil did grow at a high rate (see Table 2.2). Hence a deliberate policy on the part of the Brazilian elite to limit the availability of education does not seem plausible for that period. The low enrollment ratios observed at the end of the century therefore seem to be the result mainly of two factors: the poor initial conditions which obtained earlier in the century; and the effects of Brazil's rapid population growth in diluting the absolute increase in enrollment. As late as

1920, approximately 69 percent of all people aged 7 or older in Brazil were illiterate.[23]

The Domestic Agricultural Sector

Discussions of the Brazilian economy during the nineteenth century have generally focused on the export sector and urban-based activities. The greater availability of data for those activities, however, should not lead us to exaggerate their quantitative importance. A large portion of Brazil's population was in fact engaged elsewhere, in the 'subsistence' or domestic agricultural sector, the production of food for local consumption and the internal market.[24]

Brazil's domestic agricultural sector in the nineteenth century has been little studied. In the words of two scholars, the sector usually appears only 'between the lines' of Brazilian historiography.[25] Consequently, detailed information on this sector is scanty. Nevertheless, it was too important a feature of Brazil's economy during the nineteenth century to be ignored. On the basis of presently available information, the following statements can be advanced on the domestic agricultural sector's size and composition.

Socially, this sector comprised many of the people in Brazil's population who, in the phrase of the Brazilian historian Caio Prado, 'were not slaves but could not afford to be masters'.[26] This observation suggests one way of forming an impression of the size of the domestic agricultural sector in the Brazilian economy – an examination of the proportions of free people and of slaves in Brazil's total population. This procedure is clearly very crude. All of Brazil's slaves were not engaged in export or urban-based activities; many free people did work in those activities, and in roles other than plantation owners. Bearing this qualification in mind, then, let us see what analysis of the population in terms of its slave and free components suggests.

Brazil's social structure has sometimes been conceptualized in terms of a master/slave dichotomy. Such an approach, however, ignores the presence of a large intermediate stratum of squatters, share-tenants, and small farmers of various degrees of independence.[27] At the very beginning of the nineteenth century, at least one-half and perhaps as much as two-thirds of Brazil's population was free.[28] The vast majority of these people – poor whites, mulattoes, freedmen, and *caboclos* (half-breeds) – were not large slave-owners engaged in production for the export market. Lacking alternative opportunities in a predominantly agrarian economy, many people in this intermediate social stratum must have been involved in the production of food for domestic consumption.

Toward 1820, some 70 percent of Brazil's population was free.[29] Brazil's export activities relied heavily on slaves for most occupations, and African slaves continued to be brought to Brazil in large numbers until 1850. Consequently, until the decades after 1850, only a small percentage of Brazil's population was employed in the export activities. With the decline of slavery, free people were increasingly employed in export activities. But by that time, the free population had grown rapidly as a result of high rates of natural increase. Consequently, the number of people in the domestic agricultural sector remained large relative to the size of the country's total labor force.

The impression that a relatively large share of Brazil's labor force was not engaged in export production is corroborated if we consider disaggregated population estimates for specific locales and times during the nineteenth century. For example, in 1822 in the populous province of Minas Gerais, some 70 percent of the population was free.[30] And the economic structure of the province was such that the vast majority of these people were involved in activities oriented to the local or the domestic market. An 1837 census of the sugar and cotton district of Penedo, in the Northeast province of Alagoas, shows 82 percent of the population to have been free. This was at a time when slaves supplied most of the labor in the Northeast's export activities. Similarly, in the Rio Claro district of São Paulo, 68 percent of the population was free in 1822, and 79 percent in 1835.[31] Even in the heart of the coffee region, in 1872, fully 49 percent of the population was free; and only a small percentage of these people were plantation owners.[32] Similarly, in the sugar-producing province of Pernambuco, slaves constituted approximately 33 percent of the population *circa* 1820; 23 percent in 1840; and 11 percent in 1872.[33] A more detailed analysis of that province's 1872 census data confirms this picture of a large domestic agricultural sector. In 1872, some 58 percent of the province's population resided outside of the sugar area (*zone da mata*) or the city of Recife.[34] And even within the *zona da mata*, a non-negligible portion of the labor force was engaged in production of foodstuffs for local consumption.

Finally, the limited information available on the sectoral composition of output in Brazil also confirms this impression that a large fraction of the country's total labor force must have been in the domestic agricultural sector. At the end of this period, in the years 1911–13, exports accounted for approximately 16 percent of gross domestic product in Brazil.[35] As discussed in Chapter 5, it is unlikely that the share of exports in aggregate economic activity had been higher earlier in the nineteenth century. In addition, the value of output per worker was higher in exports than in other activities of the Brazilian economy. Hence, the export sector's share in the total labor force was even smaller than its share in GDP.

There were of course other activities in this economy besides exports and the domestic agricultural sector. In absolute terms, many people were employed in transportation, commerce, crafts, manufacturing, and government. These activities, however, were located to a great extent in cities. But as late as 1890, only 11 percent of Brazil's population resided in urban centers of 10,000 or more inhabitants.[36] In view of the foregoing discussion, then, it seems clear that a large fraction of Brazil's total labor force must have been engaged in the domestic agricultural sector during the nineteenth century.

This sector appears to have consisted of two parts. First, there were people who lived as sharecroppers, smallholders, or squatters in or near the areas of export production. Partly because of the market imperfections mentioned earlier, the factor endowments of these people prevented them from engaging in the principal export activities. Their main products were foodstuffs such as manioc, beans, and maize. Also, from the observations of contemporaries, it appears that these people took much of their total income in the form of leisure. Second, part of the labor force in the domestic agricultural sector was engaged in farming on the abundant lands in the interior of Brazil, relatively far from the areas of export production. Output consisted largely of cattle-ranching and of semi-subsistence agricultural cultivation. In the latter case, marked economies of scale do not seem to have prevailed in the technology used and in the commodities produced. Accordingly, production was mainly in the form of small-scale farming under the overlordship of a large local landowner. With labor scarce relative to land, cultivation was land-extensive. And since population in this sector was increasing relatively rapidly while abundant lands existed farther into the interior, the frontier shifted ever farther from the markets and centers of consumption. The educational level of the labor force in this sector was especially low; this circumstance probably made for particularly slow productivity growth in the domestic agricultural sector. Until the last decades of the century (see Chapter 7), there is no reason to believe that the value of output per capita in this sector grew more rapidly than, at best, an extremely modest rate.

Aside from its significance as a major structural feature of the Brazilian economy, the domestic agricultural sector is important in the present context for two reasons. Because of the sector's large weight in the overall economy, its slow economic growth lowered the pace of aggregate economic development. In addition, the sector's share in Brazil's total labor force was sufficiently large that, in principle, it might have supplied the labor which was demanded by the country's expanding 'advanced' sector. However, as we shall see in the next chapter, that was not the course that was actually followed in Brazil's economic growth during the nineteenth century. Institutional developments led to a very different pattern of economic expansion.

Additional Features

Finally, four other features of this economy are so important that they are discussed at length in the chapters which follow. I mention them here, however, to complete the present overview.

Any analysis of economic structure and change in Brazil during the nineteenth century necessarily includes a discussion of the country's international trade. It is useful, however, to put the topic of Brazilian trade and development in perspective. Much of the structural change and increased productivity that occurred in Brazil during the nineteenth century was a function of export growth. That alone would suffice to make the experience of Brazil's export sector a subject of prime importance for students of this period. In addition, the statistical information available on Brazil's foreign trade greatly exceeds the materials which pertain to most other aspects of Brazil's economic history. Moreover, other phenomena which are of major interest to historians, both intrinsically and because of their role in promoting further changes, were closely associated with the growth of Brazil's participation in the international economy. For example, foreign investment and the growth of economic infrastructure were clearly linked (both as effect and as subsequent cause) with the expansion of Brazil's foreign trade. So too was the growth of the Brazilian state; for the government's expenditure capabilities rested heavily on taxes which were levied on the country's foreign trade.[37]

For all of these reasons, Brazil's international trade in the nineteenth century merits (and has received) ample attention. But it is important to recognize that the external sector's major role in such productivity increase as the Brazilian economy achieved during this period occurred largely by default. If productivity in the domestic sector of the economy had grown at a higher rate, the place of the external sector in Brazil's economic development would have been far less important. This observation is, of course, obvious. It bears mention, however, in order to avoid a distorted perspective on the nature and sources of economic retardation in nineteenth-century Brazil.

Another major feature of Brazil's economy in the nineteenth century was the price inelasticity of aggregate output. That is, production could be expanded in this economy, but cost conditions were such that higher aggregate output often involved higher prices. Because of these supply conditions, given the pace at which aggregate domestic demand increased during the nineteenth century, Brazil experienced long-term price inflation.

The inelasticity of aggregate supply did not stem from a lack of market responsiveness in this economy.[38] Rather, the underlying causes of Brazil's inelastic aggregate supply derive from the social overhead capital conditions which we noted earlier. Land was abundantly available in nineteenth-century Brazil, and so too was the supply of labor for increasing output. But because of the poor state of the country's transportation facilities (both natural and man-made), food that was produced on more distant land involved higher market prices. Food prices were of course a major determinant of the general price level in this economy. In view of the country's adverse geographical and infrastructure conditions, then, Brazil's buoyant demand pressed on aggregate supply conditions which were inelastic with respect to price. Chapter 6 focuses on this phenomenon and some of its consequences.

A third striking feature of this economy relates to the supply of labor. As just noted, under the conditions which prevailed in nineteenth-century Brazil, higher levels of aggregate production were associated with higher prices. In marked contrast, however, labor was available under conditions such that output could be expanded with minimal increase in real wages. Thus, in the course of its expansion during the nineteenth century, the Brazilian economy faced a supply of workers which was highly elastic with respect to real labor costs. Under these conditions, it is not surprising that several decades of economic expansion could take place in Brazil with little improvement in the material lot of the mass of the country's population.

The elastic supply of labor to the Brazilian economy during the nineteenth century did not occur, however, simply as the result of market forces. Class action and political activity were also involved. Reacting to the country's initially sparse population and high land–labor ratios, Brazil's landowners used government policy to maintain institutions that would assure them an elastic supply of labor. Chapter 4 discusses these phenomena, and analyzes the effects of African slavery and subsidized immigration from Europe to Brazil.

Finally, another central feature involves the growth of productivity and living standards. To what extent was the Brazilian economy able to generate a rising level of per capita income during the nineteenth century? The next chapter considers this topic.

Notes

1   This paragraph draws on material which is presented in Nathaniel H. Leff and Herbert S. Klein, 'O Crescimento da População Não Européia antes do Início do Desenvolvimento: O Brasil do Século XIX,' *Anais da História*, vol. 6 (1974). For a discussion of early population estimates in Brazil, see Maria Luiza Marcílio, 'Evolução da População Brasileira Atraves dos Censos Até 1872,' *Anais da História*, vol. 6 (1974). Demographic structure and dynamics in nineteenth-century Brazil are discussed in Leff and Klein, 'O Crescimento,' op. cit., and in Thomas W. Merrick and Douglas H. Graham, *Population and Economic Development in Brazil, 1800 to the Present* (Baltimore: Johns Hopkins University Press, 1979), esp. Chapters III–V. Progress on many issues of Brazil's demography in the nineteenth

century probably awaits the availability of more archival data and disaggregated studies.

2   Following standard usage among economists, the 'level of technology' refers to the quantity of output that is produced with a given quantity of all inputs. Thus when one technology permits more output to be produced with the same amount of inputs as another technique, the first technology is said to reflect a higher level of technology. As this indicates, the terms 'low,' 'backward,' or 'primitive' technology do *not* refer to the degree of capital intensity in production.

3   See, for example, Viotti da Costa, *Da Senzala a Colonia* (São Paulo, 1966), pp. 183–5; Caio Prado, Jr, *The Colonial Background of Modern Brazil*, trans. by Suzette Macedo from *Formação do Brasil Contemporáneo* (7th edn, São Paulo, 1963, (Berkeley and Los Angeles: University of California Press, 1967), pp. 154–64; Stanley J. Stein, *Vassouras: A Brazilian Coffee County, 1850–1900* (Cambridge, Mass.: Harvard University Press, 1957), pp. 23–4; J. H. Galloway, 'The Sugar Industry of Pernambuco during the Nineteenth Century', *Annals of the Association of American Geographers*, vol. 68 (1968), pp. 292–5; and Peter L. Eisenberg, *The Sugar Industry in Pernambuco: Modernization without Change, 1840–1910* (Berkeley and Los Angeles: University of California Press, 1974), pp. 32–41. Richard Graham has emphasized the low level of the technology used in Brazil as compared with the much more advanced practices of the United States South during the antebellum period. This material is contained in his 'Slavery and Economic Development: Brazil and the United States South in the Nineteenth Century,' (paper presented at the Latin American Studies Association, Pittsburgh, 1979), pp. 7–8. On the illiteracy and ignorance of many coffee planters in the first half of the nineteenth century, see José Arthur Rios, 'Coffee and Agricultural Labor,' in Carlos Manuel Peláez (ed.) *Essays on Coffee and Economic Development* (Rio de Janeiro: Instituto Brasileiro do Café, 1973), p. 5. On technological borrowing from the indigenous population, see Pierre Monbeig, *Pionniers et Planteurs de São Paulo* (Paris: Armand Colin, 1952), p. 115.

4   Gerald K. Helleiner, 'Typology in Development Theory: The Land Surplus Economy (Nigeria),' *Food Research Institute Studies*, vol. 6 (1966). Martin T. Katzman, 'The Brazilian Frontier in Comparative Perspective,' *Comparative Studies in Society and History*, vol. 17 (1975).

5   See R. P. Dore, 'Agricultural Improvement in Japan, 1870–1900,' *Economic Development and Cultural Change*, vol. 9, no. 1, pt. 2 (1960); and on Australia, J. D. Gould, *Economic Growth in History* (London: Methuen, 1972), p. 88.

6   See, for example, Prado, *The Colonial Background*, op. cit., pp. 42–6. For an empirical analysis of the impact of low population densities on agricultural productivity in underdeveloped regions, see J. Dirck Stryker, 'Optimum Population in Rural Areas,' *Quarterly Journal of Economics* (May 1977). Stryker's analysis implies a gap between optimal social and private resource allocation. The existence of distortions which would lead to such an outcome in nineteenth-century Brazil is discussed in Nathaniel H. Leff, *Underdevelopment and Development in Brazil*, Vol. II: *Reassessing the Obstacles to Economic Development* (London: Allen & Unwin, 1982), Chapter 5.

7   In his paper 'How the Brazilian West Was Won' David M. Davidson has emphasized the importance of river transportation in Brazil's West. He refers, however, to transportation of soldiers for geopolitical purposes (a case where costs were presumably no object) rather than for the shipment of bulky commodities. Davidson's paper is in Dauril Alden (ed.), *Colonial Roots of Modern Brazil* (Berkeley and Los Angeles: University of California Press, 1973), pp. 61–106.

8   See Prado, *The Colonial Background*, op. cit., pp. 276–309; da Costa, op. cit., *Da Senzala*, pp. 154–69; Stein, *Vassouras*, op. cit., pp. 91–102; Eisenberg, *The Sugar Industry*, op. cit., pp. 50–1.

9   On coffee, see Warren Dean, *Rio Claro: A Brazilian Plantation System, 1820–1920*

(Stanford: Stanford University Press, 1976), p. 40. The figure on transport costs in cotton during the 1850s (not a period of low cotton prices) was calculated from data in Stanley J. Stein, *The Brazilian Cotton Manufacture* (Cambridge, Mass.: Harvard University Press, 1957), p. 221, n. 3. For a similar situation in sugar, see Eisenberg, *The Sugar Industry*, op. cit., pp. 55 ff.

10 Warren Dean, 'Latifundia and Land Policy in Nineteenth Century Brazil,' *Hispanic American History Review*, vol. 51 (November 1971); da Costa, *Da Senzala*, op. cit., pp. 73–4; Stein, *Vassouras*, op. cit., pp. 47–8.

11 See da Costa, *Da Senzala*, op. cit., pp. 71–4; and Stein, *Vassouras*, op. cit., p. 59. Conditions may have been different in the Northeast. Jaime Reis describes relatively competitive labor-market conditions for that region before 1850. See his paper 'From Banguë to Usina' in Kenneth Duncan and Ian Rutledge (eds), *Land and Labour in Latin America* (Cambridge: Cambridge University Press, 1977), pp. 372–4.

12 On the economic efficiency of sharecropping under competitive market conditions, see Steven N. S. Cheung, *The Theory of Share Tenancy* (Chicago, 1969), and Joseph Reid, 'Sharecropping in History and Theory,' *Agricultural History*, vol. 49 (April 1975). However, on the effects of factor-market imperfections such as existed in Brazil on efficiency in sharecropping, see Anthony Y. C. Koo, 'Toward a More General Model of Land Tenancy and Reform,' *Quarterly Journal of Economics*, vol. 87 (November 1973).

13 On the important role which canals and improved internal waterways played in the economic development of the United States, see Carter Goodrich (ed.), *Canals and American Economic Development* (New York: Columbia University Press, 1961).

14 The ratio of Brazil's railway trackage to its territorial size in 1890 would remain very small even if large uninhabited areas like the Amazon region were excluded from the calculation. Note, moreover, that to some extent whether an area is inhabited or not depends on the availability of low-cost transportation facilities.

15 The figures on road construction are from data presented in Annibal Villela and Wilson Suzigan, *Política do Governo e Crescimento da Economia Brasileira, 1889–1945* (Rio de Janeiro: IPEA, 1973), p. 406; and from Chapter VI of Arthur Sherwood's 'Brazilian Federal Highways and the Growth of Selected Urban Areas' (unpublished PhD thesis, New York University, 1967). The latter source gives a lower figure for the length of the total road network in 1930, 113,600 kilometers.

16 This figure was computed from data in R. P. Dore, *Education in Tokugawa Japan* (Berkeley: University of California Press, 1965), pp. 317–21. Note that the population aged 6 to 13 is used as the denominator for the ratio in Japan. Hence the enrollment ratio would be even higher if, as in Brazil, the population aged 7 to 11 had been used as the denominator.

17 This figure is from H. Passin, *Society and Education in Japan* (New York: Bureau of Publications, Teachers College, Columbia University, 1965), as cited in James I. Nakamura, 'Human Capital Accumulation in Premodern Rural Japan,' *The Journal of Economic History*, vol. 61 (June 1981), p. 277.

18 Computed from data in Laura Randall, *A Comparative Economic History of Latin America, 1500–1914*, Vol. 3: *Brazil* (Ann Arbor: University Microfilms International, 1977), p. 146.

19 For formal analysis of these issues, see R. R. Nelson and E. S. Phelps, 'Investment in Humans, Technological Diffusion, and Economic Growth,' *American Economic Review* (May 1966).

20 In discussing the causal mechanisms through which greater availability of education might have promoted economic development in Brazil, I have focused on the development and diffusion of more productive techniques. By contrast, in his treatment of the Japanese case, Nakamura ('Human Capital Accumulation') has stressed the importance of education for such conditions as 'market consciousness' and population control. There are some important differences here. Nineteenth-century Brazil was not a feudal society, and even without widespread education,

responsiveness to market forces was high (see Leff, *Reassessing the Obstacles to Economic Development,* op. cit., Chapter 3). A contrast with Japan also appears in connection with the impact of education (and ensuing microeconomic rationality) on population control. Microeconomic rationality may lead to smaller desired family size when the long-term household is the unit of decision and when institutional conditions make the adoption of a long-term perspective sensible. The extent to which such a model explains demographic behavior in nineteenth-century Brazil is not yet clear. Further, under Brazilian conditions of abundant land *in natura,* rationality at the household level may well *not* have implied population control. For most of Brazil's population, wage levels were determined parametrically. Increasing the number of workers raised family income regardless of the negative social externality which may have been involved in increasing aggregate labor supply.

21 Brazilian slaveowners did invest in the acquisition of craft skills by their human possessions, see, for example, Mary Karasch, 'From Porterage to Proprietorship: African Occupations in Rio de Janeiro, 1808–1850,' in Stanley L. Engerman and Eugene D. Genovese (eds), *Race and Slavery in The Western Hemisphere: Quantitative Studies* (Princeton: Princeton University Press, 1975).

22 Richard Graham, *Britain and The Onset of Modernization in Brazil: 1850–1914* (Cambridge University Press, 1968), p. 17.

23 To obtain some perspective, note that the 1914 figure for Argentina was approximately half that level. These data are from Roberto Borges Martins, 'Crescimento Exportador, Desigualidade e Diversificação Econômica: Uma Comparação entre o Brasil e a Republica Argentina, 1860–1930,' in *Cadernos DCP,* vol. 3 (Universidade Federal de Minas Gerais) (Março 1976), p. 85.

24 Unfortunately, the term 'subsistence' sometimes has the connotation of producing only at minimal income levels. The extent to which that condition prevailed for free workers in nineteenth-century Brazil is not certain. I prefer the term domestic agricultural sector, which more clearly indicates the nature of the goods produced and their economic destination. The domestic agricultural sector overlapped with, but was by no means coterminous with, the non-monetized or non-market sectors, terms which have also been used in this context.

25 The phrase is from Joyce Riegelhaupt and Shepard Forman, 'Bodo Was Never Brazilian,' *Journal of Economic History,* vol. 30 (March 1970), p. 103. See, however, Celso Furtado, *Formação Econômica do Brasil,* 5th edn, (Rio de Janeiro: Fundo de Cultura, 1963), pp. 143–6.

26 Caio Prado, Jr, *The Colonial Background,* p. 419, as cited by Riegelhaupt and Forman, 'Bodo,' loc. cit.

27 Prado's book, *The Colonial Background,* contains numerous observations on the people and activities of the domestic agricultural sector; but these observations are interspersed with his discussion of other topics. See, for example, pp. 183–6, 214–19, 302, 328–39, 400–2. On the *moradores* (squatters) in the Northeast, see Reis, 'From Banguê,' pp. 372–4. See also the observations in Antônio Barros de Castro, *Sete Ensaios sobre a Econômica Brasileira* (Rio de Janeiro, 1971), Vol 11, pp. 19–58.

28 The population estimates of Contreiras Rodrigues, Humboldt, and Balbi suggest that perhaps one-half of Brazil's total population was free at the beginning of the nineteenth century. These estimates are presented in Roberto Simonsen, *História Econômica do Brasil,* 4th edn, (São Paulo: Companhia Editora Nacional, 1962), p. 271. Caio Prado (*Colonial Background,* op. cit., p. 117) states that at the beginning of the century, slaves constituted one-third of the total population. That would suggest an even larger share for the domestic agricultural sector in the economy as a whole.

29 This statement is based on population estimates which are presented in Simonsen, *História Econômica,* op. cit., p. 271; Stein, *Vassouras,* op. cit., p. 294; and Alan K.

Manchester. *British Preeminence in Brazil* (Durham, NC: Duke University Press, 1933), p. 183.

30   This figure is from the data presented in Kenneth Maxwell, *A Devassa da Devassa* (Rio de Janeiro: Paze Terra, 1977), pp. 301–2. The population of Minas Gerais at that time numbered some 514,000 people, approximately 12 percent of the total for Brazil. The figure 82 percent (in following text) was computed from data cited in Riegelhaupt and Forman, 'Bodo,' op. cit., pp. 105–6.

31   Dean, *Rio Claro*, op. cit., p. 51.

32   Stein, *Vassouras*, op. cit., pp. 117–9.

33   Eisenberg, *The Sugar Industry*, op. cit., Table 22.

34   Computed from data in Tables 2 and 4 of Bainbridge Cowell, Jr, 'Cityward Migration in The Nineteenth Century: The Case of Recife, Brazil,' *Journal of Interamerican Studies and World Affairs,* vol. 17 (February 1975).

35   This figure is based on estimates of GDP which were graciously supplied by Claudio Haddad of the Fundação Getulío Vargas. In a letter dated 12 October 1976, Dr Haddad provided figures for the components of GDP which were not included in his earlier estimates of Brazilian 'Real Product' for the years 1911–13. Those estimates and the methodology which underly them are presented in Claudio Haddad, 'The Growth of Brazilian Real Output, 1900–1947,' (PhD dissertation, University of Chicago, 1974). In units of thousands of current price *mil-réis*, Haddad's estimates give the following values for Brazilian GDP in 1911, 1912, and 1913, respectively: 6,118.4; 7,237.8; and 6,570.8. These GDP estimates indicate an average export ratio of 15.6 percent in those years. The figure presented in the text is rounded to the nearest decimal place in order to avoid a spurious impression of precision. Note that GDP includes value-added which is generated in service activities (e.g. government, distribution, and finance) as well as in agriculture and industry. GDP is therefore larger than the 'Real Product' estimates other authors have presented, in which they have included only agricultural and industrial output. For this reason, those estimates of 'Real Product' in Brazil are much smaller than the figures for GDP. Similarly, export ratios computed with reference to 'Real Product' as the denominator are larger than those computed with GDP as the denominator.

36   Nicholas Sanchez-Albornoz, *The Population of Latin America: A History,* trans. by W. A. R. Richardson (Berkeley and Los Angeles: University of California Press, 1974), pp. 178–9.

37   Data and discussion on these points are presented in Leff, *Reassessing the Obstacles to Economic Development,* op. cit., Chapters 4 and 5.

38   Ibid., Chapter 3.

3
The Pace of Income Growth

Introduction

Analysis of Brazil's economic history during the nineteenth century has been hampered by the absence of national-income estimates. Moreover, the underlying data necessary to construct such estimates, such as figures for labor-force distribution and sectoral output, are also lacking. As a result, studies of Brazilian economic history have not had an adequate basis for dealing with the central question of the economy's long-run rate of income growth. Because of index-number problems and shifts in the distribution of income, per capita income growth has serious deficiencies as a measure of changes in economic welfare. Nevertheless, economists and historians sometimes find it useful to have an indicator of an economy's performance in raising output and income at a rate greater than the growth of population. For that measurement purpose, an estimate of the rate of growth of per capita income can be helpful.[1]

Monetary data are usually collected on a systematic basis before production data. Further, monetization and the growth of demand for real cash balances usually proceed in a relatively predictable manner in the course of economic development. Accordingly, a number of economists have suggested using monetary data to derive rough estimates of long-run income trends.[2] The present chapter is an application of this general approach. An additional step, however, enables us to estimate long-term income trends from *currency* data. The analysis is applied to provide estimates of the rate of income in Brazil from 1822 to 1913. The year 1822 is used as a starting point not because it necessarily constituted an economic watershed, but because it was the year in which Brazil declared its independence, and thereafter data are more plentiful.

Before beginning our analysis of per capita income growth in Brazil during the nineteenth century, it may be helpful to state its major conclusions. Through most of the nineteenth century, real per capita income in the country as a whole seems to have grown at a modest rate. Income did keep pace with the growth of Brazil's population; and aggregate output increased considerably. Moreover, the Southeast coffee region enjoyed a rate of economic growth higher than the country as a whole and laid the groundwork for subsequent development. But if one considers the economy's record in producing markedly higher incomes for the general population, the nineteenth century was not a period of major economic progress for Brazil. Some of these conclusions differ considerably from the views of earlier writers on this subject. Let us therefore present the methodology which led to these results.

The Model

The analysis starts from the Quantity Theory, $MV=PY$; where M denotes the money supply; V, the income velocity of circulation; P, the price level; and Y, national income. Dividing by P, we have $Y=(M/P)V$. In growth terms, $\dot{Y}=(\dot{M/P})+\dot{V}$. That is, the annual percentage rate of change in income over time is equal to the sum of the rates of change of the deflated money supply and of the income velocity of money. Hence, in order to estimate trends in income, we require estimates of (M/P) and $\dot{V}$. In order to utilize the data on the currency stock to derive an estimate of long-run income growth, however, we must proceed through an additional step.

We begin with identities on the income velocity of circulation, $V \equiv Y/M$; and on the share of the currency stock in the total money supply, $Z \equiv CS/M$. Writing these in logarithmic form, we have

$$\ln V = \ln Y - \ln M \qquad (1)$$

$$\ln Z = \ln CS - \ln M \qquad (2)$$

Subtracting (2) from (1) and rearranging terms, we obtain

$$\ln Y = \ln CS + \ln V - \ln Z \qquad (3)$$

Using dot notation and lower case letters to denote annual percentage rates of change in the per capita form of these variables, we observe that

$$\dot{y} = \dot{cs} + \dot{v} - \dot{z} \qquad (4)$$

That is, the rate of growth of real income per capita is equal to the rate of growth of the deflated per capita currency stock *plus* the change in velocity *minus* the change in the ratio of currency to the overall supply of money.

Because of the rough nature of the data and assumptions which must be used, this procedure can at best yield tentative conclusions concerning the likely magnitudes of income growth in nineteenth-century Brazil. Nevertheless, the advantages of the method should also not be minimized, since it does enable us to go beyond episodic impressions to provide an answer to a basic question in Brazil's economic history. Moreover, one's confidence in the technique may be enhanced by noting that it has permitted accurate replication of the estimate of Brazilian income growth in a later period, 1920–1947, for which both national income and monetary data are available.[3] In order to use expression (4) to draw conclusions from trends in the currency stock to long-term trends in income, however, we require knowledge concerning the magnitudes of $\dot{v}$ and $\dot{z}$ in nineteenth-century Brazil.

Changes in Velocity and in the Currency Ratio

Cross-section and time-series studies indicate that both Z and V are in general inversely related to Y.[4] At lower levels of per capita income and development, currency constitutes a larger fraction of the total stock of money; and velocity, the ratio of income to the money supply, is higher.[5] In addition, as John Gurley has demonstrated, larger population size (an indicator of an increased number of decentralized decision-makers who must hold cash balances to carry out their transactions) is also associated with a lower V.[6] Consequently, even without rising per capita income, growth both in the complexity of the economy and in the number of economic units would lead to increased monetization and a fall in velocity.

Data compiled by Carlos Peláez and Wilson Suzigan show that from 1830 to 1913, Z fell at a long-term rate of 1 percent per annum in Brazil.[7] A similar rate of decline is likely to have prevailed from 1822. In the first decades of the nineteenth century, Brazil was not well-developed financially.[8] Hence it is reasonable to suppose that Z was close to its upper limit of 1. If we take $Z_{1822} = .95$, and compute the long-term rate of change to the figure for Z which obtained in 1913, we also have $\frac{\dot{z}}{z} = -1.0$ percent.[9]

Observations for the years 1911–13 indicate that at the end of our period, V averaged 5.7 in Brazil.[10] Data for V in the nineteenth century are not available for Brazil. However, we can use statistics from other countries to derive lower-bound, upper-bound, and intermediate figures for V in Brazil in 1822. In the first half of the nineteenth century, V was approximately 10 in the United States.[11] This is an extreme lower limit for V_{1822} in Brazil. First, all indications are that in 1822, per capita income was lower in Brazil than in the United States. In addition, Brazil had a proportionately larger slave-labor force, for whom cash balances did not have to be held to finance wage payments. Slaves constituted approximately 30 percent of Brazil's total population at this time.[12] Moreover, since the slaves were concentrated in the activities where much of the economy's high-value output was generated, the demand for cash balances in much of the

Brazilian economy's 'advanced' sector was relatively low. Further, the Brazilian economy's quasi-subsistence sector, where little cash was used, was also proportionately much larger than in the United States.[13] Even in a market-oriented activity like cattle raising, wage payments in Brazil were often made in kind rather than in cash.[14] And even in the market centers, scrip (*vales*) was sometimes used, reducing the demand for official currency per unit of output. All of these conditions would lead to a V_{1822} that was very high in Brazil, and certainly much higher than the figure that obtained in the United States during the first half of the nineteenth century.

An upper-bound figure for V_{1822} is hard to obtain. In Mexico, as late as 1895–1897, V averaged approximately 17.[15] By contrast, Brazil in 1822 was probably more backward economically than was Mexico in the middle of the Porfirian era. The share of the export sector in aggregate Brazilian output in 1822 was much smaller than has sometimes been assumed.[16] Moreover, the population was overwhelmingly rural, and, as noted, the banking system was primitive. Finally, Brazil had been experiencing price inflation well before the beginning of our period. By increasing the cost of holding cash balances, inflation also lowered the demand for money, and thus led to a relatively high value for V_{1822} in Brazil.

On the basis of these considerations and data for contemporary less-developed countries, 25 may be considered an upper-bound assumption for V_{1822} in Brazil; 10, a lower bound; and 18, an intermediate figure.[17] (If the reader finds other assumptions for V_{1822} more plausible, he/she can of course utilize those figures in the model presented here to derive other estimates for $\dot{y}$.) For the reasons mentioned above, however, I believe that the figure of 10, which is drawn from the United States experience, is an extreme lower bound; the true figure for V_{1822} is more likely to be in the intermediate range of the figures provided. The annual figures for $\dot{v}$ which the upper-bound, intermediate, and lower-bound assumptions yield are, respectively: −1.7 percent, −1.3 percent and −0.6 percent.[18] As these figures indicate, large differences in the initial V are associated with less than proportionate variations in $\dot{v}$. Consequently, the final estimates of $\dot{y}$ are not as sensitive as might have been expected to the assumptions concerning V_{1822}.

Estimates of the Rate of Per Capita Income Growth, 1822–1913

Between 1822 and 1913, the Brazilian currency stock increased at annual trend rate of 4.6 percent.[19] On a per capita basis, the annual rate of increase of the currency stock was 2.9 percent. These figures, however, relate to the growth of the currency supply in *nominal* terms. Because Brazil experienced long-term price inflation during the

Table 3.1 *Alternative Estimates of the Annual Long-Term Rate of Growth of Nominal Monetized Per Capita Income in Brazil, 1822–1913*

$$\dot{y}=c\dot{s}+\dot{v}-\dot{z}=2.9\%+\dot{v}+1.0\%$$

(1) Assumed Value for V, 1822	(2) Implied Value for v (%)	(3) Implied Rate of Growth of Nominal Monetized Per Capita Income (%)
25	−1.7	2.2
18	−1.3	2.6
10	−0.6	3.3

Source: See the text.

nineteenth century, the pace of real currency expansion and the implied rate of real income growth were of course lower than the nominal figures for these variables.

Utilizing equation (4), the figure for $\dot{z}$ and the alternative assumptions for V_{1822} and $\dot{v}$ we obtain the upper-bound, intermediate, and lower-bound estimates for the long-term rate of growth of nominal per capita income in Brazil between 1822 and 1913. Considering the rough nature of the model used, the approximate nature of these numbers must be stressed, though the bounding procedure applied to v reduces the probability of gross error. Column (3) of Table 3.1 presents the estimates.

The estimates of Table 3.1 refer to the growth of nominal (current price) income in nineteenth-century Brazil. However, this was an economy known for its long-term price inflation. Hence, in order to draw inferences from the figures of Table 3.1 concerning the pace of real income growth, we need to know the magnitude of Brazilian inflation between 1822 and 1913. We can then subtract the rate of annual inflation from the figures of Table 3.1 to derive a range of estimates for the rate of the real per capita income growth. In Chapter 6, we present the data available for calculating the extent of price inflation in Brazil during the nineteenth century. The discussion there concludes that a likely order of magnitude for the overall rate of inflation in Brazil between 1822 and 1913 was 2.5 percent per annum.[20]

Subtracting this figure from those of Table 3.1, we arrive at lower-bound, upper-bound, and intermediate estimates for the rate of growth of real monetized income per person. These growth estimates are, respectively: −0.3 percent per annum if V_{1822} was as high as 25; +0.8 percent per annum if V_{1822} was as low as the figure prevailing in the United States in the early nineteenth century; and 0.1 percent if V_{1822} in Brazil was in the intermediate range discussed earlier.

These estimates are obviously very rough. They do, however, suggest an important general point: income per capita seems to have risen at only a moderate pace in Brazil during the nineteenth century.

In particular the intermediate figure, which is in the most likely range of the estimates, points to that conclusion. Thus, income growth in nineteenth-century Brazil probably did exceed the country's rate of population increase, 1.8 percent per annum. But on a per capita basis, income in Brazil does not seem to have risen at a high rate. The contrast with the experience of the United States is especially noteworthy. There, per capita income is estimated to have grown at an annual long-term rate of approximately 1.5 percent during the nineteenth century.[21]

As noted below, this picture of the nineteenth century as being a period of slow growth in per capita income for Brazil goes counter to earlier discussions of the subject. But the view that the country enjoyed a long period of rapid development is inconsistent with the very poor conditions which prevailed in Brazil toward the end of the period. At the conclusion of the nineteenth century, physical indices of development (e.g. life expectancy, educational enrollments, and urbanization) stood at very low levels in Brazil.[22] Also, as discussed in Appendix I of this chapter, the picture of slow per capita income growth in Brazil during the nineteenth century is corroborated by estimates based on another economic indicator, the country's export receipts. Finally, the picture that we derive from monetary analysis is also supported by a discussion of Brazilian economic growth which is formulated in terms of production theory (see Chapter 7, below).

In fact, our figures overstate the pace of income growth in nineteenth-century Brazil. The estimates of income growth which can be derived from equation (4) necessarily relate only to the monetized sector, rather than to income (and output) in the economy as a whole. The latter of course is a weighted average which comprises both monetized and non-monetized income. In the course of the nineteenth century, monetized output increased more rapidly than did non-monetized output in Brazil; and reflecting on these differential rates of growth, the share of non-monetized output in the economy as a whole declined. Because of this compositional shift, the rate of growth of total income in this economy was lower than the estimates for monetized income which are presented above.[23]

The direction of bias in our estimates, then, is clear. And, as noted, physical indicators also support the picture of only meager development in per capita terms during the nineteenth century. Consequently, the general conclusion seems warranted that per capita income in Brazil rose at only a modest rate during the nineteenth century.

Further Discussion

Aggregate income rose considerably in Brazil between 1822 and 1913. During that period, the country's population increased approximately fivefold. Hence substantial economic expansion would have been required just to keep the level of per capita income from declining. As these considerations indicate, the large increases of aggregate output which took place in nineteenth-century Brazil do not controvert the picture of a poor growth experience in per capita terms. We focus on the latter, however, because of its greater relevance as an index of productivity change and welfare gain.[24]

The large slave importations which occurred in Brazil between 1800 and 1850 have sometimes been taken as an indication of rapid economic growth.[25] Such an interpretation, however, neglects some pertinent demographic conditions. Natality and mortality rates among Brazil's slaves were so poor that the natural rate of population increase was very low, if not negative. Consequently, a large flow of slave imports was necessary merely to support a moderate growth in the country's stock of slaves.[26]

It must be emphasized, however, that our estimates relate to the growth of monetized per capita income growth in the country considered as a whole. As such, the estimates reflect the diverse experiences of Brazil's various sectors and regions. There is evidence that these fared very differently over the century. The Southeast coffee region did achieve considerable economic progress.[27] But in Brazil's large domestic agricultural sector, which employed a considerable portion of the country's labor force, the value of per capita output was probably unchanged until the end of the century. And in the Northeast, where some 52 percent of Brazil's population resided in 1822, the nineteenth century was a period of economic stagnation and perhaps even of decline.[28]

Notwithstanding the diversity of regional growth experiences, a meager increase of per capita income in nineteenth-century Brazil cannot be dismissed as reflecting no more than the special case of the Northeast. First, the plight of the Northeast cannot simply be dismissed as irrelevant and a minor affair. It hardly speaks well for a country's economic achievement if a region with half the country's population does as poorly as the Northeast in the nineteenth century. And even if we exclude the Northeast from the analysis, nineteenth-century Brazil does not emerge as an economic success story. Estimates of the rate of growth of per capita income in the rest of Brazil (excluding the Northeast) are derived in Appendix II of this chapter. As expected, those estimates for the rest of Brazil show an economic growth rate which is higher than the figures for the country as a whole. Nevertheless, the Appendix also indicates that monetized per capita income in the rest of Brazil rose at a rate well below that of the United States during the nineteenth century.

A Possible Periodization of Brazilian Income Growth in the Nineteenth Century

Our growth estimates must also be disaggregated over time. Although the estimates are expressed in terms of annual rates, they should not be interpreted as implying a uniform trend and an absence of fluctuations. On the contrary, there are clear signs that in various decades Brazilian income growth proceeded at rates that were either above or below the long-term trend. This variation is clear if we fit a trend equation to the annual observations for the deflated currency stock over the time span 1822–1913. Such an equation shows a pattern of residuals which are distributed in fairly discrete sub-periods. Thus income growth and/or monetization conditions were present in those years which led to the expansion of demand for real cash balances at a rate above or below the long-term trend value.

This observation suggests an approach to the question of periodizing Brazilian income growth in the ninety-one years before 1913. After inspection of the pattern of the residuals for the years 1822–1913, trend equations were fitted for different intervals in an effort to identify relatively homogeneous sub-periods. We cannot place great emphasis on such variations in the rate of growth. Still, if the growth of demand for cash balances varied substantially in distinct periods, this fact should be mentioned. Material which would not be worth noting for a well-charted terrain is of interest as a suggestion for further investigation in what is now virtually a *terra incognita*.

Table 3.2 shows the statistical results for the sub-period equations which gave the best fits. That is, the *t*-ratios for the trend term in these equations indicate the existence of relatively well demarcated sub-periods. The results presented in Table 3.2 relate to the series in which the currency stock was deflated by a purchasing-power-parity price index.[29] Broadly similar results were also obtained when another price index was used as the deflator.[30]

Table 3.2 suggests a period of relatively high growth from 1900 to 1913. This conclusion is consistent with the data on Real Output, exports, central government expenditure, and foreign investment, all of which show a spurt (from a cyclical trough) toward the turn of the

Table 3.2 *Annual Percentage Trend Rate of Growth of the Deflated Currency Stock, Selected Periods*

Period	Trend Rate of Growth	t-Ratio of Trend Term	Period	Trend Rate of Growth	t-Ratio of Trend Term
1822–35	6.3	4.58	1879–88	−3.6	2.82
1836–62	2.3	10.21	1889–99	−1.0	0.89
1863–78	6.0	8.13	1900–13	5.0	7.90

Source: Computed by least-squares regression from data discussed in the text.

century.[31] Similarly, the rapid growth of the period 1822–35 is supported by the export figures for those years. Another noteworthy feature of Table 3.2 is the poor growth experience evident for the twenty years after 1878. To some extent, the economic decline indicated for the years 1879–88 reflects the plight of the Northeast, which suffered from severe drought. Finally, the 1890s seem to have been a period with no statistically significant trend.

Further research is clearly needed on the periodization of Brazilian income growth during the nineteenth century, as the results presented in Table 3.2 are at best only tentative suggestions. Still, the information now available does point to a conclusion of general interest. As will be discussed in Chapter 8, from 1900 onward Brazil was able to achieve sustained economic development. This structural shift does not seem to have been preceded, however, by a period of steadily rising aggregate economic growth. On the contrary, in the decades before the onset of sustained development in Brazil, the country appears to have had below average aggregate growth. Note further that the picture of a poor per capita growth experience in the decades preceding 1900 is corroborated by estimates from another source. Using monetary data but different techniques from those employed here, Claudio Contador and Claudio Haddad have prepared estimates of Brazilian per capita income for the years 1861–99.[32] Their series shows a slight decline in per capita income between 1861 and 1899.[33] Thus the post-1899 transition to sustained economic development in Brazil apparently did not conform to a pattern of monotonic progression from an initial state of stagnation through successive stages of accelerating growth.

Earlier Views

As emphasized earlier, the periodization and the range of estimates proposed above for the growth of per capita income can be considered only rough approximations. Nevertheless, we note that the picture of nineteenth-century Brazilian economic growth which these estimates suggest differs considerably from the earlier view, frequently cited in the literature, which has its origin in the pioneering work of Celso Furtado. Furtado suggested that real per capita income declined in Brazil in the first half of the nineteenth century. He also concluded that Brazilian per capita income rose at a steady rate of approximately 1.5 percent per annum during the fifty years after 1850.[34]

In view of the incomplete information available, no one would insist on the precision of either picture of income growth in nineteenth-century Brazil. Nevertheless, the difference between Furtado's estimates and those presented here is so great that some clarifying discussion seems necessary. The substantive issues include a major revision of views concerning Brazilian economic growth in the nineteenth century. In particular, the estimates presented here suggest that a substantial increase in per capita income occurred only toward the turn of the century, fifty years later than Furtado proposed. Also involved are issues of general perspective, and, not least, of the research agenda which nineteenth-century Brazil poses for economists and historians. The questions to be answered are clearly very different for an economy characterized by minimal per capita income growth, as compared with an economy whose per capita income is believed to have been growing for half a century at the same long-term rate as the United States in its prime years.

The methodology underlying Furtado's estimates is not completely clear.[35] He seems to have used the export data as a macroeconomic indicator without taking much account of conditions in the domestic sector of the economy. A problem with that approach is that the economic growth experience of the export sector may have differed substantially from the growth experience of the domestic sector. By contrast, the methodology used here employs the data on the currency stock as a macroeconomic indicator. That series is more comprehensive; for it reflects conditions both in the domestic and in the export sectors. Also, our inclusion of a long-term downward trend in V allows for changes in the share of the monetized sector. By contrast, Furtado's methodology appears to assume a constant share for the export sector. Finally, Appendix I of this chapter analyzes the currency stock and export data together, to see what these series imply for income growth in nineteenth-century Brazil. The estimates derived there are similar to the (low) growth figures presented above. Consequently, even considering the rough nature of the estimates we have derived, they suggest the need for a very different view of per capita income growth in Brazil during the nineteenth century.

Conclusions

This chapter has utilized a model based on increasing monetization and demand for cash balances to derive a range of estimates for the rate of income growth in Brazil during the nineteenth century. Because of the limitations of the available data, the principal conclusion of this 'quantitative' analysis is qualitative: namely, that Brazil experienced only a relatively modest increase in per capita income between 1822 and 1913. A consideration of the export statistics leads to the same conclusion. In discussing the pace of economic growth in nineteenth-century Brazil, however, we have stressed the need for disaggregation. For some purposes, a meaningful picture of income growth in nineteenth-century Brazil requires separate discussion of the Southeast and Northeast regions – which had very different experiences in their export activites – and the domestic agricultural sector.

The low rate of per capita income growth in the country as a whole during the nineteenth century also sheds light on the origins of the income gap which now separates Brazil from the economically advanced countries. During the twentieth century, Brazil's long-term rate of per capita income growth has not been below that of the United States and the other more developed countries.[36] But the long period in the nineteenth century when Brazilian per capita income grew at a rate markedly lower than that of the United States led to the widening of the international gap. Consequently, Brazil began its modern economic growth from a relatively low level of per capita income, far behind international income comparisons.[37] The fact that Brazil's income gap had its origins in the country's poor economic experience before the twentieth century has been noted before.[38] But as we have seen, sustained growth in Brazilian per capita income began approximately half a century later than has sometimes been proposed. This observation increases the importance of the nineteenth century as a focal period for Brazilian historical studies. And because of the long delay before Brazil experienced economic progress at a pace similar to that of the economically advanced countries, the nineteenth century can be called a period of economic retardation for Brazil.

Finally, since our analysis of Brazil's economic growth during the nineteenth century contrasts sharply with earlier views, it suggests the need for a new perspective in research on Brazil's economic history during this period. *Why* Brazil did not achieve a higher rate of economic development in the nineteenth century is one of the subjects of the chapters which follow.

Appendix I: The Evidence from Exports on Income Growth In Brazil, 1822–1913

The purpose of this appendix is to utilize the available data on the value of Brazilian exports in order to see what light these statistics shed on the country's overall rate of income growth between 1822 and 1913. Such an alternative analysis is all the more necessary because, as mentioned earlier in this chapter, the export statistics have previously been taken as indicating that nineteenth-century Brazil experienced rapid growth in per capita income. Our point of departure is the identity

$$X/Y = X/CS \cdot CS/Y \qquad (6)$$

where X denotes exports; Y, national income; and CS, the currency stock. All variables are expressed in *nominal* terms. Using dot notation and lower case letters to denote the annual percentage rates of change in the per capita form of these variables, we have:

$$\dot{x} - \dot{y} = (x/cs + (cs/y)) \qquad (7)$$

Equation (7) shows two determinants of changes in the country's export coefficient: movements in the ratio of exports to the currency stock, and changes in the ratio of the currency stock to national income. In the present context, although the nominal value of exports rose at a rate slightly above the growth of the currency stock, we know from equation (4) above that, because of increasing monetization, the per capita currency stock probably expanded more rapidly than per capita income. Transposing terms, we observe that

$$\dot{y} = \dot{x} - (x/cs) - (cs/y) \tag{8}$$

The data on the nominal per capita *mil-reis* value of exports show $\dot{x}$ and $(\dot{x}/cs)$ to have been 2.7 percent and -0.2 percent, respectively. Using the value for $\dot{z}$ and the intermediate figure for $\dot{v}$, we have $(cs/\dot{v}) = 0.3\%$. Hence, equation (8) indicates that in nominal *mil-reis*,

$$\dot{y} = 2.7\% + 0.2\% - 0.3\% = 2.6\%$$

This is the same as the estimate of nominal per capita income growth which was derived in the text of the chapter when we utilized, as in the present procedure, the intermediate figure for $\dot{v}$ (see Table 3.1). We can use other values of $\dot{v}$ and $(cs/\dot{y})$ in expression (8) to derive alternative income-growth estimates from Brazil's export data. By the nature of the underlying identities, these calculations yield nominal income-growth figures similar to those of Table 3.1.

These estimates based on the export data must also be deflated by a general price index; for as discussed in Chapter 6, prices in the economy as a whole rose at a higher rate than the exchange rate depreciated. Overall price inflation at the 2.5 percent annual rate cited in the chapter reduces the rate of real income growth to those presented in the text. Hence the export data confirm the earlier conclusion that Brazil probably experienced only moderate growth of per capita income between 1822 and 1913.

Appendix II: Income Growth in The Northeast and in the Rest of Brazil

As noted in the text, Brazil's large Northeast region experienced a rate of per capita income growth during the nineteenth century which was well below the pace of economic progress in the rest of Brazil. This observation raises some important questions: to what extent does the modest rate of per capita income growth in Brazil during the nineteenth century reflect nothing more than the poor experience of the Northeast? It is conceivable that the low aggregate rate for the country as a whole may be masking buoyant economic expansion in the rest of Brazil, excluding the Northeast. Perhaps per capita income in the rest of Brazil did in fact grow at an annual long-term rate similar to the 1.5 percent which the United States enjoyed during the nineteenth century?

In order to answer these questions, we will adapt a model proposed by Simon Kuznets for computing the rate of income growth in economic units whose parts, such as regions, experience very disparate rates of economic progress.[39] First, however, we require some additional notation. We will write a to denote the share of the Northeast in Brazil's total population; $(1-a)$ to denote the population share of the rest of Brazil; y, the level of real, monetized, per capita income in the country as a whole; y_{NE}, the level of real, monetized, per capita income in the Northeast; and y_{RB}, the level of real, monetized per capita income in the rest of Brazil. We observe that in any year:

$$y = a y_{NE} + (1-a) y_{RB} \qquad (9)$$

Data are available on the regional population shares, a and $(1-a)$, in 1822 and 1913. In addition, Claudio Haddad has provided an estimate of the level of y in 1911–13. And the growth rate estimates presented in the text of this chapter can be extrapolated back to 1822 to provide figures for y in that year. Consequently, if we have information on regional income differentials (the ratio of y_{RB} to y_{NE}) in 1822 and in 1913, we can solve equation (9) for the numerical value of y_{RB} in the initial and terminal years. Growth rates for y_{RB} during the nineteenth century can then be computed.

Because of the rough nature of the data used, this procedure can obviously provide only crude orders of magnitude in answer to the questions we have posed. However, the alternative to using a formal model with explicit parameter values is to base one's view of $\dot{y}_{RB}$ during the nineteenth century on casual impressions. These are usually derived from an informal model and implicit parameter values. Although such impressions can be helpful, credence is enhanced if the procedure and assumptions are explicit, so that they can be assessed for their logical consistency and plausibility. The reader can of course utilize the model developed here in conjunction with parameter values which he may find more plausible, and derive his own estimates of $\dot{y}_{RB}$.

The available data indicate that in 1822, some 52 percent of Brazil's population was in the Northeast.[40] In 1913, the figure was approximately 38 percent.[41] Haddad's estimate for Brazil's per capita GDP in 1911–13 has already been noted.[42] This figure can be extrapolated backward to 1822 by means of the growth rates presented in this chapter (−0.3 percent, +0.1 percent, and 0.8 percent) to derive estimates of the level of y in 1822. Initial and terminal figures for the per capita income regional differential, the ratio of y_{RB} to y_{NE}, are more difficult to obtain, however, and require a more extended discussion.

In 1939, the first year for which national income estimates are available for Brazil's individual states, per capita income in the rest of Brazil was twice as high as in the Northeast.[43] This was after almost three decades in which the rest of Brazil, particularly the Southeast and the South, had enjoyed agricultural and industrial expansion at rates higher than the Northeast.[44] Consequently, in 1913 a lower ratio of y_{RB} to y_{NE} must have prevailed. We will use a value of 1.75. This may overstate the terminal ratio, for it includes in the 'rest of Brazil' a populous state like Minas Gerais, whose development level in 1913 was well below that of São Paulo and Rio de Janeiro. If anything, then, the value utilized for the regional income disparity in 1913 would bias upward our estimates for the rate of growth of y_{RB}.

For the beginning of the nineteenth century, Roberto Simonsen speaks of the Southeast as being in serious economic crisis, a condition which suggests that income levels in the Northeast may have been ahead of those in the rest of the country.[45] However, information on regional slave importations and tax collections suggests that by 1822, at any rate, the situation may have changed. Because of these uncertainties concerning the initial regional income differ-

Table 3.3   *Estimates of the Annual Long-Term Rate of Growth of Real Monetized Per Capita Income in Brazil Outside of the Northeast,* y_{RB}, *1822–1913*

Assumed Initial Ratio of y_{RB} to y_{NE}	Alternative Values for $\dot{y}$ (%)		
	−0.3	+0.1	+0.8
	Implied Rates of Per Capita Income Growth Outside the Northeast (%)		
(1)	(2)	(3)	(4)
1.25	−0.2	0.2	0.9
1.0	−0.1	0.3	1.0
0.91	nil	0.4	1.1

Note: The values for $\dot{y}$ are from pp. 32–3. For the other parameter values, see the text.

ential, we will use a range of figures for the 1822 ratio of per capita income in the Northeast to per capita income in the rest of Brazil: that y_{NE} was 10 percent greater than y_{RB}; that the two were equal; and that y_{RB} was 25 percent greater than y_{NE}. Using the parameter values just discussed, we can solve equation (9) for the value of y_{RB} in 1822 and in 1913. We can then compute the annual long-term rate of growth of y_{RB} between the initial and terminal years. These estimates of the rate of per capita income growth in Brazil excluding the Northeast are presented in Table 3.3.

As expected, Table 3.3 shows rates of per capita income growth for the rest of Brazil which are higher than the estimates for the country as a whole. However, the only growth rates in Table 3.3 which are relatively high are those shown in column 4, which are derived from the 0.8 percent figure for aggregate $\dot{y}$. As discussed above, that value is based on an extreme lower bound (and highly unlikely) assumption concerning the level of V_{1822} in Brazil.[46]

Further, all of the estimates of Table 3.3 are well below the 1.5 percent annual growth rate enjoyed by the United States. Hence, Table 3.3 indicates that even excluding the Northeast, the pace of economic progress in Brazil was relatively low during the nineteenth century. This conclusion may differ from perceptions that are based on rapid expansion in Brazil's coffee region. On a per capita basis, however, that growth was less impressive. And the 'rest of Brazil' comprised much more than the coffee zones of the Southeast.

The assumptions and data that underly the estimates of Table 3.3 are clearly open to question. However, we have available a rough check on the reliability of the results. We can use the same procedure and parameters to compute the range of growth rates of per capita income in the Northeast. Since the values for the growth of y_{NE} are the other side of the coin of our estimates for the growth of y_{RB}, we can see whether they fall within the bounds of plausibility. The result of such computations for the growth of per capita income in the Northeast are set out in Table 3.4.

Table 3.4 conveys an impression of decline or, at best, moderate growth in per capita income. This is in accordance with the range of values which might have been set on the basis of *a priori* information concerning conditions in the Northeast during the nineteenth century. In particular, the intermediate figures (see column 3), which are probably the most likely values, are consistent with the picture proposed by Celso Furtado (himself from the Northeast).

Table 3.4 *Estimates of Annual Long-Term Rate of Growth of Real Monetized Per Capita Income in the Northeast of Brazil, y_{NE}, 1822–1913*

Assumed Initial Ratio of y_{RB} to y_{NE}	Alternative Values for $\dot{y}$ (%)		
	−0.3	+0.1	+0.8
	Implied Rates of Per Capita Income Growth in the Northeast (%)		
(1)	(2)	(3)	(4)
1.25	−0.6	−0.2	+0.5
1.0	−0.7	−0.3	+0.4
0.91	−0.8	−0.4	+0.3

Source: The values for $\dot{y}$ are from pp. 32–3. For the other parameter values, see the text.

He suggested a modest decline in per capita income levels in the region.[47]

The results of Tables 3.3 and 3.4, then, indicate that Brazil's relatively poor growth experience during the nineteenth century was not due exclusively to the special case of the Northeast. That region's lower growth rate did reduce the overall rate of increase; but the growth rate for the rest of Brazil was also below (and most probably, well below) the pace of economic advance achieved in the United States. Hence even if we exclude the large Northeast region, the nineteenth century does not seem to have been a period of rapid increase in Brazilian per capita income.

Notes

1 The lack of national income estimates for periods before the twentieth century has also hampered research on the economic history of other less-developed countries. The only pre-1890 estimates for such countries of which I know are Henry C. Aubrey's 'National Income of Mexico,' *Estadística*, 8 (July, 1950): Clark Reynolds, *The Mexican Economy: Twentieth Century Structure and Growth* (New Haven: Yale University Press, 1970) Appendix B; John H. Coatsworth, *The Mexican Economy, 1800–1910* (mimeo., University of Chicago, 1978), Chapter 1; Gisela Eisner's *Jamaica 1830–1930* (Manchester University Press, 1961); and M. Mukherjee's *National Income of India* (Calcutta, 1969), as cited in Simon Kuznets, *Economic Growth of Nations* (Cambridge, Mass.: Harvard University Press, 1971), p. 33. Because of the difficult data requirements which must be met to construct national income estimates on the basis of production data, the alternative methodology developed in this chapter may also be useful for research on the economic history of other less-developed countries.

2 Ernest Doblin, 'The Ratio of Income to Money Supply: An International Survey,' *Review of Economics and Statistics*, vol. 33, no. 3 (August 1951); Milton Friedman, 'Monetary Data and National Income Estimates,' *Economic Development and Cultural Change* (April 1961).

3 Carlos Manuel Peláez and Wilson Suzigan, *História Monetária do Brasil, 1800–1973* (Rio de Janeiro: IPEA, 1976), p. 212.

4 Friedman, 'Monetary Data,' op. cit.; Doblin, 'The Ratio of Income to Money Supply,' op. cit.; J. M. Keynes, *A Treatise on Money*, Vol. I (London: Macmillan, 1930), p. 31; John G. Gurley and E. S. Shaw, 'Financial Structure and Economic Development,' *Economic Development and Cultural Change*, vol. 15 (April 1967); Jacques Melitz and Hector Correa, 'International Differences in Income Velocity,' *The Review of Economics and Statistics*, vol. 52 (February, 1970); and especially

John G. Gurley, 'Repercusión del Desarrollo Económico en las Estructuras Financieras: Estudio de Cortes Transversales,' in *Estructura Financiera y Desarollo Económico* (Buenos Aires: Instituto Torquato di Tella, 1968). In addition, Daniel J. Khazoom has presented data showing a strong positive correlation between Z and V. See his 'Covariations in the Currency Ratio and the Velocity of Money in Underdeveloped Countries,' *Journal of Development Studies*, vol. 3 (October 1966).

5 Apart from the possibility that at low income levels cash balances may be a luxury good, among the reasons adduced for an inverse relation between level of per capita income and V are: (1) the growing differentiation in the structure of the economy which interrupts the synchronization of production and requires larger cash balances; (2) the relative decline in the share of production devoted to direct use by producers, for example, in agriculture; (3) the disproportionate growth in purely financial transactions; (4) the change in payment patterns, for example, from daily to weekly payments.

6 John G. Gurley, 'Repercusión del Desarrollo Económico,' op. cit., especially pp. 138–43, 150.

7 This figure is from Carlos Manuel Peláez and Wilson Suzigan, *A História Monetária do Brasil*, op. cit., p. 370. The work of Peláez and Suzigan has now made available direct estimates of the Brazilian money supply during the nineteenth century, and thus obviates the need to include Z in the technique for computing income trends from monetary data. I have nevertheless included this step to illustrate the use of the procedure for countries where monetary data are not available, but currency data are. The estimates of Peláez and Suzigan indicate that the nominal per capita money supply grew at an annual trend rate of 3.2 per cent from 1839 to 1913.

8 For material on the Brazilian banking system in that period, see J. Pandiá Calógeras, *A Política Monetária do Brasil* (São Paulo: Companhia Editora Nacional, 1960, [trans. by Thomaz Newlands Neto from the 1910 edition of *La Politique Monétaire de Brésil*]), Chapters 2 and 3.

9 The figure for the Brazilian currency ratio in 1913 is available in Raymond Goldsmith, *Financial Structure and Development* (New Haven: Yale University Press, 1969), Table D-4.

10 These observations were computed from monetary data in Paulo Neuhaus, *História Monetária do Brasil, 1900–1945* (Rio de Janeiro: IMBEC, 1975), p. 157; and from estimates of Brazilian GDP in the years 1911–13. The GDP estimates were graciously made available by Dr Claudio Haddad who specially compiled figures for the components of GDP that were not included in his estimates of Brazilian 'real product'. The estimates of Brazilian real product are contained in his *Growth of Brazilian Real Output, 1900–1947* (PhD dissertation, University of Chicago, 1974). Haddad's GDP estimates are presented in n. 35 of Chapter 2, above.

11 I owe this information to a personal communication from Professor Raymond Goldsmith. He bears no responsibility for the present discussion.

12 See the references cited on p. 20 in Chapter 2, above.

13 On Brazil's large domestic agricultural sector see Chapter 2, pp. 20–2, above.

14 Caio Prado, Jr, *The Colonial Background of Modern Brazil*, trans. by Suzette Macedo from *Formação do Brasil Contemporáneo*, 7th edn (São Paulo, 1963; Berkeley and Los Angeles: University of California Press, 1967), p. 219.

15 Leopoldo Solis, 'La Evolución Económica de México a Partir de la Revolución de 1910,' *Demografia y Economia*, vol. 3, no. 1 (1969), Cuadro 2.

16 See pp. 20–1 in Chapter 2, above.

17 See the estimates presented in Gurley, 'Repercusión del Desarrollo Económico,' op. cit., pp. 124–7. Two considerations, however, lead me to select 25 as an upper bound for V_{1822} even though this is higher than the figures presented by Gurley for most (contemporary) underdeveloped countries. First, as noted in the text, the importance of slaves in Brazil's labor force and their concentration in the economy's

high-productivity activities would greatly lower the demand for cash balances per unit of output. This condition which raises the magnitude of V is not present in current underdeveloped countries. In addition, institutional and economic changes may well have occurred which have lowered the income–money ratio for contemporary less-developed countries as compared with early nineteenth century. On the latter point, see Rondo Cameron, *Banking in the Early Stages of Industrialization* (New York, 1967), p. 318.

18   It has sometimes been suggested that the abolition of slavery in Brazil, in 1888, led to an abrupt shift in velocity, due to the sudden need to hold cash balances to pay wages to the labor force. In fact, however, the percentage of slaves in the Brazilian population declined steadily during the century, and by the time emancipation came, the slaves constituted only some 4 percent of the population.

19   The series on the Brazilian currency supply is based almost exclusively on the country's stock of *paper* currency. The data used are from Peláez and Suzigan, *História Monetária*, op. cit., Table A. 1. Although metallic currency had also been minted in Brazil before the beginning of the period, gold and silver money had generally left the country to settle international accounts. However, I have included in the initial currency stock the small sums of pre-1822 mintings of copper money, which are believed to have remained in circulation. Data on the latter are available in Instituto Brasileira Geografia e Estatística, *Anuário Estatístico, 1939/40* (Rio de Janeiro, 1941), p. 1354. The series for the annual value of the nominal Brazilian currency stock are presented in the Statistical Appendix, below.

20   See Appendix II of Chapter 6, below. As discussed there, serious conceptual problems attend any effort to derive a rate of price inflation for the country as a whole. In the context of an economy as unintegrated (horizontally as well as vertically) as nineteenth-century Brazil, aggregation is not an obvious procedure. However, focus on the nation as the unit of study is compelling and, for some purposes, useful. The estimates here are presented within that perspective.

21   Robert Gallman, 'Gross National Product in the United States, 1834–1909,' in *Output, Employment, and Productivity in the United States After 1800* (New York: National Bureau of Economic Research Publication, 1966), pp. 9–10; and Paul A. David, 'The Growth of Real Product in the United States before 1840: Some Controlled Conjectures,' *The Journal of Economic History*, vol. 28 (June 1967), p. 155.

22   See pp. 213–15 in Chapter 9, below.

23   Another way of seeing how equation (4) overstates the rate of growth for the entire economy is as follows. Writing Y for income and N for population, and using subscripts 1 and 2 to denote the monetized and non-monetized sectors, respectively, we can express the growth rate of per capita income in the economy as a whole as:

$$\left(\frac{\dot{Y}}{N}\right) = \left(\frac{\dot{Y_1 + Y_2}}{N_1 + N_2}\right) = \left(\frac{\dot{Y_1}}{N_1 + N_2}\right) + \left(\frac{\dot{Y_2}}{N_1 + N_2}\right) \tag{5}$$

The numbers given in Table 3.1 for the growth of monetized per capita income relate to $Y_1/(N_1+N_2)$. This is less than (Y_1/N_1) because, due to labor inflows from abroad and labor-force reallocation within Brazil, population in the monetized sector was growing at a rate higher than total population. The usual expectation for subsistence agriculture is of stagnant per capita output; that is, $(Y_2/N_2) \approx 0$. Because of the differential rates of population growth, population in the non-monetized sector was increasing at a rate lower than total population. That is, $\dot{N_2} < (N_1 + N_2)$; and therefore, $Y_2/(N_1+N_2) < Y_2/N_2$. Consequently, the last term on the right-hand side of (5) is negative. Thus the rate of growth of per capita income in the economy as a whole is less than the figures presented in Table 3.1, which relate only to monetized income.

24   Problems exist of course with using per capita income growth as a measure of

welfare gain for the broad population. For example, as James Meade notes in his *The Growing Economy* (London: Allen & Unwin, 1968), p. 64, the latter question requires consideration of changes in the distribution of income. We discuss that issue in Chapter 7, pp. 141–3, below. Note, however, that evaluation of welfare gains is less ambiguous in a situation where per capita income does *not* increase.

25 Information on the magnitude of slave importations to Brazil during this period is presented in David Eltis, 'The Export of Slaves from Africa, 1821–1843,' *Journal of Economic History*, vol. 37 (June 1977), p. 416.

26 Viotti da Costa presents data indicating that in 1830 the rate of natural increase of the slave population in São Paulo was −2.1 percent. See her *Da Senzala a Colonia* (São Paulo, 1966), p. 257. Peter Eisenberg cites negative rates of natural increase of 2–5 percent for the slave population of Pernambuco in the second decade of the century, with negative rates persisting thereafter. See his *The Sugar Industry of Pernambuco* (Berkeley and Los Angeles: University of California Press, 1974), p. 151, n. See also pp. 54–6, in Chapter 4.

27 Within the Southeast, however, there were important *intra*-regional shifts. The impact of rapid expansion in the new coffee-producing areas such as São Paulo was partly offset by the decline of the older coffee areas within the Southeast. On this decline, see Stanley J. Stein, *Vassouras: A Brazilian Coffee County, 1850–1890* (Cambridge, Mass.: Harvard University Press, 1957), pp. 213–49.

28 The especially poor economic experience of the Northeast during the nineteenth century is discussed in Nathaniel H. Leff, *Underdevelopment and Development in Brazil*, Vol. II, *Reassessing the Obstacles to Economic Development* (London: Allen & Unwin, 1982), Chapter 2. Analysis of nineteenth-century Brazil's development in terms of the disparate experiences of the Northeast, the domestic agricultural sector, and the Southeast coffee region is proposed in Celso Furtado, *Formação Econômica do Brasil*, 5th edn (Rio de Janeiro, 1963), p. 168.

29 This price index is discussed in Appendix I of Chapter 6, below. The price deflator cited in the next sentence of the text is discussed on pp. 98–100 of that chapter.

30 Some of the periods presented in Table 3.2 are relatively short. Hence one may wonder whether the full impact of inflation on the nominal currency stock can be captured by deflating annual observations. As discussed in Chapter 6, however, Brazil's inflation during the nineteenth century was characterized by a fairly swift adjustment process.

31 Data and discussion of Claudio Haddad's estimates of Real Output in Brazil are presented in Chapter 8, pp. 165–6, below. Information on the growth of Brazil's exports during various decades of the nineteenth century is presented in Table 5.1 of Chapter 5.

32 Claudio Contador and Claudio Haddad, 'Produto Real, Moeda, E. Precos: A Experiência Brasileira No Período 1861–1970,' *Revista Brasileira de Estatística*, vol. 36 (July 1975).

33 The time series presented by Contador and Haddad, 'Produto Real,' op. cit., Table 1 shows a decline at an annual trend rate of −0.4 percent. The absolute value of the *t*-ratio on the trend coefficient was 2.17. However, in reflection of the fluctuations around the trend during these four decades, the R^2 of the trend equation was only .12.

34 Furtado, *Formação Econômica do Brasil*, op. cit., Chapters 19 and 25, especially pp. 130–1 and 175–6. Furtado's estimates of income growth in Brazil during the nineteenth century have frequently been quoted for the picture they give of the Brazilian economy during this period. See, for example, William H. Nicolls, 'The Transformation of Agriculture in a Semi-Industrialized Country: The Case of Brazil,' in Erik Thorbecke (ed), *The Role of Agriculture in Economic Development*, National Bureau of Economic Research (New York: Columbia University Press, 1969), pp. 319–20. Furtado's estimates have also been cited in the form of the level of per capita income which his growth figures, extrapolated backward, imply for

1850. See, for example, William P. McGreevy, 'Recent Research on the Economic History of Latin America,' *Latin American Research Review*, vol. 3 (Spring 1968), p. 98, Table 11.

35 See Furtado, *Formação Econômica*, op. cit., Chapters 19 and 25.

36 See pp. 165–6 in Chapter 8.

37 One may wonder how Brazilian per capita income stood relative to per capita income in the United States at the beginning of our period, in 1822. The index-number problems – over time and across space – are so great as to deprive such a comparison of much welfare content. But in view of the concern and analytical interest many people have in the international income gap, the exercise to compute relative income levels in 1822 may be worthwhile. The estimates of Simon Kuznets (*Economic Growth and Structure* [New York, 1965], p. 305) and of Paul David ('The Growth of Real Output,' op. cit.) suggest that in 1822, per capita income in the United States was approximately 253 dollars (1950 prices). Our benchmark estimate of per capita GDP in Brazil is for 1911–13. This estimate is due to Claudio Haddad (see n. 35 in Chapter 2, above), and shows a figure of 215 dollars (1950 prices) in those years. Using the intermediate growth-rate figure of 0.1 percent per annum to extrapolate backward, we obtain an estimate of 196 dollars (1950 prices) for the level of Brazilian per capita income in 1822. This was some 78 percent of the US figure for that year. In the course of the nineteenth century, the difference in income levels widened steadily because of the large difference in rates of per capita income growth.

38 Furtado, *Formação Econômica*, op. cit., pp. 175–6.

39 See Simon Kuznets, 'Problems in Comparing Recent Growth Rates for Developed and Less-Developed Countries,' *Economic Development and Cultural Change*, vol. 20 (January 1972), pp. 192–9. A similar approach can be derived from Edmar L. Bacha, 'El Economista y el Rey de Belindia: Una Fabula para Tecnocratas,' *El Trimestre Económico*, vol. 42 (July 1975).

40 This percentage was computed from data which are presented in Stein, *Vassouras*, op. cit., p. 296. Following the convention of the Brazilian Institute of Geography and Statistics, the Northeast comprises Maranhão, Piauí, Ceará, Rio Grande do Norte, Paraíba, Alagoas, Sergipe, Bahia, Fernando Noronha and Pernambuco.

41 This figure is approximate, derived by interpolating between the Northeast's population share in 1890, 42 percent and its share in 1940, 35 percent. These data are from Ministério de Planejamento, *Demografia* (Rio de Janeiro, 1966), p. 78.

42 See n. 37, above.

43 This figure was computed from data presented in Douglas H. Graham, 'Divergent and Convergent Regional Economic Growth and Internal Migration in Brazil, 1940–1960', *Economic Development and Cultural Change*, vol. 18, no. 3 (April 1970), p. 380.

44 See, for example, the comparative growth data which are presented in John Wirth, *Minas Gerais in The Brazilian Federation, 1889–1937* (Stanford: Stanford University Press, 1977), p. 33.

45 See his *História Econômica do Brasil*, 4th edn (São Paulo: Companhia Editora Nacional, 1962), pp. 375, 380.

46 See pp. 31–2, above.

47 *Formação Econômica*, op. cit., pp. 117–8, 175.

4
Slavery, European Immigration, and the Elastic Supply of Labor

An economy in which output and the demand for workers can expand over long periods without putting upward pressure on real wages is said to face an elastic supply of labor. As we will see below, nineteenth-century Brazil was such an economy; and the consequences for the country's development were profound. Two institutions were of central importance in maintaining Brazil's elastic supply of labor: slavery and, later in the century, subsidized mass immigration from Europe. Because of their centrality in the country's pattern of economic expansion, these institutions require special discussion.

Slavery and the Demand for Labor Within Brazil

From the viewpoint of economic development, both the level of wages and their rate of increase over time are important. Slavery constrained each of these key variables during much of the nineteenth century. In fact, two distinct aspects of Brazilian slavery are relevant in this context. First, the possibility of importing slaves from Africa meant that Brazil's plantation owners could satisfy their growing demands for labor with relatively little utilization of workers from the domestic agricultural sector. Consequently, the export activities could increase their output substantially without bidding up wages within the Brazilian economy. During the first half of the nineteenth century, the British government attempted to stop the international flow of slaves to Brazil. Particularly after the 1820s, these efforts seem to have raised the price of slaves above the level that would otherwise have prevailed.[1] Nevertheless, the overall supply of imported slaves remained sufficiently abundant that, as discussed below, the real costs of slave labor for Brazil's 'advanced' sector remained virtually unchanged.

In addition to its effects on the course of wages over the period, at any point in time slavery permitted the planters to enjoy a lower level of labor costs than would otherwise have prevailed. Had it not been for slavery, Brazil's plantation owners would have had to pay their workers wages at the level of their opportunity cost – the income that free workers could obtain in their best alternative occupations. Because of the coercion inherent in the institution, however, slavery enabled the planters to keep their implicit wage costs below the opportunity cost of labor elsewhere in the economy. The effects of slavery on wages and the demand for free workers were especially important in nineteenth-century Brazil, for slaves were used in the economy's higher-productivity activities throughout the country. This experience contrasted with the situation in the United States, where slavery was concentrated in one region, the South, and did not directly influence labor-market conditions in the rest of the economy.

In order to understand why Brazil's planters generally preferred to employ slaves rather than workers from the domestic agricultural sector, it helps to consider some of the conditions that were involved in the comparison. Free workers were not considered more efficient than slaves, and slave labor was a close substitute for unskilled (as well as for skilled) free labor in many production activities.[2] The user cost of slave labor services was determined by: (1) the costs of capturing and transporting slaves from Africa; (2) the interest rate on the capital employed in the stock of slaves; and (3) the maintenance costs of slaves. Interest costs appear to have been relatively high in Brazil. Thus, in Rio de Janeiro, medium-term rates to coffee planters with ample collateral seem to have been approximately 12 percent in the 1850s and 1860s.[3] And in the Northeast, *short-term* rates for prime commercial paper averaged 16 percent between 1835 and 1841; and 11 percent between 1857 and 1869. The standard of living provided for slaves, however, was low. More generally, the supply price of slaves was apparently very low in relation to the discounted net income stream which was produced with their labor. This is suggested by the tenacious resistance of Brazil's plantation owners to British efforts at stopping the slave trade, and by the large number of slaves who were in fact imported in Brazil. Between 1800 and 1852, when the British navy forced suspension of slave imports, approximately 1.3 million slaves were brought to Brazil.[4]

The supply price of free labor was determined primarily by the opportunity cost of the income forgone in its alternative occupations. This labor was mainly confined to the domestic agricultural sector where, for the reasons discussed in Chapter 2, its productivity was not high. Nevertheless, people in that sector apparently had an income (which included leisure as well as the returns to their capital and entrepreneurship) which was appreciably above the user costs of slave labor.[5] This is attested by the fact that slaves were used in preference to free workers in Brazil's major export activities during most of the century. In addition, when proposals were discussed for replacing slave labor in Brazil, it was usually in terms of importing indentured workers from Europe or the Orient (or, occasionally, in terms of forced impressment of workers from Brazil).[6] The wages necessary to attract free workers from the domestic agricultural sector were considered too high.[7]

To obtain a clearer picture of the benefits which slavery afforded Brazil's planters, it would be useful to have quantitative information on the private returns to slaveowning. Pedro Carvalho de Mello has collected primary material from Rio de Janeiro (the country's largest slave market) which are valuable in this context. His data on slave rental rates and slave prices can be used to determine whether the net income which slaves generated was high or low relative to the level of slave prices.[8] The ratio of slave rental fees to slave prices is not equivalent to the rate of return to capital engaged in slaveholding.[9] To compute the latter, capital gains (or losses) and the 'depreciation' due to slave mortality must also be taken into account. However, if we abstract from mortality conditions for the moment (see below), and confine the analysis to the pre-1880 years, before expectations of abolition led to a decline in slave prices, Mello's data can be used to form a rough impression of the private returns which the planters derived from their use of slave labor (see Table 4.1).

Two points emerge from Table 4.1. First, the data suggest that slaveownership and the use of slave labor permitted relatively high private returns to slaveowners in nineteenth-century Brazil. For example, if we assume the average life expectancy of a slave to have been as low as four years and utilize Table 4.1's mean rental price ratio, 23.5 percent, the internal rate of return on an investment in slaves was 16 percent.[10] (Slaveowners' returns would of course be larger to the extent that life expectancy of their slaves exceeded four years.) Similarly, working with a more elaborate methodology, Dr Mello has also reached the conclusion that slavery was highly profitable for the slaveowners. Utilizing the Fogel–Engerman approach for computing the returns on investments in slaveowning and his own estimates of slave longevity in 1873, Mello has computed the rate of return for that particular year at 13 percent. This was well above the returns available

Table 4.1 *Estimates of Net Slave Rental Rates Divided by Slave Prices in Rio de Janeiro, 1835–1879*

Period	Percent	Period	Percent
1835–44	35.2	1863–66	21.1
1845–49	26.7	1867–70	21.7
1851–54	21.1	1871–74	24.7
1855–58	17.8	1875–79	23.1
1859–62	19.9		

Source: Computed from data in Pedro Carvalho de Mello, 'The Economics of Labor in Brazilian Coffee Plantations, 1850–1888,' (PhD dissertation, University of Chicago, 1977), p. 50, Table 16; p. 66, Table 19. See also n. 8, p. 72.

on most other investments in the Brazilian economy at the time.[11]

Table 4.1 also contains information pertinent in the context of our focus on changes *over time* in the private profitability of slaveowning. The data indicate no evidence of a long-term decline in private profitability for the planters. More generally, slave prices in current *mil-réis* rose sharply following the suspension of the overseas slave trade; Mello's data show an increase at a trend rate of 1.7 percent per annum between 1850 and 1878.[12] But during the same period, the rental rates for slaves (which reflected the marginal productivity of slave labor) also rose. Indeed, the increase in rental rates was even higher, 2.2 percent per annum. Thus, perhaps in response to the rise in slave prices, the planters seem to have adopted new practices which increased the productivity of slave labor.[13] Moreover, the rate of increase in the value of output per slave apparently exceeded the rise in slave prices. Consequently, the planters' advantage in using slave labor continued despite the increase in slave prices.

Finally, although this analysis relates to changes in the cost of slave labor in Rio de Janeiro, a similar situation seems to have prevailed in the Northeast. Data available on Pernambuco slave prices in current *mil-réis* indicate no statistically significant upward trend between 1852 and 1880.[14] Thus slavery was privately profitable for slaveowners in Brazil's higher-productivity activities at the beginning of the nineteenth century; and at least until the decade before emancipation (which came in 1888) became a real possibility, the planters' economic gains from using slave labor do not seem to have declined.

An Alternative Interpretation and the Actual Course of Events

The preceding discussion has stressed the relevance of purely economic considerations in determining the employment of slaves rather than of free workers in Brazil's advanced sector. This interpretation contrasts with some earlier treatments, which have focused instead on sociocultural factors. Thus it has been suggested that the planters were reluctant to use indigenous wage workers as a major source of labor supply because of social and ideological considerations. For example, the demand for free workers is alleged to have been limited because the planters preferred the seigneurial social relations permitted by slavery.[15] And on the supply side, Brazilian workers are also said to have preferred not to work on the plantations. Here the limitations reputedly derived both from the social stigma attached to activities that were associated with slavery, and from the high value which free workers accorded to leisure.[16]

Such attitudes may well have existed, raising the level of the wages that would have been necessary to attract workers from the domestic agricultural sector to Brazil's export activities. Nevertheless, the key condition in this context seems to have been the fact that the planters did in fact have available the lower-cost alternative of utilizing slaves. Had it not been for that option, it is unlikely that the preferences cited would have precluded larger-scale employment of workers from the domestic agricultural sector. As noted, the existence of slavery reduced the demand for free workers and the wages that were available to them. This consideration must be borne in mind when assessing a hypothetical situation of behaviour in the absence of slavery. The choices that Brazilian workers made between income and leisure (or other values) in the presence of low wages cannot be used to assess the trade-offs which they would have reached with the option of higher wages. Even with unchanging preferences, it is likely that increased demand for labor and higher wages would have evoked a larger supply of labor from the domestic agricultural sector. Similarly, product markets in Brazil's advanced sector were reasonably competitive. Hence, regardless of the discriminatory preferences of the planters, it is likely that in the absence of slavery competitive pressures would have led to the employment of free workers.[17]

These theoretical expectations are supported by a relevant empirical experience: the post-abolition course of events in the areas within Brazil which lacked the option of shifting to the utilization of European immigrant workers. Sociocultural preferences similar to those just discussed also existed in Brazil's Northeast and in the province of Minas Gerais. But those areas were unable to attract large-scale immigration, and the transition to a labor system employing free indigenous workers occurred smoothly.[18] This experience suggests that had the alternative of using low-cost slaves not been available earlier in the century, Brazil's planters would have expanded their output by employing free workers from the local economy.

In the historical course which Brazil actually followed through the first half of the nineteenth century, however, labor demands in the country's higher-productivity activities were supplied largely by low-cost slaves imported from Africa rather than by indigenous workers. The impact of slave importations on the incremental demand for free labor and wage levels within Brazil was far from trivial. The 1.3 million slaves imported into Brazil between 1800 and 1852 constituted more than one-fifth of the total increase in the country's population.[19] Moreover, because of the age selectivity of slave importation and the slaves' higher participation rates, their share in the growth of the country's labor force was much greater. Thus labor incomes were low in nineteenth-century Brazil not only because of the state of labor productivity but also because of the prevalence of slavery.

With the ending of overseas importation of slaves, the internal price of slaves rose.[20] The country's dwindling slave population was then reallocated to the activities (mainly coffee production on fertile new lands in São Paulo) where, because the marginal value-product of labor was greatest, the highest prices could be paid for slaves. At the same time, free labor was increasingly employed in the lower-productivity activities in the export sector. By the 1870s, free workers outnumbered slaves on the sugar plantations of Pernambuco.[21] The planters also began adopting rationalization practices and labor-saving techniques on a wider scale.[22]

The way in which Brazil dealt with the long-term labor situation posed by the abolition of slavery, however, reversed this movement and resulted in a reversion to the earlier pattern. As pressures for the end of slavery increased and the percentage of slaves in the Brazilian labor force declined, large-scale European immigration to Brazil began. This immigration was not attracted, however, by rising wages in Brazil. Rather, the Brazilian government subsidized the immigrants' transportation costs, thus increasing the net private returns to immigration (see below).[23] The inflow of workers from abroad was so great that real wages of the immigrants in São Paulo coffee sector apparently did not rise between the 1880s and 1914, a period of rapid economic expansion in that region.[24]

Economic Causes of the Decline of Brazilian Slavery

Other studies have discussed the political process by which slavery was gradually limited in Brazil until the achievement of abolition in 1888.[25] Some economic aspects of this process are also of interest, particularly as they contrast with the experience of the United States.

Table 4.2 presents estimates of Brazil's slave population during the nineteenth century. These figures suggest that the absolute number of slaves in Brazil rose from 1819 until mid-century, when overseas importation of slaves was stopped. The percentage of slaves in Brazil's population fell sharply, however, throughout this period. In 1819, slaves constituted approximately a third to a quarter of the country's population; in 1872, the figure was down to some 15 percent. Other estimates indicate a larger initial percentage of slaves in the country's

Table 4.2 *Estimated Slave Population of Brazil During the Nineteenth Century*

Year	Slave Population (thousands)	Year	Slave Population (thousands)
1819	1,107	1872	1,511
1823	1,148	1880	1,368
1850	2,500	1888	500
1864	1,715		

Source: Estimates cited in Stanley J. Stein, *Vassouras: A Brazilian Coffee County, 1850–1900* (Cambridge, Mass.: Harvard University Press, 1957), p. 294.

total population, and an even steeper decline.[26] By the time abolition came to Brazil, in 1888, the percentage of slaves in the total population was very small, approximately 4 percent.

The decline in the percentage of slaves was partly due to the high rates of natural increase which prevailed among Brazil's free population during the nineteenth century.[27] The fall in the absolute number of slaves after 1871 is also not entirely surprising, for in that year legislation was enacted which emancipated the children of slaves. In practice, however, that legislation was often evaded.[28] More generally, the decrease in the absolute number of slaves between 1850 and 1871 requires clarification. This decline was especially significant because of its consequences. The fall in the number of slaves had the important effect of reducing political support for slavery in some regions of the country. This shift, in turn, facilitated the move to complete abolition without compensation.

Several possible explanations might account for the absolute and relative decline of the slave population in Brazil. First, it may be suggested that the relative rate of return in the economy's slave-intensive activities fell during the century. The fall in the percentage of slaves would then reflect a sectoral shift in the composition of output within the economy. That hypothesis is not sustainable, however. The share of exports – the activities in which slaves were concentrated – did not decline in Brazil during the nineteenth century.

Another possible explanation might be that because of high supervision costs and lack of incentives, slave labor was relatively expensive, and hence employers preferred free labor to slaves. As indicated by our earlier discussion, however, that was not the case in nineteenth-century Brazil. Further, some historical evidence is available for comparing the relative costs of slaves and of free labor in efficiency units. During the 1850s efforts were actually made in Brazil to replace slaves with indentured European immigrants. Those experiments failed to justify the claim that such a labor system would be as profitable for the plantation owners as slavery.[29] And in view of the predominance of the planters in Brazil's political and social life, the relevant issue was the labor system which maximized planter profits.[30]

It may also be suggested that slavery declined in Brazil because the discounted net income stream generated by the output of slaves fell below their supply price. As we saw earlier, however, slavery continued to be privately profitable in the coffee sector until the early 1880s.[31] Indeed, the continuing rise in the price of slaves reflected the fact that use of slave labor remained profitable for the planters. And despite the rise in slave prices, the absolute number of slaves in the coffee zones of Rio de Janeiro and São Paulo continued to increase until 1883.[32] The experience with respect to manumission is also relevant in this context. Relative to the size of the total slave population, there was little manumission of productive slaves in Brazil until just before abolition. This observation, too, goes counter to an interpretation that slavery had become economically unviable.[33]

Finally, the decline in the number of slaves after 1850 might be attributed simply to the cessation of overseas slave imports. That is not a sufficient explanation, however. In the southern United States, overseas importation of slaves was also stopped by outside political forces. Nevertheless, as Conrad and Meyer have shown, the supply of slaves rose notably because of natural and/or market-induced demographic increase.[34]

In fact, slave breeding did not occur in Brazil after 1850. Quite the contrary, some slave children were manumitted at birth. More generally, the absence of slave rearing is indicated by information concerning the age structure of the slave population of the coffee plantations which were situated on depleted lands in Rio de Janeiro province. These plantations would have provided an ideal locus for slave rearing. Nevertheless, after overseas slave imports were stopped, the average age of the slave population on these plantations showed a steady increase rather than the decline which would have come with the institution of slave breeding.[35]

The absence of slave breeding in Brazil should not be surprising, for demographic and economic conditions were very different from those in the southern United States. Because of the relatively long period (approximately ten years) before 'investments' in slave rearing yield positive income, the discount rate for analyzing these investments is crucial. Conrad and Meyer cite 6–8 percent as relevant rates of interest for the ante bellum South. As noted earlier, however, interest rates in Brazil were much higher. Further, mortality rates for slaves were greater than in the United States. This condition, too, would have lowered the potential returns from rearing slaves: first, by increasing the costs of producing a surviving slave; and second, with lower life expectancy, by reducing subsequent income flows. Demographic conditions were so poor for slaves in Brazil during the nineteenth century that the death rate seems often to have exceeded the birth rate. Hence, the natural rate of increase for slaves may even have been negative.[36]

This was due both to the natality and to the mortality conditions of Brazil's slave population. Natality rates were low because of the high male–female ratio which derived from the sex selectivity of importation during the pre-1852 period, when males were the main object of importation. In 1872, there were approximately 114 males per 100 females in the total slave population.[37] This ratio prevailed two decades after the cessation of large-scale importation of slaves from abroad; hence it reflected nearly a generation of movement toward sex ratios which were demographically more normal than those which had obtained earlier. Consequently, in preceding decades the male–

female ratio must have been even higher, lowering the natality rate among the slave population. In addition, mortality rates for Brazil's slaves seem to have been higher, particularly for infants and children, than for the rest of the population. There are many reports of inhumane treatment, which would have increased death rates among the slave population. Significantly, such practices continued despite the end of overseas importation and the rise in slave prices after 1852.[38]

The overworking and poor maintenance conditions which led to high slave mortality rates in the post-importation period have sometimes been interpreted as evidence of economic irrationality on the part of Brazilian slaveowners. However, mortality rates need not be considered as determined completely by exogenous or non-economic conditions.[39] High mortality rates may have been the planters' response to high interest rates, and hence a low present value to the income that slaves would generate in the distant future. Under such conditions, overworking may have reflected an effort on the part of slaveowners to modify the time profile of their income stream, to obtain more output earlier, even at the cost of higher death rates for slaves and the sacrifice of later production.[40] Because of the discount rate and, relatedly, the demographic conditions of nineteenth-century Brazil, then, high rates of natural increase for the slave population were not economical for the planters. Hence in a marked contrast with the United States, once the overseas importation of slaves was stopped, the absolute number of slaves fell, and *a fortiori* so too did the percentage of slaves in Brazil's total labor force.

The ultimate abolition of slavery in Brazil was of course the result of a political process. But the balance of forces in that conflict was also affected by the economic changes we have considered. For the reasons discussed, the total number of slaves in Brazil fell after 1852. At the same time, one of Brazil's major regions, the Southeast, was experiencing rapid economic expansion while the other, the Northeast, was not. Coming together with the decline in the country's aggregate stock of slaves, the disparity in regional rates of development led to a major reallocation of Brazil's slave population. In 1823, approximately 39 percent of Brazil's slaves were located in the Southeast coffee provinces. By 1872, however, the figure had risen to 59 percent; and by 1886/7, to 67 percent.[41]

During the nineteenth century, Brazilian politics had a strong regional component.[42] What is important in the present context is that the geographical realignment of the slave-labor force weakened the political support for slavery within Brazil's regionally-based political system. First, by the 1880s the Northeast had made the transition to an economy which could rely on free labor. Hence the region did not offer diehard resistance to the abolition of slavery in Brazil. The erosion of the Northeast's commitment to slavery was important; for the region was a major source of support for the country's imperial regime. The economic changes we have discussed also altered political positions on slavery within the Southeast. The country's declining stock of slaves implied a sharp rise in the coffee planters' incremental labor costs (see below). This situation led to policy adjustments which ultimately changed political alignments within the powerful coffee sector. Facing the prospect of a large and discontinuous increase in their labor costs, the São Paulo coffee planters developed a new source of low-cost workers in subsidized European immigration. With the new arrangements operating effectively, by the middle 1880s, São Paulo, at least, could afford to accept rather than resist abolition. We will consider the *Paulistas'* policy response shortly. First, however, let us consider some other effects of the process we have analyzed.

Some Effects of the Decline of Slavery

The process we have discussed involved a gradual decline, spread over decades, for slavery in Brazil. This gradualism facilitated the country's economic adjustment to alternative labor-market institutions. In addition, as just noted, the fall in the number of slaves helped smooth Brazil's course through the political crisis engendered by the campaign for abolition. Although slavery remained privately profitable until the end, the economic implications of emancipation were not drastic enough to cause a major upheaval. Consequently, Brazil was spared the terrible human, political, and economic costs which the shift from slave to free labor helped provoke in the United States.

The extent to which Brazil's former slaves improved their monetary incomes as a result of emancipation is not completely clear.[43] In principle, the freedmen should have benefited because of the alternative opportunities afforded by the availability of abundant land in Brazil's interior. In practice, large-scale migration to these lands was often limited by the capital-market imperfections, high transport costs and illiberal land policy noted in Chapter 2. Following abolition, the former slaves often left their previous plantations and moved in search of better conditions within their immediate localities.[44] Such labor mobility and the shift to a more competitive labor market may have enabled workers to receive higher incomes than would have been possible – other conditions remaining the same – under the previous system of predatory wage determination. The problem was that other conditions did not remain the same. Wages in the coffee region were very much affected by the onset of mass immigration from Europe which came with the decline of slavery. Moreover, the connection between the demise of slavery and the beginning of large-scale European immigration was causal and purposeful rather than mere circumstantial (see below). Finally, in the Northeast, the freedmen's opportunities for economic betterment were constrained by the region's special macroeconomic difficulties.[45]

In addition to wages, however, other conditions may have entered the freedmen's utility functions; their welfare was also affected by the new opportunities for leisure, uncertainty, and liberty. If we take these other considerations into account, the welfare effects of abolition appear less ambiguous. After emancipation, the former slaves had to share in the risks and uncertainties of changing market conditions. But as slaves they had also suffered from the risks and instability inherent in the possibility of being sold to other owners. The former slaves do seem to have valued highly their new opportunities for increased leisure, and for self-determined rates of labor-force participation.[46] Another benefit which accrued to the freed slaves was social and psychological: the possibility of a family life free of the constraints imposed by individual slaveowners or by the slave system.[47]

Further, even considering the limits to personal and economic freedom which former slaves faced in Brazil, the intrinsic value of human liberty must also be taken into account. And presumably the assessment of the welfare changes which accompanied the freedom from the inhumanities of slavery should be made in terms of the values of the people immediately concerned. Brazil's slaves made clear their own preferences on this issue; in the year preceding abolition, mass slave escapes from bondage occurred with increasing frequency. Moreover, the fact that the number of flights accelerated over time suggests that they were not based on imperfect information concerning the costs and benefits of freedom. Though abolition may have been 'nearly painless' for the planters, it hardly follows (as some historians have concluded) that the erstwhile slaves did not also benefit.[48]

Abolition thus seems to have had important personal consequences for the slaves who were freed. The effects on Brazil's economic structure and development were less significant. In itself, the change from slave to wage labor seems to have altered little in the economy. The impact on output levels was minimal as free workers, including immigrants, substituted easily for slave labor. And contrary to what has sometimes been suggested, it is not clear that the shift to wage labor affected the level and composition of final demand.[49] These were determined mainly by the level of wage income or implicit labor costs, regardless of the institutional channel through which sustenance was provided. The movement to cash wage payments might in principle have brought the benefits of increased monetization.[50] But abolition was followed by the inflationary upsurge of the *encilhamento*, which led to severe 'financial repression' in the subsequent decade. The decline of slavery did stimulate Brazil's efforts to attract European immigration. Here too, however, the structural effects seem to have been less far-reaching than has sometimes been suggested.

European Immigration

Table 4.3   *Gross Non-Slave Immigration to Brazil, 1820–1909*

Period	Annual Average of Immigrants Over the Decade	Period	Annual Average of Immigrants Over the Decade
1820–29	640	1870–79	20,780
1830–39	570	1880–89	47,890
1840–49	620	1890–99	118,170
1850–59	11,300	1900–09	66,650
1860–69	9,850		

Source: Imre Ferenczi and Walter F. Wilcox, *International Migrations,* Vol. I (New York: National Bureau of Economic Research, 1929), pp. 236–7.

With the cessation of overseas importation of slaves and the downward pressure which they had exerted on wages, European immigration to Brazil accelerated (see Table 4.3). Brazil could not compete with the United States for mass immigration, however, and the flow was numerically small. By the mid-1870s, it was apparent to some of the coffee sector's political leaders that, from the viewpoint of maximizing planter returns, they faced a potential labor-supply problem.[51] The extension of the railway network to new production zones in São Paulo indicated that a large increase in coffee output could be expected, and with it, a large increase in the demand for labor. Competitive bidding for the country's remaining stock of slaves, however, would lead to a sharp increase in labor costs. Accordingly, some *Paulista* political leaders sought a monopsonistic, class solution which would shift downward their aggregate labor-supply schedule, and thereby minimize the *fazendeiros'* (coffee planters') wage costs.

The coffee sector's labor market, *circa* the mid-1870s, is depicted schematically in Figure 4.1. The current annual demand for labor is represented by the curve D_1. Its intersection with the slave-labor supply curve ABC gives an implicit unit labor cost of w_1. The country's fixed stock of slaves, however, imposed a kink in the labor-supply schedule at B. Thereafter, the expansion of coffee production and the ensuing shift of the demand for labor to D_2 would intersect with the higher supply schedule of free laborers from within Brazil, FG. This intersection would lead to a higher average (and *a fortiori*, marginal) unit labor cost of w_2. By promoting a flow of subsidized immigration from Europe, however, the planters could transform the situation. Such measures would in effect shift the relevant labor-supply curve for the D_2 period from ABG to ABE, with the lower unit labor cost of w_3.[52]

Recognizing that they would otherwise face a sharp increase in their labor costs, the planters pressed Brazil's central government and the

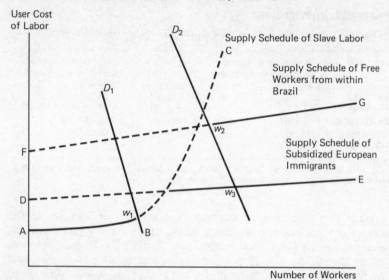

Figure 4.1   *The Coffee Sector's Labor Market circa the Mid-1870s*

government of São Paulo province to pay the transportation costs of immigrants from Southern Europe. Such subventions had two effects on potential European emigrants. First, without raising wage levels in Brazil, transportation subsidies raised the net private returns to immigration to Brazil. Second, the subsidies overcame the capital-market imperfection which would otherwise have prevented destitute Europeans from emigrating at all. Thus, by paying transportation costs Brazil could attract immigrants who, if they could have financed their own immigration, might have gone to the United States or Argentina, where wages were higher.

On the supply side, immigration to Brazil was facilitated by the crisis in Italian agriculture. Also, occasional economic downturns in the United States and in Argentina enabled Brazil to increase its share in the total supply of European immigrants in some years.[53] As a result of these conditions, the flow of Europeans to Brazil increased sharply. The change was most dramatic in the case of the São Paulo coffee sector. Between 1880 and 1885, an average of 4,300 immigrants entered São Paulo. In 1886, the figure was 9,500; and in 1887, the year before abolition, the figure was 33,000. Overall, between 1885 and 1909, some 2.8 million European immigrants entered Brazil. Almost all of these people went to the Southeast.

Some other aspects of this process are also noteworthy. As already indicated, immigration was facilitated by the Brazilian policy of subsidizing transportation costs, thus overcoming the capital-market imperfection which restricted emigration by impoverished Europeans to the New World. The immigrants were not drawn by a high level of wages, which was not offered them in Brazil. Local labor markets, however, were reasonably competitive. In addition, the *Paulistas* developed innovations in labor contracts which relieved workers of much of the risk that they would have borne under a pure share-cropping system.[54] Nevertheless, living conditions for the immigrants were so poor that in 1902 the Italian government attempted to ban subsidized emigration to Brazil. The flow of immigrants continued, however, because of the possibilities that Brazil offered for eventual upward mobility, including ownership of land.

Between 1885 and 1913, São Paulo province and Brazil's central government spent some £11 million on immigration subsidies.[55] Since these funds came largely from taxes levied on the coffee sector, they did not involve a government 'giveaway'. One may wonder, therefore, why the planters preferred to have their resources utilized for subventions rather than apply them directly in paying higher wages. The answer is straightforward. By using subsidies to shift downward their labor-supply schedule, the planters saved on their marginal and on their inframarginal labor costs, both current and future.

European immigration yielded some major benefits for Brazil's economic development. Immigrants (and their children) were to play an important role in the supply of entrepreneurship for industrialization and in modernization of the rural sector of the Southeast.[56] The immigrants also had a higher educational level than the native-born Brazilian population. Thus the 1920 census showed an illiteracy rate of 56 percent for immigrants as compared with 73 percent for the native-born population of São Paulo state.[57] Some of the gains which are alleged to have stemmed from immigration, however, seem to have been overstated. For example, immigrants came to account for a disproportionately large share of the workers in São Paulo's manufacturing sector. This may simply have reflected the immigrants' greater mobility at the time the *Paulista* industrial sector was emerging. The immigrants' heavy participation in the local industrial work force did not occur because they constituted a trained and disciplined industrial labor force. Most of the immigrants were uneducated peasants who came from rural zones of southern Europe rather than from the technologically more advanced European areas. For the same reason, European immigration probably did not make as large an absolute contribution to the Brazilian human-capital stock as did nineteenth-century immigration to the United States.[58]

More generally, European immigration to Brazil has often been credited with developmental effects for which it was neither a necessary nor a sufficient condition; and which probably would have occurred in a similar fashion in the absence of immigration. Thus the advent of the European immigrants with their 'advanced' consumption habits has sometimes been considered an important factor in the growth of an internal market for manufactured goods in Brazil.[59] This interpretation, however, neglects the austere consumption standards which many immigrants adopted in their effort to accumulate savings for remission abroad or for purchase of land in Brazil.[60] Even more importantly, the main force behind the growing demand for manufactures in Brazil was the growth of the domestic market which accompanied the expansion of coffee exports and the spread of railways within the Southeast.[61] No special cultural impact of European immigrants was needed; numerous studies of diverse societies have in fact demonstrated a consistent pattern in the close relationship between higher income levels and the demand for manufactured goods.[62] And as discussed below, wage incomes (which were the main element in the emergence of a market for basic industrial products in Brazil) might well have been higher without European immigration.

Similarly, Brazil's urbanization and particularly the growth of the city of São Paulo have also been attributed largely to immigration. But it is difficult to imagine how such urban growth would have occurred without other economic changes, such as industrial development. The latter owed little to European immigration *per se* (see Chapters 8 and 9 below). The experience of the Northeast, which did not attract much European immigration, offers a comparative perspective which is useful in this context. Transportation facilities were no more developed in that region than in Brazil's Southeast, nor were cultural attitudes likely to have been more conducive to mobility. But in the absence of immigration's deplacement effect, native-born workers in the Northeast displayed considerable labor mobility – both to the city of Recife and to the more distant Amazon region – in response to economic incentives. Thus Bainbridge Cowell's study of parish registers in Recife has shown that in the 1870s, approximately 26 per cent of the city's population had come from other parts of Pernambuco or from neighbouring provinces.[63] In the 1890s and 1910s, the figure was up to 39 percent. Further, internal migration in Brazil was not limited, as has sometimes been supposed, by political constraints. Between 1872 and 1910, hundreds of thousands of Northeasterners emigrated to the Amazon region.[64] In the light of these indications of substantial labor mobility within Brazil, it appears likely that if overseas immigrants had not been available, the supply of labor to fill the growing demand for industrial workers in São Paulo and Rio de Janeiro would have come from domestic sources.

European immigrants certainly provided some entrepreneurship and human capital which facilitated Brazil's economic development. But to end the discussion with those conclusions would be misleading. For it would ignore the fact that the massive immigration of unskilled workers also increased the supply of labor, and thus led to a lower general wage level than would otherwise have prevailed.[65]

The Elastic Supply of Labor

Large-scale European immigration, then, guaranteed the continuation of two structural features of the Brazilian economy which had earlier existed with the importation of slaves from Africa. By bringing in workers from overseas, Brazil's planters were able to maintain wage levels in the advanced sector below the opportunity cost of labor elsewhere in the economy. Further, the possibility of importing labor directly in response to the growing demand for workers in the advanced sector also had another important consequence. Both slave importation and the program for subsidized immigration meant that shifts in the demand curve for labor in effect determined shifts in the supply schedule of workers.

We can now examine the available historical material to see whether slavery and subsidized European immigration did in fact ensure an elastic supply of workers in Brazil during the nineteenth century. That is, could output and employment in the 'advanced' sector of the economy expand over the long term with minimal upward pressure on real wages and labor costs? Apart from its other effects, an elastic labor supply was important for the distribution of income in nineteenth-century Brazil. The elasticity of substitution in this economy was probably below unity (see Chapter 7). Hence, if wage levels had been higher, the share of labor in the country's national income would have been greater.

As noted earlier, despite the extraordinary expansion of output and in the demand for labor which occurred in São Paulo between 1880 and 1914, real wages in the coffee sector do not seem to have increased. Similarly, in the Northeast, domestic demographic and economic conditions led to a situation in which real wages of field hands may even have fallen between 1876 and 1896.[66] For the preceding half-century, the data collected by Pedro Carvalho de Mello on slave rental rates and slave purchase prices enable us to consider the long-run course of labor costs in Rio de Janeiro. This was an area where the demand for labor was expanding vigorously between 1835 and 1888, and where rising labor costs might well have been expected. Table 4.4 presents the results of trend regressions which use Dr Mello's data.

Table 4.4 shows that between 1835 and 1888, slave rental rates in nominal *mil-réis* rose at an annual trend rate of 1.8 percent (see row 1). For slave purchase prices, the rate of increase was 2.0 percent per annum. These data, however, relate to rates of increase in current prices, uncorrected for inflation. It is likely that the rate of price increase in Brazil during this period was at least 2 percent per annum.[67] If this was indeed the case, then the data of Table 4.4 indicate that

Table 4.4   *Trend Rates of Change in Nominal Slave Rental Rates and Purchase Prices in Rio de Janeiro, 1835–1888*

Period	Annual Percentage Trend in:	
	Rental Rates	Purchase Prices
	(Percentage points per annum)	
(1) 1835–88[a]	1.8*	2.0*
	(11.79)	(5.80)
(2) 1835–49	−1.9*	1.5*
	(3.43)	(4.22)
(3) 1850–88[a]	1.4*	−0.2
	(7.03)	(0.48)

Notes: These regressions were computed from data in current prices. Absolute values of the *t*-ratios are in parentheses. Asterisks denote trend coefficients significantly different from zero at the .01 level.

[a] The period for the trend in slave prices terminates in 1887 rather than in 1888.

Source: Computed using least-squares regression with data presented in Pedro Carvalho de Mello, 'The Economics of Labor in Brazilian Coffee Plantations, 1850–1888', (PhD dissertation, University of Chicago, 1977), p. 50, Table 16; p. 66, Table 19.

real labor costs did not rise during the half century preceding 1888.

This conclusion is reinforced if we consider the results of some other regression equations which, to avoid obfuscation, are not presented in Table 4.4. In those equations we use the *mil-réis* price of coffee to deflate Mello's data, and then compute the trends in the 'real' slave hire rates and purchase prices.[68] The trend rates of change during the period 1835–88 is: −0.3 percent per annum for the deflated series of slave rental rates (with a *t*-ratio of 1.43); and −0.1 percent for the deflated observations of slave purchase price (with a *t*-ratio of 0.39) between 1835 and 1887. Thus neither deflated series of labor costs shows an increase over this period. We noted earlier that between 1880 and 1913 real labor costs apparently did not rise in São Paulo (the area in which the demand for labor was expanding most vigorously in *that* period). Taken together with our present findings, then, we can conclude that at least from 1835 to 1913, Brazil's 'advanced' sector faced a highly elastic supply of labor.

Table 4.4 also shows the trend rates of change in nominal labor costs for two distinct sub-periods. These are divided at 1850, the year in which large-scale importation of slaves from Africa was stopped.[69] In the pre-1850 years, the supply of slaves increased so rapidly that rental rates actually fell (see row 2). Slave prices in current *mil-réis* rose, however, reflecting capital gains in anticipation of the impending cessation of imports. By contrast, from 1850 to 1888, slave prices showed no overall trend (a consequence of the rise following 1850 and the fall preceding abolition). However, rental rates, which provide a purer measure of actual labor costs, show a 1.4 percent annual trend rate of increase. This was probably below the pace of price inflation in Brazil.

The elastic supply of labor to Brazil during the nineteenth century depended heavily, as we have seen, on the importation of low-cost workers from abroad.[70] This pattern of labor supply had important effects both on the 'advanced' and on the 'backward' sectors of the Brazilian economy. In the advanced sector, low wage levels led to lower capital–labor and land–labor ratios than would otherwise have prevailed. And over time, the elastic labor supply dampened pressures for capital deepening and labor-saving technical progress. As noted earlier, some shifts in the latter direction did in fact occur during a brief interval in the 1870s. But the onset of mass immigration permitted a return to the earlier pattern, with its consequences for factor proportions, wage levels, and income distribution.

The elastic supply of overseas labor also had important consequences for Brazil's backward sector. Because of the alternative source of labor supply from abroad, the expansion of output in Brazil's higher-productivity activities did not lead to a large-scale absorption of workers from the domestic agricultural sector, with, ultimately, rising real wages. These workers might have come initially from the numerous free population residing in and near the zones of export production and, later, from more distant areas. The domestic agricultural sector's labor force was large relative to the size of the export and urban-based activities, and was fully capable of supplying the advanced sector's labor demands.[71] But this 'natural' pattern of economic development was not permitted to unfold. The planter class intervened with political action, first in resisting British pressures to restrict the importation of slaves, and subsequently in instituting the program of mass immigration.

The similarities between Brazil's experience and W. Arthur Lewis's model of economic development under conditions of 'unlimited supplies of labor' are clear.[72] The major difference from the Lewis model is that in Brazil, the 'unlimited supply' of labor to the expanding, more productive sector came mainly from overseas. In this respect, the Brazilian case resembles the model discussed by Myint and others in connection with the 'opening' of Africa and Asia in the nineteenth century.[73] Further, the implications for wages, the distribution of income, and structural economic change in Brazil seem to have been similar to the colonial pattern, even though a foreign power was not present in this instance. The contrast is with a country like Australia in the last half of the nineteenth century. There, government efforts to ease upward pressures on wages through subsidized immigration lagged behind government capital formation, and were subsequently dropped.[74] Those conditions led to higher capital–labor ratios and rising real wages. In addition, with labor scarcity emerging as a feature of Australian life, a powerful trade union movement developed, which was to exert a major influence on the country's subsequent economic and political evolution.

Our discussion has noted the effects which continuing large increases in the supply of labor had on Brazil's economic development. An important question remains to be answered. Partly as a result of large-scale immigration, the population of the United States, too, increased at a rapid pace during the nineteenth century. Thus between 1860 and 1910, the US population grew at a rate of approximately 2.2 percent per annum.[75] If a high rate of demographic growth dampened upward pressures on wages in Brazil, why did not the same result occur in the United States? These two economies differed in other important respects, however. Consequently, it should not be surprising that rapid population growth led to different outcomes in the two cases.

First the relevant measure in this context is not the rate of population increase *per se*, but rather the magnitude of population growth relative to the pace of capital formation and technical progress. Those productivity-augmenting conditions rose more buoyantly in the United States than in Brazil during the nineteenth century.[76] In addition, other differences derived from the circumstance that income levels and the economic opportunities for immigrants were generally greater in the United States than in Brazil. As the preferred destination for voluntary emigrants from Europe, the United States had greater access to skilled and educated workers through immigration. Accordingly, the positive impact of immigration on the quality of the labor force was greater in the United States. Further, because Brazil was not as attractive a destination as the United States, relatively little of the population movement to Brazil was self-financed. That is, the vast majority of international immigrants who could pay their own transportation and resettlement costs, and who could therefore decide on their own destinations generally did not come to Brazil in this period. Consequently, most of the labor importation to Brazil during the nineteenth century was financed by Brazilian capitalists. (In earlier decades, the financing mechanism operated through the market for African slaves, and later via the subsidized immigration program.) Because of these financing arrangements, a larger fraction of the people brought to Brazil were workers rather than dependents. Hence, a given amount of population in-movement to Brazil meant a larger increase in the supply of labor than in the United States. The effects on wages and capital formation were correspondingly greater.

Finally, the fact that, in contrast to the situation in the United States during the nineteenth century most of the population movement to Brazil was financed by local capitalists, also had another implication. This financing condition made for tight links between changes in the demand for workers in Brazil and changes in the supply through importation. With an abundant supply initially of captive Africans and, subsequently, of impoverished southern Europeans, the magnitude and timing of labor in-movements to Brazil were closely governed by shifts in Brazil's demand for labor. Consequently, disequilibrium states in which the demand for workers exceeded the supply of workers in local labor markets – with ensuing upward pressure on labor costs – were relatively brief. For this reason, a self-reinforcing dynamic in which higher wages induced capital deepening and technical progress is noticeable mainly for its absence in nineteenth-century Brazil.

As this discussion indicates, the economic context within which immigration and population growth took place in nineteenth-century Brazil was very different from that of the United States. The effects of these demographic conditions on economic development were also different in Brazil. The historical results of this economic process in Brazil are summarized in Table 4.4. The information presented there concerning negligible increase in real wages over half a century (coming together with indications of a similar experience in subsequent decades) is all the more poignant because it relates to the most prosperous and expansionary sector of Brazil's economy during the nineteenth century.

A Postscript

Our earlier discussion also implied a suggestion concerning welfare judgments on population growth and large-scale labor importation to Brazil in the nineteenth century. In considering those phenomena, it is important to distinguish between the interests of the planters and those of the rest of the population. The interest of the *fazendeiros* (planters) in securing an elastic supply of low-cost labor is clear. The rest of Brazil's population, however, might well have benefited from a reduction in the supply of unskilled labor from overseas.

One can readily understand the planters' concern to avoid the adjustment costs and the higher wages that would have been involved in a transition to generalized use of local workers. And in view of the *fazendeiro's* social and political influence in nineteenth-century Brazil, it is not surprising that the government and elite opinion, too, considered that such a shift would entail a 'labor crisis'. Contemporary intellectual perceptions were also colored by racial preconceptions prevalent in the nineteenth century, which doubted the capacities of the *caboclos* (half-breeds) and mulattoes of Brazil's domestic agricultural sector.[77] What is surprising, however, is that more recent observers have often adopted the perspective of Brazil's dominant class in its concern about a 'labor shortage'. Similarly, later scholars, too, have sometimes failed to consider more carefully the possibility that Brazil could have experienced a development pattern based on domestically supplied labor.[78] Had it not been for the continuing large in-movements of population, which kept labor cheap relative to capital, Brazil might have followed a very different course in its economic (and social) development.

It may be suggested that the higher wages necessary to attract workers from the domestic agricultural sector would have slowed the expansion of Brazil's higher-productivity activities. Many observers, however, would consider higher wages rather than export growth to be the essence of economic development. Moreover, in some instances, low wages in the present may be acceptable on general welfare grounds because they permit capital formation and higher wages in the future. In the Brazilian case, however, the elastic supply of low-cost labor from abroad continued for generations. In addition, putative long-term gains which may have accrued to Brazilian workers as a result of labor importation must be assessed with a positive discount rate, in reflection of time preference. Assessed in these terms, the gains to Brazil's workers appear to have been negative.

Further, the extent to which higher wages would have slowed growth in Brazil's advanced sector is itself not clear. As noted earlier, the planters might well have offset increased labor costs with capital deepening and technical progress, and thus maintained profits and expansion despite higher wages. Moreover, Brazil's coffee exports depended far more on the country's specific land and climate conditions than on cheap labor. Similarly, in the Brazilian manufacturing sector, ample tariff protection and the larger domestic market made possible by higher wages could well have permitted comparable rates of industrialization despite higher wage payments. These considerations suggest an important conclusion: Brazil's economic growth might have proceeded unimpaired, but with a different development pattern in wages and income distribution, if the advanced sector had utilized internally-supplied workers more extensively rather than drawing so much of its labor supply from overseas.[79]

As noted earlier, during the nineteenth century Brazil had a large, native-born labor force which could have supplied the labor demands of the expanding, higher-productivity sector.[80] In addition, this counter-factual suggestion is supported by a later experience which occurred in the 1930s. Nationalist motivations led the Brazilian government to restrict large-scale immigration of unskilled labor from abroad. Nevertheless, the flow of workers from the São Paulo hinterland and from other regions within Brazil was sufficiently large that the modern sector in the Southeast continued its expansion without impediment.[81] There is a final irony here. By the time the government curtailed overseas immigration, the rate of natural population increase in Brazil had risen sharply. As a result, despite the slackening in immigration, the growth of the country's labor force actually accelerated.[82] Consequently, Brazil's pattern of economic expansion with a highly elastic labor supply continued.

Conclusions

Nineteenth-century Brazil had an abundance of land, but institutional conditions acted to prevent 'real' factor endowments from inducing a form of agricultural development which was characterized by high labor productivity. Thus government land policy and capital-market imperfections limited access to land. Similarly, the prevalence of slavery throughout the economy's advanced sector meant that labor costs to the plantation owners were kept below the opportunity costs of labor in the rest of the local economy.

As this discussion indicates, agricultural productivity in Brazil may have suffered from static factor-market imperfections. But even more important from the viewpoint of economic development was the capacity of the country's planters to shift downward their labor-supply schedules in response to their own growing demands for workers. By continuing the importation of slaves despite British opposition, and later, by instituting subsidized mass immigration from Southern Europe, the planter class in effect linked increases in the supply of labor directly to increments in the demand. Historically, these conditions seem to have led to an expansion pattern in which the economy's advanced sector could grow for almost a century without rising real wages.

The elastic supply of labor meant that the growth of the labor force in Brazil's advanced sector was high relative to the pace of capital formation and technical progress. The flow of low-cost workers from overseas also limited the absorption in higher-productivity activities of workers from Brazil's large domestic agricultural sector. This displacement effect occurred because the inflow of imported labor was large relative to the growth of demand for workers in Brazil's advanced sector (see the Appendix to this chapter). There were two potential sources of raising labor incomes within this economy: reallocation of workers from the backward to the advanced sector, and rising wages within the advanced sector itself. The country's highly elastic supply of labor from overseas had a negative impact on both.

The elastic supply of labor affected factor proportions, technical progress, and the distribution of income in nineteenth-century Brazil. In addition, feedback effects were also present, as the absence of significant upward pressures on real wages dampened movements toward increasing capital–labor ratios or labor-saving technological change. Because of the impact of the continuing flow of low-cost labor from overseas on wage levels, such events as the abolition of slavery and the onset of European immigration did little to change the basic pattern of the country's economic and social development. Although continuing importation of unskilled labor enabled the planters to maintain their private returns, the consequences for the rest of the population and for the country's overall development were prejudicial. This experience also suggests that conclusions concerning the welfare effects of population growth in nineteenth-century Brazil may be a function of the observer's class perspective. Indeed, class interests were so disparate in this case as to raise serious questions concerning the validity of using the nation as a unit of analysis. For this reason, little objective meaning can be attached to questions concerning the optimal rate of population increase for 'Brazil' during the nineteenth century.[83] Finally, the persistent feature of a highly elastic supply of labor from overseas during the nineteenth century has an important implication for comparative economic analysis. Because of this structural feature, Brazil's experience in nineteenth-century economic expansion was closer to the model of foreign-colonized areas in Asia and Africa than to the case of a region of recent settlement like Australia.

Appendix: Mass Immigration and Wages in the São Paulo Coffee Sector, 1885–1913

As mentioned earlier, Michael Hall's study suggested that real wages did not rise in the São Paulo coffee region between 1880 and 1913.[84] Since that was a period of rapid economic expansion in Brazil's leading development region, the absence of an upward trend in real wages is important for confirming the hypothesis that even after the abolition of slavery, Brazil's advanced sector faced an elastic supply of labor. The purpose of this appendix is to see whether the data which are available on the increment of labor supply from immigration, and on the growth of labor demand derived from the expansion of coffee production during this period, are consistent with constant real wages.

Between 1880 and 1890, the stock of coffee trees in São Paulo increased by some 113.7 million trees.[85] Production conditions were such that one worker was required to tend and harvest each additional 2,000 trees. Hence the expansion of coffee output generated an increased demand for approximately 56,850 workers.

Between 1880 and 1890, some 223,000 immigrants arrived in São Paulo. This number cannot, of course, be identified with the increment in labor supply. Not all immigrants remained in Brazil; not all who stayed went to the coffee sector; and of the latter, only a fraction was in the labor force. Estimates of the coefficients necessary to make these three adjustments are, respectively: .68, .79, and .63.[86] Applying these coefficients to the gross flow of 223,000, we find that immigration increased the supply of labor to the São Paulo coffee sector by approximately 75,500 workers. This figure is clearly a rough estimate. Nevertheless, plausible modifications are unlikely to change the basic impression that during the 1880s, a period of extremely rapid expansion of coffee output, the supply of labor increased at least as much as did the demand.[87] Indeed, 'over-importation' of workers may in fact have occurred. Such a phenomenon was certainly consistent with the interests of the planters who controlled the agencies which promoted immigration from overseas.

A similar labor-market situation appears to have prevailed over the longer-term period from 1890–92 to 1911–13. During those years the number of coffee trees in the São Paulo area increased from a base of 100 to an index of 354.[88] The expanding output made possible by this increasing capital stock generated a demand for approximately 271,000 additional workers. During the same period, however, the gross flow of immigrants to São Paulo amounted to some 1,451,200 people. Information is not available on the coefficients necessary to adjust this figure in order to estimate the net increment of labor supply to the coffee sector during this period. Nevertheless, immigration clearly did lead to a large increase in the supply of labor. (For example, application of the coefficients cited in the previous paragraph would yield an increment of some 491,000 workers.) Further, over this entire period, Brazil's native-born population (and labor force) were also increasing rapidly. Under these conditions, it appears plausible that the supply of workers grew sufficiently to keep pace with labor-market demand, mitigating upward pressure on wages.[89]

Notes

1 Phillip LeVeen, 'A Quantitative Analysis of the Impact of British Suppression Policies on the Volume of the Nineteenth-Century African Slave Trade,' in Stanley Engerman and Eugene Genovese (eds), *Race and Slavery in The Western Hemisphere* (Princeton University Press, 1975), esp. p. 71.

2 See Viotti da Costa, *Da Senzala a Colonia* (São Paulo, 1966), pp. 83–94; and Michael M. Hall, 'The Origins of Mass Immigration in Brazil, 1871–1913' (PhD dissertation, Columbia University, 1969), Chapter 3.

3 These are the estimates of Lacerda Werneck and Ferreira Soares, as cited by Pedro Carvalho de Mello, 'The Economics of Labor on Brazilian Coffee Plantations, 1850–1888' (PhD dissertation, University of Chicago, 1977), p. 145. Stanley J. Stein cites higher rates. See his *Vassouras: A Brazilian Coffee Country, 1850–1900* (Cambridge, Mass.: Harvard University Press, 1957), pp. 19–20. Real rates of interest were lower, however, to the extent that inflation (which was likely at a rate of 2–3 percent per annum on a long-term basis) was also occurring. The short-term rates cited below for the Northeast are from the *Diário de Pernambuco*, as presented in Peter L. Eisenberg, *The Sugar Industry in Pernambuco: Modernization without Change, 1840–1910* (Berkeley and Los Angeles: University of California Press, 1974) p. 64. David Denslow has suggested 18 percent as a mean representative figure for long-term interest rates in the Northeast. This estimate is presented in his study 'Sugar Production in Cuba and Northeast Brazil, 1850 to 1914' (mimeographed, 1972), Chapter 3.

4 This estimate is based on sources which are presented in da Costa, *Da Senzala*, op. cit.; Phillip D. Curtin, *The Atlantic Slave Trade; A Census* (Madison, Wisc.:

University of Wisconsin Press, 1969), pp. 207–40, 269; and Leslie Bethell, *The Abolition of The Brazilian Slave Trade* (Cambridge University Press, 1970), p. 390.

5 See, for example, Warren Dean, *Rio Claro: A Brazilian Plantation System, 1820–1920* (Stanford: Stanford University Press, 1976), p. 194.

6 See da Costa, *Da Senzala*, op. cit., pp. 126–8, 139–44; and Eisenberg, *The Sugar Industry*, op. cit., pp. 194–7.

7 Stein, *Vassouras*, op. cit., pp. 59–62; Eisenberg, *The Sugar Industry*, op. cit., pp. 194–8. For a similar situation in nineteenth-century Ghana, another economy with abundant land available, see Steven H. Hymer, 'Economic Forms in Pre-Colonial Ghana,' *The Journal of Economic History*, vol. 30 (March 1970), pp. 47–9.

8 Pedro Carvalho de Mello, 'The Economics of Labor,' p. 50, Table 16; p. 66, Table 19. These samples are for slaves aged 16 to 50 (ibid., pp. 48, 64). For the year 1873, Mello has computed the ratio of the net rental income received by slaveowners to the gross rental rate. Because of search costs, taxes, and other expenses borne by the lessor, the ratio amounted to 65.2 percent (ibid., pp. 159–61). I have used this adjustment figure in computing the ratio of net rental fees to gross hire rates for all years in the period.

9 Robert Evans, Jr, 'The Economics of American Negro Slavery, 1830–1860,' in National Bureau of Economic Research, *Aspects of Labor Economics* (Princeton University Press, 1962).

10 Note also that net rental fees reflect the slaveowners' reservation price. They accepted this fee only if their slaves could not generate a higher yield working on the slaveowners' own land. For this reason, the data of Table 4.1 may understate private returns.

11 See Mello, 'The Economics of Labor,' op. cit., pp. 170 ff. Mello's model follows the methodology developed by Robert Fogel and Stanley Engerman, *Time on The Cross: Evidence and Methods* (Boston: Little, Brown, 1974), pp. 80–1.

12 The trend regressions reported here were computed using annual observations of data in Mello, 'Economics of Labor,' op. cit., pp. 50, 66.

13 Some empirical support for the suggestion that labor productivity was raised *in response to* the rise in slave prices comes from a regression using Mello's data on nominal rental fees (R) and purchase prices (P) for the years 1850–88. Regressing ΔR on ΔP lagged one year yields a positive regression coefficient on the ΔP_{-1} term, with a t-ratio of 1.90 and a Durbin–Watson statistic of 2.31. Increased overworking may have been among the techniques utilized by the planters in response to higher slave prices. See Celso Furtado, *Formação Econômica do Brasil*, 5th edn (Rio de Janeiro: Fundo de Cultura, 1963), p. 142.

14 This statement is based on a regression using observations in Eisenberg, *The Sugar Industry*, op. cit., Table 25. Eisenberg does not present data on rental rates.

15 On planter attitudes, which this literature often terms 'pre-capitalistic', see, for example, Dean, *Rio Claro*, op. cit., p. 123. Dean calls such attitudes an 'immense paradox'; for the planters did act as capitalists in the markets for land, credit, and other inputs. Another theme here has been the planters' class interest in maintaining a docile and economically unintegrated sub-class. That such conditions restricted the demand for free workers seems unlikely, however. On the contrary, the planters do not seem to have been able to collude effectively on the demand side of the labor market. See, for example, Jaime Reis, 'From Banguë to Usina,' in Kenneth Duncan and Ian Rutledge (eds), *Land and Labour in Latin America* (Cambridge University Press, 1977), p. 374.

16 On worker attitudes, see, for example, José Arthur Rios, 'Coffee and Agricultural Labor,' in Carlos Manuel Peláez (ed.), *Essays on Coffee and Economic Development* (Rio de Janeiro: Instituto Brasileiro do Café, 1973), p. 15; and Furtado, *Formação Econômica*, op. cit., pp. 143–6.

17 Gary Becker, *The Economics of Discrimination* (Chicago: University of Chicago Press, 4th impression, 1968), Chapters 3 and 4.

18 The experience of Minas Gerais is mentioned in Thomas H. Holloway, 'Immigration and Abolition: The Transition from Slave to Free Labor in the São Paulo Coffee Sector,' in Dauril Alden and Warren Dean (eds), *Essays Concerning the Socioeconomic History of Brazil and Portuguese India* (Gainesville, Fla.; University of Florida Press, 1978). The experience in the Northeast is discussed in detail in Eisenberg, *The Sugar Industry,* op. cit., Chapter 8.

19 Nathaniel H. Leff and Herbert S. Klein, 'O Crescimento da População Nao-Europeía Antes do Início do Desenvolvimento: O Brasil do Século XIX,' *Anais de História,* vol. 6, (1974), Tables 1 and 3.

20 Stein, *Vassouras,* op. cit., p. 65.

21 J. H. Galloway, 'The Sugar Industry of Pernambuco during The Nineteenth Century,' *Annals of The Association of American Geographers,* vol. 57 (1968), p. 298. By contrast, the coffee plantations of Rio de Janeiro and São Paulo were able to purchase enough slaves so that their work force was overwhelmingly non-free until the early 1880s. See da Costa, *Da Senzala,* op. cit., pp. 84–90, 145; and Hall, 'The Origins,' op. cit., p. 27.

22 See da Costa, *Da Senzala,* op. cit., pp. 100, 177–86; Stein, *Vassouras,* op. cit., pp. 47, 91, 165, 173; Hall, 'The Origins,' op. cit., p. 27.

23 Higher wages in themselves might not have sufficed to attract a large flow of European immigration to Brazil. The point is that implementation of the subsidy program attracted so large a number of immigrants that wages did not in fact rise.

24 This is Hall's conclusion ('The Origins,' op. cit., pp. 139–40). See also the estimates of the supply of immigrants relative to the incremental demand for labor which are presented in the appendix to this chapter.

25 See, for example, Leslie Bethell, *The Abolition of the Brazilian Slave Trade: Britain, Brazil, and The Slave Trade Question, 1807–1869,* (Cambridge University Press, 1970); Robert Conrad, *The Destruction of Brazilian Slavery, 1850–1888* (Berkeley and Los Angeles: University of California Press, 1972); and Robert B. Toplin, *The Abolition of Slavery in Brazil* (New York: Atheneum, 1972).

26 See the figures presented in Roberto C. Simonsen, *História Econômica do Brasil,* 4th edn (São Paulo: Companhia Editora Nacional, 1962), p. 271.

27 Leff and Klein, 'O Crescimento', op. cit.

28 See Stein, *Vassouras,* op. cit., pp. 67–9.

29 See, for example, da Costa, *Da Senzala,* op. cit., pp. 67–9.

30 Warren Dean (*Rio Claro,* op. cit., Chapter 4) suggests that export-agricultural production would have been economically feasible using free labor. As indicated in the text, however, the planters were concerned with maximizing their private returns rather than with feasibility of a free-labor system.

31 See also Stein, *Vassouras,* pp. 65, 228, 231; and da Costa, *Da Senzala,* pp. 137–49.

32 Mello, 'The Economics of Labor,' op. cit., pp. 76–7.

33 Brazilian slavery has sometimes been discussed as a case in which manumission was common. However, research by Herbert Klein indicates that two special conditions were present in most cases of manumission: (1) the freed person was a newly-born infant, (2) who was freed by his (free) father, presumably for affective reasons. See Herbert Klein, 'The Colored Freedman in Brazilian Slave Society,' *Journal of Social History,* vol. 3 (March 1969), pp. 38–45. Hence the economic inferences which can be drawn from such manumission are very different from other cases where manumission occurred in the absence of these two conditions. On other limiting features of manumission in Brazil, see Carl N. Degler, 'Slavery in Brazil and the United States: An Essay in Comparative History,' *American Historical Review,* vol. 75 (April 1970), pp. 1010–12. See also Jacob Gorender, *O Escravismo Colonial* (São Paulo: Editora Atica, 1978), pp. 340–8; the discussion there pertains mainly to the post-independence period. Katia M. de Queirós Mattoso's study of

manumissions in Bahia between 1819 and 1888 is also relevant here – 'A carta de Alforria como Fonte Complementar para O Estudo da Rentabilidade da Mão-de-Obra Escrava Urbana,' in Carlos Manuel Peláez and Mircea Buescu (eds), *A Moderna História Econômica* (Rio de Janeiro: APEC, 1976). Her data indicate that manumission was not very common, and that in cases where it did occur, women and children were disproportionately the beneficiaries. Further, in cases where affective motives were not present, manumission seems to have reflected the slave's capacity to muster the purchase price rather than the economic non-viability of slavery from the viewpoint of the slaveowner.

34   A. H. Conrad and J. R. Meyer, 'The Economics of Slavery in the Antebellum South,' *Journal of Political Economy*, vol. 66 (May 1958).

35   Stein, *Vassouras*, op. cit., pp. 227–9.

36   Furtado, *Formação Econômico*, op. cit., pp. 140–3; da Costa, *Da Senzala*, op. cit., p. 257; Eisenberg, *The Sugar Industry*, op. cit., p. 151; Degler, 'Slavery in Brazil,' op. cit., pp. 1017–18.

37   Stein, *Vassouras*, op. cit., p. 155, n; pp. 76–7. See also Klein, 'The Colored Freedman,' op. cit., p. 41; Dean, *Rio Claro*, op. cit., p. 57; Gorender, *O Escravismo Colonial*, op. cit., pp. 332–40.

38   See Eisenberg, *The Sugar Industry*, op. cit., pp. 173–5; Degler, 'Slavery in Brazil,' op. cit., p. 1018; Stein, *Vassouras*, op. cit., p. 186, *n*.

39   This was first pointed out to me by Stanley Engerman.

40   The analysis here assumes an asymmetry: that the slaveowners obtained higher net returns.from overworking than from efforts to reduce slave mortality. In view of the poor medical and public-health conditions which prevailed in nineteenth-century Brazil, that assumption appears amply justified.

41   Mello, 'The Economics of Labor,' op. cit., p. 74; and more generally on the regional economic shift in nineteenth-century Brazil, see Chapter 2 in Nathaniel H. Leff, *Underdevelopment and Development in Brazil, Vol. II: Reassessing the Obstacles to Economic Development* (London: Allen & Unwin, 1982).

42   To note that Brazilian politics had a strong regional component is not to ignore the powerful centralizing pressures which were also present. Indeed, one was a response (and a stimulus) to the other. Aspects of the regional/centralization issue in Brazilian politics and economic development are analyzed in Leff, *Reassessing the Obstacles*, op. cit., Chapter 5.

43   Cf. the discussion in Furtado, *Formação Econômica*, op. cit., Chapter 24.

44   Stein, *Vassouras*, op. cit., pp. 256–63; 279–80; Eisenberg, *The Sugar Industry*, op. cit., pp. 179–82.

45   Leff, *Reassessing the Obstacles*, op. cit., Chapter 2.

46   On the high value accorded leisure, see Furtado, *Formação Econômica*, op. cit., p. 166.

47   As discussed in Leff and Klein, 'O Crescimento,' op. cit., birth rates were much higher for free blacks than for slaves in nineteenth-century Brazil. This difference in behavior provides an empirical basis for evaluating the suggestion that slavery involved frustrated preferences, with ensuing emotional and personal costs.

48   The quotation (from Eisenberg, *The Sugar Industry*, op. cit., p. 179) suggests the zero-sum game approach with which this question has often implicitly been treated.

49   For a different view, see Furtado, *Formação Econômica*, op. cit., Chapter 26. Also, see pp. 61–3, below.

50   On the benefits of increased monetization in underdeveloped countries and their negation because of inflation and ensuing 'financial repression', see Edward S. Shaw, *Financial Deepening in Economic Development* (New York: Oxford University Press, 1973); Ronald McKinnon, *Money and Capital in Economic Development* (Washington: The Brookings Institution, 1973).

51   For an excellent historical account of the process analyzed here, see Thomas H. Holloway, 'Immigration and Abolition,' op. cit. The discussion that follows is not

meant to imply that the São Paulo planters thought explicitly in terms of the models presented. However, this conceptual framework is useful in understanding the pattern of their actual behavior.

52 The curve DE is drawn below the curve FG. This is because Hall ('The Origins of Mass Immigration,' op. cit., p. 161) makes it clear that the supply price of subsidized immigrants was less than the cost of free workers from within Brazil. Mello ('The Economics of Labor,' op. cit., pp. 93–102) has presented an interesting counter-factual analysis. He suggested that with continuing reallocation of the country's slave-labor force from other activities to coffee production, the number of slaves in Brazil would physically have sufficed to attain the output levels reached as late as 1902. However, the economic aspects of such a process must also be considered. In fact the planters found it more economical to subsidize large-scale immigration from Europe than to provoke the rise in prices that would have been required to draw the country's remaining slaves to coffee. On possible effects of labor scarcity and European immigration on labor costs in Rio de Janeiro during these years, see n. 70 below.

53 This point is brought out in Douglas H. Graham, 'Migração Estrangeira e a Questão da Oferta de Mão-De-Obra No Crecimento Econômico Brasileiro, 1880–1930,' *Estudos Econômicos*, vol. 3, no. 1 (1973), pp. 38–44.

54 On both points, see Thomas H. Holloway, 'The Coffee Colono of São Paulo: Migration and Mobility, 1880–1930,' in Kenneth Duncan and Ian Rutledge (eds), *Land and Labour in Latin America*, op. cit.

55 This figure was computed from data presented in Graham, 'Migração Estrangeira,' op. cit., p. 35.

56 On industrial entrepreneurship, see the data cited in Graham, 'Migração Estrangeira,' op. cit., p. 52. For information on rural modernization, I am indebted to a personal communication from Warren Dean.

57 These data are cited in Graham, 'Migração Estrangeira,' op. cit., p. 51.

58 Contrary to some impressions, the absolute level of the skills and education of the immigrants to the United States in the nineteenth century was high, almost as high as that of the native-born population. This point is documented in Peter J. Hill, 'The Economic Impact of Immigration to the United States' (unpublished PhD thesis, University of Chicago, 1970), especially Appendix B.

59 Concerning the role attributed to immigrants, with their European consumption habits, in the growth of the industrial market in Brazil, see, for example, Graham, 'Migração Estrangeira,' op. cit., pp. 47–8. On the alleged causal significance of immigrants for Brazil's urban growth and industrialization, discussed below, see ibid., pp. 46–54.

60 Holloway, 'The Coffee Colono,' op. cit.

61 See pp. 144–51 in Chapter 7.

62 See, for example, H. S. Houthakker, 'New Evidence on Demand Elasticities,' *Econometrica*, vol. 33 (September 1965), pp. 277–88; and D. A. Humphrey and H. S. Oxley, 'Expenditure and Household-Size Elasticities in Malawi: Urban-Rural Comparisons, Demand Projections, and A Summary of East African Findings,' *Journal of Development Studies*, vol. 12 (January, 1976).

63 Bainbridge Cowell, Jr, 'Cityward Migration in The Nineteenth Century: The Case of Recife, Brazil,' *Journal of Interamerican Studies and World Affairs*, vol. 7 (February, 1975), Table 3.

64 Furtado, *Formação Econômica*, op. cit., pp. 156–7; Cowell, 'Cityward Migration,' op. cit., p. 17.

65 In terms of its relevance to present less-developed countries, Brazil's historical experience does not indicate the undesirability of immigration. This may of course be a low-cost source of needed skills, education, and entrepreneurial qualities. Rather, this experience demonstrates the consequences for wages and income distribution of an infinitely elastic supply of unskilled labor, from whatever source.

66   Eisenberg, *The Sugar Industry*, op. cit., Table 26.

67   See pp. 123–4 in Chapter 6, below. The rate of increase of food prices in Rio de Janeiro (the P_E index discussed in Chapter 6) was 5.0 percent per annum during this period.

68   Another possible deflator for the nominal slave rental and purchase-price series would be the ratio of coffee prices to the price of Brazilian imports. That procedure would indicate trends in labor costs relative to the value of the imported goods which could be purchased with labor's output. Export prices of Great Britain, Brazil's major overseas supplier, fell during the nineteenth century (see Chapter 5). Consequently, if the nominal labor-cost series were deflated in the manner just described, the 'real' labor-cost series would exhibit a *downward* trend.

69   Until 1852, slaves continued to be imported to Brazil in numbers exceeding 1,000 per annum. However, large-scale importation was stopped in 1850.

70   The trend equation fitted to the slave rental data for the years 1850–88 showed an interesting pattern in its residuals (the difference between actual observations and the values predicted by the trend equation). From 1870 through 1880, all residuals were positive. That is, actual hire rates were above their long-term trend values, suggesting a situation of labor scarcity. Beginning in 1881, however, all residuals were negative. The latter situation may reflect the increased labor supply made available by immigration.

71   See pp. 20–2 in Chapter 2, above. Concerning the size and the geographical mobility of the population in Brazil's domestic agriculture sector, see pp. 60–2 above, and pp. 50–1 in Leff, *Reassessing the Obstacles*, op. cit., Chapter 3.

72   W. A. Lewis, 'Economic Development with Unlimited Supplies of Labour,' *Manchester School of Economic and Social Studies*, vol. 23 (May 1955). Furtado has also emphasized the importance of the elastic supply of labor to the advanced sector. However, he seems to have assumed that wage levels were higher there than in the rest of the economy. See his *Formação Econômica*, op. cit., Chapter 26, p. 179.

73   See Hla Myint, 'The Gains from International Trade and the Backward Countries,' *Review of Economic Studies*, vol. 32 (1954–1955), p. 135; Brinley Thomas, 'The Alleged Exploitation of The Underdeveloped Countries: A Review of The Evidence,' *Proceedings of the Thirty-Third Conference of the Western Economic Association*, 1956; Jonathan Levin, *The Export Economies* (Cambridge, Mass.: Harvard University Press, 1961), Chapter 3.

74   Noel G. Butlin, 'Colonial Socialism in Australia, 1860–1900,' in H. G. J. Aitken (ed.), *The State and Economic Growth* (New York, 1959), esp. pp. 62–71.

75   This figure was computed from data in US Department of Commerce, *Long-Term Economic Growth, 1860–1965* (Washington: GPO, 1966), pp. 182–3.

76   The slow pace of technical progress and capital accumulation in Brazil during the nineteenth century are discussed in Chapter 7, below.

77   A rare source of information on these attitudes during a later period, the 1920s, is presented in Robert M. Levine, 'Some Views on Race and Immigration during the Old Republic,' *The Americas*, vol. 27, no. 4 (April 1971). This article analyzes the results of a questionnaire survey in which the Sociedade Nacional de Agricultura elicited the views of its members on race and immigration in Brazil.

78   For example, Furtado (*Formação Econômica*, op. cit., Chapters 21–24) devotes four chapters to the general heading of 'The Labor Problem'. Furtado himself indicates that the 'problem' involved was payment of the higher wages necessary to attract internally-supplied workers.

79   It may be suggested that with higher wages in Brazil, foreign investment would have been lower. Most capital imports, however, went either directly to the government or were attracted by government interest guarantees. Moreover, under normal production-function conditions, the marginal productivity of labor (and wages) would not have fallen proportionately even if capital formation had been lower. As

noted in the text, however, capital deepening would have been a more likely consequence of higher wages.

80 See pp. 62–3, above. Other evidence on labor mobility in response to economic incentives in nineteenth-century Brazil is presented in Leff, *Reassessing the Obstacles*, op. cit., Chapter 3.

81 See Chapters 8 and 9 below. Transportation costs within Brazil had fallen since the 1880s, and thus the costs of internal migration had declined. But following a social-demand approach to the provision of economic infrastructure, internal transportation facilities could have been provided earlier if the option of importing labor from abroad had not been followed.

82 Because of the rise in the rate of natural demographic increase, Brazil's population growth accelerated from 2.1 percent per annum in 1920–40 to 2.4 percent per annum in 1940–50 and 3.0 percent per annum in 1950–60. These figures are from Ministério de Planejamento, *Demografia* (Rio de Janeiro, 1966), p. 39.

83 Cf. the perspective on optimal population growth proposed by A. Sauvy, in A. J. Coale (ed.), *Economic Factors in Population Growth* (New York: Wiley, 1976), p. 84.

84 Michael Hall, 'The Origins of Mass Immigration in Brazil,' op. cit., pp. 139–40.

85 This figure from Holloway, 'Immigration and Abolition,' op. cit. That paper is also the source for the other data used in this and in the next paragraph, except for the coefficient for the percentage of immigrants remaining in Brazil during the 1880s. The latter figure is from G. Mortara, 'Alcuni Data Sull' Immigrazione Italiana in Brasile,' *L'Industria*, no. 3 (1950).

86 The .63 figure utilized for the labor-force participation rate reflects the age and sex selectivity of immigration to Brazil. Holloway (loc. cit.) suggests figures of 63–75 percent, in reflection of the fact that women and children older than 12 joined the workforce at the harvest.

87 Coffee expansion also led to indirect labor demand (e.g. in transport); and the planting of additional coffee trees also required labor. The latter, however, was done largely at times other than the harvest period which generated the peak labor demand. Adding these other sources of increasing demand for labor would not change the overall supply–demand picture presented in the text, particularly if the increment to the local labor force from natural increase is also taken into account.

88 This paragraph is based on data presented in Thomas H. Holloway, 'Condições do Mercado de Trabalho e Organização do Trabalho Nas Plantações da Economia Cafeeira de São Paulo, 1885–1915,' *Estudos Econômicos* (São Paulo) vol. 2, no. 6 (December 1972).

89 Holloway has also documented the substantial upward mobility of immigrant workers, and the fact that a non-negligible percentage of the immigrants were able ultimately to establish themselves as independent farm operators. The possibilities for achieving the latter status depended, however, on wage levels, savings propensities, and land prices rather than on rising wages *per se*.

5
International Trade

Involvement in the world economy entailed more than the importation of labor for nineteenth-century Brazil. Trade in commodities also took place; and exports and imports of goods (and of capital) had important effects on income growth and structural change in Brazil during the nineteenth century. We leave for later a discussion of international capital movements to Brazil in this period.[1] In this chapter, we consider the expansion of international trade in commodities and some of its consequences for the Brazilian economy. Before beginning the analysis, however, it will be useful to place the discussion explicitly in its broader intellectual context.

The Broader Context

Perceptions concerning nineteenth-century trade and its effects in tropical countries like Brazil have provided an implicit background to many analytical models of trade and development. Impressions concerning the historical experience have also influenced later thinking about development strategy;[2] but the actual record concerning nineteenth-century trade and development in many less-developed countries, however, is not always clear. In his classic discussion of nineteenth-century trade and development, Ragnar Nurkse focused on the temperate zone countries; and simply stated that the tropical countries had remained 'outsiders', relatively neglected by the process.[3] At the same time, Cairncross and other writers have advanced strong *a priori* reasons why rising exports *could* have been a major source both of income growth and of some of the structural changes associated with development.[4] Empirical studies have also presented different perspectives on the actual historical experience in tropical trade and development. For example, W. Arthur Lewis suggested that through growing trade, 'the tropics were transformed during the period 1880 to 1913'.[5] By contrast, Irving Kravis has noted that some tropical countries experienced considerable expansion of their exports during the nineteenth century, but did not achieve substantial economic development.[6]

This chapter seeks to clarify the historical picture through an examination of Brazilian trade and development during the nineteenth

century. Apart from intrinsic historical interest, Brazil's experience
has also attracted more general theoretical attention. Thus the country
has sometimes been cited as a classic instance of the failure of expanding exports to lead to a 'take-off' in economic development. As Charles
Kindleberger phrased this view:[7]

> Brazil, for example, has had separate booms in sugar, rubber,
> cotton, and coffee, each of which under different conditions might
> have been expected to lead to a 'natural' process of economic
> growth. However many times the plane went down the runway it
> had not, prior to World War II, effected a takeoff.

Further, the failure of expanding foreign trade to promote widespread development in Brazil is of interest on wider analytical grounds.
This is because many of the conditions which have elsewhere been
cited as crucial for constraining a process of export-led development
were not present in this case. For example, in many underdeveloped
countries, the export activities operated within an enclave whose
structure minimized the spill-over effect of export growth on the rest of
the economy.[8] In Brazil, however, the conditions present reduced such
limitations on the foreign-trade multiplier. Nevertheless, rising
exports clearly did not lead to generalized economic development in
nineteenth-century Brazil. In fact, the apparent inadequacies of a
model of export-led development have seemed so striking in this case
as to stimulate a paradigmatic shift on the part of some observers. Thus
André Gunder Frank's perception of the Brazilian experience helped
him to elaborate the 'development of underdevelopment' conceptual
framework.[9] In that perspective, Brazil is viewed as a prototypical case
in which growing exports and involvement in the world economy
necessarily fail to promote generalized development.

Before discussing the impact of international trade on Brazil's
economic development, it is useful to consider some data which show
what actually happened in Brazil's foreign trade during the nineteenth
century. These data provide an empirical basis for discussing such
issues as the stability of export expansion, trends in the terms of trade,
and the magnitude of export growth.

An Aggregate View

Between 1822 and 1913, the *mil-réis* value of Brazil's exports rose at a
trend rate of 4.5 percent per annum. On a per capita basis, nominal
export receipts increased at an annual trend rate of 2.7 percent. Since
Brazil experienced price inflation during this period, the pace of export
growth in constant domestic prices was of course slower than these
nominal figures might suggest. In current sterling prices, the value of

Table 5.1 *Annual Sterling Value of Brazilian Exports, Total and Per Capita, Decadal Averages*

Period	Sterling Value of Total Exports at Current Prices (thousands of £)	Per Capita Sterling Value of Exports at Current Prices (£)	Sterling Value of Total Exports at Constant (1880) Prices (thousands of £)	Per Capita Sterling Value of Exports at Constant (1880) Prices (£)
1822–31	3,816	.763	2,123	.422
1832–41	5,350	.909	3,785	.642
1842–51	5,899	.854	5,432	.784
1852–61	10,887	1.357	10,022	1.251
1862–71	15,431	1.658	12,191	1.308
1872–81	20,492	1.870	18,403	1.669
1882–91	21,772	1.626	24,886	1.855
1892–1901	30,715	1.855	37,826	2.288
1902–11	50,700	2.428	57,642	2.765

Source: The decadal averages in constant sterling prices were computed using as a deflator the export price index of Great Britain, Brazil's principal foreign supplier during the nineteenth century. This series is from Albert H. Imlah, *Economic Elements in the Pax Britannica* (Cambridge, Mass.: Harvard University Press, 1958), pp. 94–8.

aggregate export receipts rose at an annual trend rate of 3.1 percent; and on a per capita basis, at 1.3 percent per annum.

Table 5.1 presents more detailed information on the sterling value of Brazil's exports during the nineteenth century. In order to show the size of the country's exports relative to its population, the data are also presented in per capita terms. And to convey an idea of the overseas purchasing power of Brazilian exports, Table 5.1 also shows the export values expressed in constant (1880) sterling prices. The latter series was constructed using as a deflator the export-price index of Great Britain, Brazil's principal foreign supplier.

As the data indicate, Brazil began the period with a relatively low level of exports. Total export receipts averaged less than £4 million in current prices during the 1820s. On a per capita basis, the figure was less than £1. (During most of this period, £1 was worth approximately $4.87.) To gain some comparative perspective, note the contrast with the United States. Between the 1820s and the 1890s, the value of per capita exports in the United States was some 75 percent higher than in Brazil.[10] This differential is especially noteworthy because in the United States productivity was rising in many sectors during the nineteenth century; and hence the country's economic development was much less dependent on foreign trade than was the case in Brazil.

The contrast with the United States is even greater if we consider the absolute level of exports. This question is of special importance because in both Brazil and the United States, the central governments relied heavily on taxes that were levied on foreign trade. Consequently, the absolute level of exports provides an indication of the size of a tax base which was vital for public-sector expenditure and investment programs. From the 1820s through the 1850s, total export receipts were five times greater in the United States than in Brazil. In the subsequent four decades, the ratio was even higher, 6.8 to 1. As these figures indicate, the central government in the United States could draw on a much larger public-finance base to support its expenditure and infrastructure programs.

Table 5.1 also shows that the low level of per capita exports in Brazil persisted until the end of the century. Because of the country's rapid population growth, the rise in per capita export values was much less than the rise in total exports. Thus from the initial decade to the last decade of the period, Brazil's aggregate export receipts increased by a factor of 13.3 in current sterling prices. Expressed in constant sterling prices, the increase in the value of aggregate exports was even greater: the growth factor here was 27.2. However, the growth factors for the corresponding per capita series are considerably smaller: 3.2 and 6.6, respectively.

As just indicated, the increase in Brazil's exports is larger when the value of the country's exports is expressed in constant prices. This difference reflects the fact that Brazil experienced favorable international price trends during the nineteenth century. World prices of manufactured goods, Brazil's major import, generally declined during the period. Thus, reflecting the lower costs that came with the Industrial Revolution, British export prices fell at a trend rate of 0.8 percent per year between 1822 and 1913.[11] At the same time, sterling prices for most of Brazil's exports were generally higher in the course of the century than they had been in the 1820s. Table 5.2 presents data on both of these price movements. First, the table shows the evolution of p_x, an index of the sterling prices of Brazil's exports. In addition, Table 5.2 presents an index of Brazil's international barter terms of trade, the ratio of the country's export prices to the prices of its imports, p_x/p_m. The latter series was computed using British export prices as a rough proxy for Brazil's import prices.

Perhaps the most important feature of the p_x series in Table 5.2 is what it does *not* show. There is no evidence of long-term declining prices in the index of Brazil's exports. On the contrary, the annual observations of the p_x series display a very modest but statistically significant upward trend. The magnitude of this trend is miniscule, 0.1 percent per annum. Nevertheless, the direction of the trend is worth mentioning in order to correct any perception that in general, Brazil's export prices fell during the nineteenth century.

Table 5.2 also shows that Brazil's international terms of trade were usually much better during the century than at the beginning of the

Table 5.2   *Index of the Sterling Prices for Brazil's Exports and Index of Brazil's Barter Terms of Trade, 1826–1910*

		(Indices: 1826–30=100)			
Period	p_x	p_x/p_m	Period	p_x	p_x/p_m
1826–30	100	100	1871–75	117	156
1831–35	113	131	1876–80	106	174
1836–40	106	128	1881–85	101	183
1841–45	103	149	1886–90	135	271
1846–50	116	182	1891–95	111	229
1851–55	127	206	1896–1900	129	274
1856–60	122	187	1901–05	127	254
1861–65	127	170	1906–10	130	244
1866–70	94	127			

Source: For the index of Brazilian import prices, p_m, the export price index of Great Britain were used. This series was taken from Albert H. Imlah, *Economic Elements in the Pax Britannica* (Cambridge, Mass.: Harvard University Press, 1958), pp. 94–8. For the series on Brazilian export prices, p_x, an index was constructed from the data on the unit value of exports. As discussed below, the composition of Brazilian exports changed drastically during this period. Consequently, an export price index using fixed weights would give a very misleading picture of the evolution of Brazilian export prices at any point at all far from the base-period weights. The approach adopted was to use a moving base. The weights used were the share of the individual commodity in the value of aggregate Brazilian export receipts during the current and the preceding four years. For this reason, the series begins in 1826.

period. The annual observations of the terms-of-trade index presented in Table 5.2 rose at an annual trend rate of 0.9 percent per annum. Further, this series understates the rising trend in Brazil's terms of trade. This is because data limitations prevented the inclusion of information on the impact which declining international freight rates had on Brazil's import costs. During the nineteenth century the cost of ocean shipping fell sharply, so Brazil's import prices could decline by more than the index of British export prices.[12] Moreover, the improvement in the terms of trade would come across even more dramatically if Brazilian data permitted computation of the index from the beginning of the century. British export prices fell 50 (!) percent between 1808, the year in which Brazil was opened to direct trade with countries other than Portugal, and 1826, the initial year of Table 5.2.[13] Note, finally, that the improvement in Brazil's barter terms of trade during the first half of the century was not erased during the second half. Indeed, the terms of trade showed a long-term improvement after the 1870s.

We can bring together in another measure the figures just considered on the barter terms of trade and on the growth of Brazil's export receipts. This measure is the income terms of trade; it indicates the amount of imports which a country's exports could purchase, and is computed as the value of export receipts deflated by the index of import prices (V_x/p_m). Between 1822 and 1913, Brazil's income terms of trade rose at an annual trend rate of 4.0 percent. On a per capita basis, the income terms of trade increased at an annual trend rate of 2.2 percent.

Disaggregation by Period and by Commodity

The trend equations just cited for Brazil's income terms of trade can also be used for another purpose. Inspection of the residuals for those equations indicated substantial variations in the growth of Brazil's income terms of trade in the years between 1822 and 1913. The distribution of these residuals above and below the trend line suggested the existence of fairly discrete time periods within this ninety-two-year span. This observation suggested a procedure for periodizing Brazil's foreign-trade experience during the nineteenth century.

Following this approach, trend regressions were fitted for the sub-periods which were suggested by the pattern of the residuals in the 1822–1913 equations. The results which gave the best statistical fit, indicating the existence of relatively homogeneous periods, are presented in Table 5.3. This procedure and the sub-periods derived from it are necessarily crude. But as the results of Table 5.3 indicate, this approach is more accurate than viewing the years 1822–1913 as a uniform period for the growth of either Brazil's total or per capita income terms of trade.

Table 5.3 shows a respectable rate of expansion for Brazil's income terms of trade between 1822 and 1849. But in the almost half-century from 1850 to 1896, the pace of growth was relatively low. In per capita terms, the income terms of trade rose at a trend rate of only 1.6 percent per annum. This long period of slow growth had important cumulative effects on the level of Brazilian trade and development. Finally, the data of Table 5.3 also show that after 1897, Brazil's per capita income terms of trade rose at a truly buoyant rate. Before then, however, the value of Brazil's per capita exports grew much more slowly than might

Table 5.3 *Periods in the Increase of Brazil's Income Terms of Trade, Aggregate and Per Capita*

Period	Annual Trend Rate of Growth of v_x/p_m (%)	R^2 of Trend Equation	Annual Trend Rate of Growth of Per Capita V_x/p_m (%)	R^2 of Trend Equation
1822–49	4.2 (11.7)	.83	2.8 (7.0)	.64
1850–96	3.3 (26.8)	.94	1.6 (14.0)	.81
1897–1913	5.6 (11.3)	.89	3.5 (7.1)	.76

Note: The *t*-ratios for the trend parameters are in parentheses.

Source: The data on the value in current sterling of Brazilian exports was recomputed in constant (1880) sterling prices, and trend equations were estimated for this series. The sterling price index used as a deflator was the export price index of Great Britain. This series was taken from Albert H. Imlah, *Economic Elements in the Pax Britannica* (Cambridge, Mass.: Harvard University Press, 1958), pp. 94–8.

have been considered typical for the nineteenth-century expansion of world trade.

We can also disaggregate Brazil's export experience by commodity. Data are available on the country's eight major export products, which accounted for more than 90 percent of all export receipts. These data permit a more detailed analysis of Brazilian exports. And since some of these commodities were produced within specific regions of the country, a disaggregated view also helps provide insight into the pattern of regional development in nineteenth-century Brazil. Table 5.4 sets out information on the growth of value, quantity, and unit value (henceforth referred to as price) for these products. For each commodity's sterling value and price series, the British export price index was used as a rough proxy for a Brazilian import price series, to compute also the trends in the individual commodities' income and barter terms of trade. The data are divided into two periods, breaking at 1873, the year of the onset of a major depression in the nineteenth-century world economy.

The data of Table 5.4 do not indicate the presence of chronic instability or of sharp cyclical fluctuations in most of Brazil's commodities.

Table 5.4 *The Quantum, Value, and Price Trends of Brazil's Eight Major Export Commodities, 1822–1913*

			Annual Trend Rate of Growth (in %) of:			
			Sterling Price		Sterling Value	
					(Current	(Constant
		Quantum	(Current	(Constant	Sterling	Sterling
Product	Period	Exported	Sterling)	Sterling)	Prices)	Prices)
Cotton	1822–73	2.5	0.7	1.4	3.2	4.1
	1874–1913	−1.9	1.2	1.7	−0.7	−0.2
Sugar	1822–73	2.2	−0.6	*	1.6	2.4
	1874–1913	−6.4	−0.7	*	−7.1	−7.0
Coffee	1822–73	5.3	*	1.0	5.2	6.2
	1874–1913	3.8	−0.9	*	2.9	3.6
Leather	1822–73	2.5	−0.6	*	2.0	3.0
	1874–1913	2.0	1.4	2.0	3.4	4.3
Tobacco	1822–73	3.0	1.5	2.4	4.5	5.7
	1874–1913	1.1	1.2	1.7	2.3	2.8
Cocoa	1822–73	3.2	2.7	3.5	5.9	6.8
	1874–1913	5.5	*	*	5.2	5.9
Rubber	1828–73	10.0	2.1	2.6	12.1	12.6
	1874–1913	5.7	2.6	3.5	8.3	9.1
Erva Maté[a]	1831–74	6.4	1.2	1.8	7.7	8.2
	1874–1913	5.3	1.6	2.2	6.9	7.7

[a]Erva Maté is a South American tea.

Note: The asterisks indicate the *t*-value of the trend term is not significant at the 5-percent level. The series used to compute the value of each product's sterling price and export value in constant-value sterling (1880) prices, p_m, is the British export price index, from Albert H. Imlah, *Economic Elements in the Pax Britannica* (Cambridge, Mass.: Harvard University Press, 1958), pp. 94–8.

Table 5.5 *Share (in percent) of Individual Products in Total Brazilian Export Receipts*

Product	1821–23	1871–73	1912–14	Product	1821–23	1871–73	1912–14
Cotton	25.8	16.6	2.9	Tobacco	3.2	3.2	2.6
Sugar	23.1	12.3	0.3	Cocoa	0.6	0.8	2.9
Coffee	18.7	50.2	60.4	Rubber	0	5.3	17.4
Leather	13.5	6.4	4.7	Erva Maté	0	1.6	3.3

Note: Columns may not sum to 100 percent because the Brazilian data source does not report figures for some products which accounted for a very small portion of total export receipts during the period.

Rather, the fact that the parameter estimates for almost all of the trend coefficients are statistically significant above the 0.05 level indicates steady long-term movements in the price, quantity, and value of most Brazilian exports over these extended periods. In addition, the information on price trends in constant sterling values does not suggest a pattern in which exports of most individual commodities expanded in the face of declining terms of trade. As this observation indicates, a model of 'immiserizing' export growth generally does not fit Brazil's historical experience during the nineteenth century.[14]

Table 5.4 showed important differences in the rates at which the value of individual export commodities grew. Because of the very different pace of growth in the various commodities, the composition

Table 5.6 *A Periodization of Export Growth for Some Individual Commodities: Growth of Export Values in Current Sterling Prices*

Product	Period	Annual Trend Rate of Export Growth	R² of Trend Equation
Cotton	1822–48	−4.0 (6.1)	.77
	1849–59	*	n.a.
	1860–71	12.5 (2.2)	.58
	1872–99	−4.0 (2.7)	.47
	1900–13	*	n.a.
Sugar	1822–84	1.5 (8.3)	.73
	1885–1913	−9.8 (6.8)	.75
Coffee	1822–50	5.7 (7.7)	.83
	1851–88	3.2 (11.5)	.89
	1889–1902	*	n.a.
	1903–14	6.9 (3.6)	.75
Cocoa	1822–55	6.4 (5.1)	.67
	1856–97	3.0 (8.6)	.80
	1898–1913	7.1 (7.3)	.89
Rubber	1827–49	9.3 (4.9)	.73
	1850–86	6.2 (11.5)	.89
	1887–1913	8.2 (9.9)	.89

Note: The numbers in parentheses are the *t*-ratios for the trend parameters. n.a. indicates not applicable. The asterisks indicate the *t*-value for the trend term is not significant at the .05 level.

of Brazil's export receipts changed markedly during the century. Table 5.5 presents information on this transformation. As the data indicate, cotton and sugar, which had earlier accounted for nearly half of Brazil's total export value, showed a sharp decline. Cocoa, erva maté, and rubber appeared as new export commodities. Coffee increased its share, and grew to dominate Brazil's foreign trade. Coffee was produced in Brazil's Southeast (principally Rio de Janeiro and São Paulo), while sugar and cotton were produced mainly in the country's Northeast region. The very different rates at which exports of these products grew during the nineteenth century led to the emergence of a significant regional disparity in Brazil's economic development.[15]

Finally, because of the special importance of some commodities within individual regional economies, it would be helpful to have more information on the periodization of their export growth. In connection with Table 5.3 above we discussed a method for distinguishing distinct periods in long-term series. Table 5.6 presents the periodization which this method suggests for some major regional export products during the nineteenth century.

Demand and Supply Conditions

Several factors lay behind the rising quantum and value that we have observed for most of Brazil's export commodities in the nineteenth century. First, as mentioned, were the favorable terms of trade for most of these products. Growing demand and, for most products, rising prices provided an important condition for the expansion of Brazil's exports during the century. Thus the sharp rise in the country's income terms of trade between 1897 and 1913 (see Table 5.3) owed much to the worldwide economic expansion during that period. However, it would be misleading to regard Brazil's export growth during the nineteenth century as simply demand-determined, and a passive response to conditions in the main centers of the world economy. Favorable supply conditions were also necessary for Brazil to take advantage of international demand. These supply conditions within Brazil reflected both market responsiveness and government promotional policies.[16]

One feature that contributed to the country's increasing supply capacity was the growth, particularly after the 1870s, of the country's railways. This expansion lowered transportation costs and facilitated bringing new areas into cultivation. In addition, the export sector's force of low-cost workers was being constantly augmented by in-movements of workers from overseas. As we saw in Chapter 4, such importation of workers was maintained to the point that the export activities faced a highly elastic supply of labor through the nineteenth century. Government policies were important in stimulating both railway construction and the importation of labor. Although its record in promoting the economic development of the country as a whole was not very impressive in the nineteenth century, the Brazilian govern-ment did help provide favorable conditions for export expansion. This focus is not surprising. The export interests were very influential in Brazilian politics during the nineteenth century. In addition, Brazil's fiscal system was such that the state depended heavily on foreign-trade taxes for its revenues.

Despite the conditions which aided export growth, the rate at which Brazil's export receipts increased during most of the century was not very high. As noted earlier, Brazil's aggregate income terms of trade rose at an annual trend rate of 4.0 percent between 1822 and 1913. On a per capita basis, however, the figure was only 2.2 percent. Similarly, use of the export-price index presented in Table 5.2 suggests that the quantum of Brazil's exports rose at an annual trend rate of 3.0 percent. In per capita terms, the rate of increase was 1.2 percent per annum.

Two sets of conditions help explain the relatively slow growth of Brazil's aggregate exports during the nineteenth century. First, the pace of output growth in some export activities seems to have been constrained by the inelasticity of the local food supply. As will be discussed in Chapter 6, rapid expansion of export production was often hampered by a rise in the relative price of foodstuffs.[17] Second, Brazil's aggregate export expansion was limited by the poor experience of cotton and sugar. Those commodities had been the country's major exports at the beginning of the period (see Table 5.5). Consequently, the adverse effect of their slow growth (see Table 5.4) on the country's overall rate of export expansion was specially large.

Trade and Structural Change

Thus far we have focused only on the growth of income which came from expanding exports and improving terms of trade. Growing foreign trade also led to important structural changes in the Brazilian economy. Although total export receipts grew more slowly than might have been presumed, income in Brazil's external sector does seem to have risen at a rate higher than in the rest of the economy. As a result, it is likely that the share of export production in the Brazilian economy's aggregate output increased somewhat during the nine-teenth century.[18] Another important change followed from the close connection between the value of the country's foreign trade and the fiscal resources available to the government. Because of this linkage, as the foreign trade sector expanded, so too did the Brazilian state.[19]

Growing foreign trade also led to other structural changes. In some commodities, rising export receipts in Brazil were partly due to rising prices. Consequently, the backward-linkage effects stemming from higher export volumes were smaller than the trends in export values imply. In general, however, structural changes were facilitated by the fact that most of the entrepreneurship and fixed capital employed in the country's export activities were supplied from domestic sources. In this respect, Brazil differed notably from some colonial or comprador economies. Also, in contrast with export production in some enclave economies, the technology used in Brazil's export sector relied heavily on inputs that were locally produced. Thus nineteenth-century Brazil was not a classic export economy. The conditions which in other underdeveloped countries made for large external leakages and a small spill-over effect from expanding foreign trade on the domestic economy were much mitigated in Brazil.

Because of these historical features, export growth promoted important structural changes in Brazil's economy during the nineteenth century. The growth of domestic incomes based on exports enlarged the internal market for manufactured products. As a result, with the necessary supply conditions also satisfied, industrial development began during the second half of the nineteenth century in southeastern Brazil, the region which experienced increasing exports and rising incomes on a large scale.[20] Further, expanding exports also promoted growth in Brazil's domestic agricultural sector. Growing income and the substitution of export production for subsistence cultivation increased the size of the internal market for foodstuffs. This market was increasingly supplied by domestic producers whose factor proportions prevented them from producing the principal export commodities. In addition to these forward-linkage effects, the expanding markets and higher returns made possible by growing international trade also led to increased railroad construction. Almost all of these railways, moreover, were financed by foreign investors or by the Brazilian government (whose revenues, as noted earlier, depended heavily on taxes levied on foreign trade). Investment resources on this scale were available only because of the country's growing exports and foreign-debt servicing capacity. Although the first railways were built mainly in the areas of export production, they also assisted the domestic agricultural sector by reducing internal transportation costs, and by providing the basis for subsequent railway construction reaching further into the hinterland.[21]

These developments involved structural changes of enormous importance for the Brazilian economy. The overall impact of trade on development would have been much greater, however, if nineteenth-century Brazil had not differed in significant ways from some standard two-sector models of economic development. In contrast with closed-economy models, Brazil's economic expansion took place in the context of a relatively open economy. Also, as compared with models of unlimited labor supply, in Brazil unimproved land was initially the surplus factor. Analysis of the dynamics of a land-surplus economy involves more than a simple relabeling of the variables to reach essentially the same conclusions as those obtained for a labor-surplus model. For in the context of an open economy, the relatively scarce factors of capital and labor can be imported, whereas international factor movements are not possible for land. This possibility is of course recognized in work on closed two-sector models.[22] Historically, however, it was not an unusual case, but rather the essence of the story for many underdeveloped countries.

In the event, the overseas supply of capital to Brazil was much less elastic than the overseas supply of labor. Coming together with Brazil's natural demographic increase, the importation of labor led to relatively high rates of population growth. As a result, the increments to the country's labor force were large compared to the growth of demand for workers in Brazil's 'advanced' sector. Moreover, the process of drawing on the international economy to increase the supply of labor was especially important for the country's export sector, for that was the destination of most of the imported labor. Thus the availability of imported workers made labor a relatively abundant factor in Brazil's advanced sector. And as we saw in Chapter 4, the consequences for development in the context of this two-sector model were far-reaching.

Furthermore, just because aggregate productivity levels in the export activities were higher than in the rest of the economy, export expansion contributed to the formation of a dualistic pattern in Brazil. That is, dualism was the direct result of the relative absence of development in the country's internally-oriented activities. Under these conditions, generalized economic growth could begin only when output per capita in Brazil's domestic agricultural sector began to increase. Railway construction, which was promoted by export expansion, did eventually help stimulate growth in the country's domestic agricultural sector. It was a long time, however, before this process had substantial effects. Political as well as economic responses were required, and each system was subject to its own constraints.[23] A more generalized development pattern involving non-negligible magnitudes did not begin in Brazil until late in the nineteenth century.

The Benefits from Trade

The major short-term benefit from export growth in Brazil was higher income. This in turn seems to have been due largely to improvements in static allocational efficiency. That is, the composition of output was changed to take advantage of the opportunities offered by specialization and the international terms of trade. By contrast, some of the dynamic gains expected in models of trade and development do not appear to have been prominent in nineteenth-century Brazil.

Perhaps because of the low level of the country's human-capital stock, the export activities seem to have used in production (if not in processing) essentially the same primitive techniques as were employed in Brazil's domestic agricultural sector. Moreover, very large intrasectoral productivity gains – due, for example, to rapid shifts in production functions, or economies of scale in the export activities – do not seem to have occurred. Similarly, the expansion of international trade in nineteenth-century Brazil was not accompanied by large gains due to a 'vent-for-surplus' process.[24] These involve the net benefits which accrue to labor as workers who had previously been idle begin producing for the export market. As noted above, much of the labor employed in Brazil's export came from abroad. Despite the absence of these dynamic effects, the composition of Brazilian output in many areas seems to have shifted toward greater emphasis on export production during the nineteenth century. This compositional shift suggests how welcome the static efficiency gains were to Brazilian producers.

Another possible consequence which must be considered in evaluating the gains of Brazil's trade expansion is that the growth of imports may have destroyed domestic import-competing cottage industries.[25] In fact, such a decline in local craft production and the impoverishment of the factors engaged in these activities does not seem to have occurred on a large scale in nineteenth-century Brazil. The country had been a Portuguese colony before its independence, and Portugal had already limited local craft and manufacturing production. In this respect, Brazil avoided the serious dislocations which affected other underdeveloped countries as they increased their participation in the world economy during the nineteenth century.[26]

Notwithstanding the promotional conditions discussed earlier, the growth of Brazil's foreign trade during the nineteenth century clearly did not lead the country to generalized economic development. That much is evident from the low levels of the development indices which prevailed in Brazil at the beginning of the twentieth century. First, the fact that export expansion in the Southeast's coffee-producing region was accompanied by very slow growth of exports in Brazil's large Northeast region did not make for generalized development. Partly because of the Northeast's poor export experience, the country's overall rate of export growth was, as we have seen, low. Since the rate of export growth is expected to be the propelling force in a process of export-led development, it is not surprising that such a process did not operate on a wide scale in Brazil. Further, the relative size of the export sector whose growth was supposed to pull the rest of the economy forward was also not very large. In 1911–13, exports averaged approximately 16 percent of gross domestic product in Brazil.[27] During the nineteenth century, the share of the export sector in aggregate Brazilian output had probably been smaller.[28]

We can contrast these conditions with those implicit in perspectives which have viewed nineteenth-century trade as an 'engine for development'.[29] Expressed in terms of that metaphor, Brazil suffered from two limitations. The size of the engine (the export sector) was small relative to the object which was to be pulled forward (the rest of the Brazilian economy). Further, the engine's power (the rate of export growth) was also not very great. Coming in conjunction with the elastic supply of labor from overseas, these conditions were crucial in limiting the success of a generalized process of export-led development in nineteenth-century Brazil.

Other Issues

The income growth that was generated by export expansion was not distributed equally in Brazil. Much of the new income accrued to landowners with relatively low transportation costs, who obtained quasi-rents for their land and entrepreneurship. That landowners gained more than workers is not surprising. Brazil's exports were land-intensive; and pressures for higher wages in the expanding export sector were dampened by the elastic supply of labor. Under these conditions, the growth in incomes consequent upon export expansion probably led to an increase in the inequality of income distribution within each export region. In addition, a significant degree of inter-regional inequality emerged because of the disparate export experiences of the Southeast and of the Northeast. Thus this process of trade and development also had important consequences for the distribution of income in Brazil. The lion's share of the increased income from exports did not go, however, to foreign capitalists. In contrast with the plantations and mines of many other underdeveloped countries, Brazil's exports were produced by domestic capitalists. The most important role which foreigners took in this process was through their investment in Brazil's railroads. Part of the railway construction, however, was financed through fixed-interest bonds floated by the Brazilian government. In addition, the government regulated railway rates, and itself owned a significant portion of the country's railway trackage.[30] Rather, the most important distributional effects were those that occurred within the country.

Nineteenth-century Brazil's pattern of economic expansion, with its orientation toward international trade and comparative advantage, has been criticized on numerous grounds. For example, it has been suggested that expanding foreign trade did not create an economy that was directed toward satisfying the material needs of the mass of the country's population.[31] The absence of such a mass-welfare orientation in nineteenth-century Brazil's economy is clear. Our earlier discussion suggests that Brazil's expansion pattern reflected the country's initial distribution of land, and the large-scale importation of unskilled labor from overseas.[32] Those conditions, rather than any intrinsic deficiencies of primary product exportation, seem to have been the underlying causes of the economy's subsequent distribution of income and consumption.[33] As the efforts of Fidel Castro to increase sugar exports in post-revolutionary Cuba indicate, export growth along lines of comparative advantage need not be inherently incompatible with a mass-welfare orientation.

Brazil's expanding foreign trade has also been criticized for serving 'extraneous objectives', and for functioning in terms of 'international circumstances'.[34] External market conditions, however, generally offered Brazil the advantage of a growing market and of favorable price trends (see Tables 5.2 and 5.4). And if international trade served the interests of foreign ('extraneous') producers and consumers, it hardly follows that Brazilians did not also benefit. Both parties can gain from trade. In the nineteenth century, with its falling prices for manufactures and rapidly expanding demand for tropical commodities, the gains from moving to international price ratios were large.[35] For this reason, the income losses which autarky would have involved for Brazil would have been especially severe.

Finally, it has been suggested that growing foreign trade made Brazil vulnerable to economic and political pressures emanating from the international economy. These pressures are believed to have distorted the country's development and introduced rigidities which were to restrict its subsequent progress. Questions of imperialism and dependency in nineteenth-century Brazil are so important, however, that they require an extended discussion and a separate chapter.[36]

Conclusions

One can evaluate Brazil's experience with international trade and economic development during the nineteenth century in two very different ways. It is important to recognize that these interpretations need not be considered mutually exclusive. On the contrary, they provide insights which are complementary rather than competitive.

On the one hand, we have seen that international trade had only limited effects in promoting generalized development in the Brazilian economy during the nineteenth century. At the same time, expanding exports, coming concurrently with improved terms of trade, were the major source of productivity increase in an economy that was otherwise relatively stagnant in terms of per capita income growth. Furthermore, growing foreign trade led to important structural changes in Brazil. In creating both a domestic market as well as the necessary conditions on the supply side, export growth helped stimulate Brazilian industrialization. Also, the growing internal market and railway construction engendered by expanding exports eventually led to development in the domestic agricultural sector. The effects of export expansion on economic development in Brazil stand out dramatically if we compare the nineteenth-century growth and structural change of southeastern Brazil, which experienced relatively high rates of export growth, with the Northeast, which did not.

The contrast between the Southeast and the Northeast also eases the apparent paradox of these conflicting interpretations. Although expanding foreign trade did not function as an engine for the entire train, it did pull one important car. The divergence between the Southeast and the Northeast also underlines the obvious point that large-scale export growth is a necessary condition for a process of export-led development. And as the disparate regional experience indicates, this condition was not always satisfied in nineteenth-century Brazil's international trade. Much has been said of the export booms which have occurred in Brazil's economic history. But over the period 1822–1913, the value of the country's exports increased at an annual rate of only 2.2 percent on a per capita basis. As this figure suggests, a major limitation with international trade as a source of economic development in nineteenth-century Brazil was the small scale of the country's export expansion.

We can gain further insight into the importance of foreign trade for economic development in nineteenth-century Brazil from a broader perspective. Export expansion, where it occurred, permitted Brazil to enjoy income growth and economic development *without* many of the structural changes which have sometimes been considered essential preconditions ('prerequisites') for economic progress in a backward economy. Breaking out of a situation of stagnant per capita income by means of exogenous international trade and investment has of course been the standard process in most underdeveloped countries. For this reason, the closed-economy models of 'self-starting' development which predominate in the theoretical literature are not empirically relevant for analyzing the onset of economic development in most countries of the world.

In another sense, however, such models are directly relevant. What they provide, in effect, is a basis for counterfactual analysis. That is, these models show how serious were the internal structural barriers which underdeveloped countries would have had to face if they had been restricted to the development possibilities of a closed economy. By the same token, such models indicate how important for development were the opportunities which international trade opened for a country like nineteenth-century Brazil.

Notes

1 Nathaniel H. Leff, *Underdevelopment and Development in Brazil*, Vol. II: *Reassessing the Obstacles to Economic Development* (London: Allen & Unwin, 1982), Chapter 4.

2 See, for example, the statement by Raúl Prebisch: 'For a century now our economies have been linked to the international economy and 50% of our population is still stagnating in pre-capitalist conditions. . . .'. This is from Prebisch's *Toward a Dynamic Development Policy for Latin America*, as quoted in Stanley J. Stein and Barbara H. Stein, *The Colonial Heritage of Latin America: Essays on Economic Dependence in Perspective* (New York: Oxford University Press, 1970), p. 188.

3 See his *Equilibrium and Growth in the World Economy*, Gottfried Haberler and Robert Stern (eds) (Cambridge, Mass.: Harvard University Press, 1962), p. 289.

4 A. K. Cairncross, 'International Trade and Economic Development,' *Economica* (August 1961).

5 W. Arthur Lewis, *Aspects of Tropical Trade, 1883–1965* (Uppsala: Almquist and Wiksell, 1969), pp. 7–12.

6 Irving Kravis, 'Trade as a Handmaiden of Growth: Similarities between the Nineteenth and Twentieth Centuries,' *The Economic Journal*, vol. 80 (December 1970), esp. pp. 850–5. See all John Hanson II, *Trade in Transition: Exports from the Third World, 1840–1900* (New York: Academic Press, 1980).

7 Charles P. Kindleberger, *International Economics* (Homewood, Ill.: R. D. Irwin, 1953), p. 375. Note that Kindleberger's statement was advanced before the availability of the statistical information (presented in Chapter 8, below) on Brazil's sustained economic development since 1900. That information provides the empirical basis for a radically different interpretation of Brazil's nineteenth-century experience with trade and development.

8 The standard study here is Jonathan V. Levin, *The Export Economies* (Cambridge, Mass.: Harvard University Press, 1960).

9 André Gunder Frank, 'Capitalist Development of Underdevelopment in Brazil,' in his *Capitalism and Underdevelopment in Latin America: Historical Studies of Chile and Brazil* (New York: Monthly Review Press, 1967), esp. pp. 162–71. On the prominent role of Great Britain in Brazil's foreign trade and investment during the nineteenth century, see Alan K. Manchester, *British Preeminence in Brazil* (Durham, NC: Duke University Press, 1933).

10 The figures presented here and below on the value of US exports during the nineteenth century were computed from data in the US Department of Commerce, *Historical Statistics of the United States, Colonial Times to 1957* (Washington: GPO, 1960). The implications of the Brazilian's state's heavy dependence on foreign trade taxes during the nineteenth century (mentioned in the next paragraph) are discussed in Leff, *Reassessing the Obstacles*, op. cit., Chapter 5.

11 This trend was computed from data in Albert H. Imlah, *Economic Elements in the Pax Britannica* (Cambridge, Mass.: Harvard University Press, 1958), pp. 94–8. For evidence on a long-term decline in the prices of manufactured products in the United States, see Dorothy Brady, 'Relative Prices in the Nineteenth Century,' *Journal of Economic History*, vol. 24 (June 1964).

12 Thus Douglass C. North has presented estimates indicating that total factor productivity in ocean shipping on the North Atlantic rose at an annual rate of some 3.5 percent between 1814 and 1860. See his paper 'Sources of Productivity Change in Ocean Shipping,' *Journal of Political Economy*, vol. 76 (September 1968), esp. p. 965. Identical gains may not have accrued on the shipping routes to Brazil, but the direction of price change must have been similar. Note also that the productivity increases cited above occurred *before* the large gains which obtained in the post-1860 shift from small sailing vessels to larger, steam-powered ships. Further

information on the decline of international shipping costs during the nineteenth century is presented in Gerald S. Graham, 'The Ascendancy of the Sailing Ship, 1850–1885,' *Economic History Review* N. S. vol. 9 (1956–67), pp. 74–88.

13 Imlah, *Economic Elements*, op. cit., pp. 94–8. Britain had flexible exchange rates from 1808 to 1819 and import prices also declined in those years, but not as rapidly as the index of export prices.

14 Jagdish Bhagwati, 'Immiserizing Growth,' *Review of Economic Studies*, vol. 25 (June 1958).

15 This topic, and the causes of the poor experience of Brazil's sugar and cotton exports during the nineteenth century are discussed in Leff, *Reassessing the Obstacles*, op. cit., Chapter 2.

16 Empirical evidence on market responsiveness in the supply of individual Brazilian exports during the nineteenth century is presented in Table 3.1 of Leff, *Reassessing the Obstacles*, op. cit., Chapter 3.

17 See pp. 115–16 in Chapter 6, below. Empirical support for the importance of that pattern is suggested by the supply-response equations which are cited in note 16. The dependent variable in those equations is the deviation of the logarithm of each commodity's export quantum from its long-term trend. Despite the detrending, the residuals for most of the supply-response equations show strong evidence of positive serial correlation. This observation confirms the importance of cycles around trend such as would be provoked by inelastic local supply of foodstuffs to the export activities.

18 The model and data presented in Appendix I of Chapter 3 above permit us to derive estimates of the change in the aggregate export coefficient, X/Y, between 1822 and 1913. The ratio of export receipts to the currency stock declined at an annual trend rate of 0.2 percent during this period. Inserting this value and the intermediate figure for the change of velocity into the aforementioned model, we find that the ratio of export income to monetized income rose at an annual rate of 0.1 percent between 1822 and 1913. Of greater quantitative significance was the fact that monetized income in nineteenth-century Brazil increased at a higher rate than did income in the non-monetized sector (see Chapter 3, pp. 33–4). Hence, the share of exports in total output rose even more than relative to monetized output.

19 On the close connection between the expansion of Brazil's foreign trade and the growth of government expenditure during the nineteenth century, see pp. 84–5 in Leff, *Reassessing the Obstacles*, op. cit., Chapter 4, and pp. 112–13 in Chapter 5, below. For a general discussion of linkages between export growth and development, see Albert O. Hirschman, 'A Generalized Linkage Approach to Development, with Special Reference to Staples,' *Economic Development and Cultural Change*, vol. 25, Supplement (1977).

20 See Chapters 8 and 9 below; and Warren Dean, *The Industrialization of São Paulo, 1880–1945* (Austin: University of Texas Press, 1969), Chapter 1. Rapid growth in income from exports was not, of course, a sufficient condition for regional industrialization. Necessary input supply conditions had also be to be satisfied. In addition, as the case of rubber indicates, the income generated and the market created by export growth had to reach a sufficiently large scale. The value of rubber exports grew at a higher long-term rate than coffee, but because rubber started from a much smaller base, the absolute magnitude of the income generated was much lower. During the 1850s, the value of coffee exports was twenty-two times greater than the value of rubber exports. By the first decade of the twentieth century, the disparity in scale had narrowed greatly, but the value of coffee exports was still twice as large as the value of rubber exports.

21 See pp. 144–51 in Chapter 7.

22 See, for example, Dale W. Jorgenson, 'The Development of a Dual Economy,' *The Economic Journal*, vol. 71 (June 1961), p. 334.

23 Leff, *Reassessing the Obstacles*, op. cit., Chapter 5.

24 Hla Myint, 'The Classical Theory of International Trade and the Under-developed Countries,' *The Economic Journal*, vol. 68 (March 1958).

25 See, for example, Staffan B. Linder, *Trade and Trade Policy for Development* (New York, 1966), pp. 144–5 for an emphasis on this possibility in the trade of under-developed countries.

26 For example, for a discussion of this process in Asia, see Stephen Resnick, 'The Decline of Rural Industry Under Export Expansion: A Comparison among Burma, Philippines, and Thailand, 1870–1938,' *The Journal of Economic History*, vol. 30 (March 1970).

27 The numbers underlying this figure are presented in n. 35 of Chapter 2, above.

28 On the rising share of the export sector in aggregate Brazilian output during the nineteenth century, see n. 18 above. The information presented here may conflict with perceptions of nineteenth-century Brazil as being an economy in which the export sector accounted for a large share of GDP. Those impressions probably reflect the fact that much of the country's economic *growth* occurred in that sector. Also because of the greater availability of data, much of the writing on nineteenth-century Brazil has focused on the export sector. Finally, this perception may be due to a loose application of views based on the large share of the export sector during the middle of the *eighteenth* century. From 1760 to 1814, however, per capita exports had declined and resources were slowly shifted into domestically oriented activities such as subsistence agriculture. On the latter shift in the half-century preceding our period, see Roberto C. Simonsen, *História Econômica do Brasil*, 4th edn (São Paulo: Companhia Editora Nacional, 1962), pp. 383, 271, 292–3.

29 See, for example, Nurkse, *Equilibrium and Growth*, op. cit. Roberto Borges Martins has presented an interesting analysis of Brazil's trade experience in the context of the broader issues raised at the beginning of this chapter. His discussion may be found in 'A Interpretação do Crescimento com Liderança de Exportações: Modelos Teóricos e A Experiência Brasileira,' in Carlos Manuel Peláez and Mircea Buescu (eds), A *Moderna História Econômica* (Rio de Janeiro: APEC, 1976). Unfortunately, his analysis was prepared without the availability of the information, presented above, on the role of the low rate of export growth and on the elastic supply of labor in constraining a process of export-led development in Brazil.

30 In 1889 the Brazilian government owned approximately 30 percent of the country's railway trackage; and in 1914, approximately 60 percent. See Julian Duncan, *Public and Private Operation of Railways in Brazil* (New York: Columbia University Press, 1932), pp. 40, 66. Part of this ownership resulted from nationalizations which were implemented in an effort to reduce the burden of servicing fixed foreign obligations.

31 See, for example, the prominent Brazilian historian, Caio Prado, Jr, *The Colonial Background of Modern Brazil* trans. by Suzette Macedo from *Formação do Brasil Contemporáneo*, 7th edn (São Paulo, 1963) (Berkeley and Los Angeles: University of California Press, 1967), p. 145.

32 See Chapters 2 and 4, above.

33 Another question is whether, given the initial distribution of wealth, nineteenth-century Brazil would have been better off with an alternative development pattern which did not emphasize foreign trade. That issue is discussed in Leff, *Reassessing the Obstacles*, op. cit., Chapter 4.

34 Caio Prado, *Colonial Background*, loc. cit.

35 See, for example, the estimates for Japan which are presented in J. R. Hubner, 'Effects on Prices on Japan's Entry into World Commerce after 1858.' *Journal of Political Economy*, vol. 79 (May 1973).

36 Leff, *Reassessing the Obstacles*, op. cit., Chapter 4.

6

Inflation and the Inelastic Supply of Output

Our discussion in Chapter 4 noted that nineteenth-century Brazil had an elastic supply of labor. By contrast, the supply of goods in this economy was relatively inelastic. That is, higher levels of real output generally involved higher costs, and the country's prices rose in a secular inflation. In this respect, Brazil differed from the world economy, which experienced long-term price stability during the nineteenth century. The present chapter seeks to analyze this special feature of the Brazilian economy. Our focus, however, goes beyond the phenomenon of inflation *per se*. The existence of generalized price increases also sheds light on some broader economic relations and their change in nineteenth-century Brazil.

In principle, Brazil's inflation during the nineteenth century might have been the side effect of a process in which expanding aggregate demand generated rapid growth in real output. In practice, the country's long-term inflation reflected a different situation. Nineteenth-century Brazil generally had loose money policies. These led to a buoyant demand for goods; but in reflection of the country's inelastic supply conditions, a major result was higher prices rather than mainly higher output. Why this was so and what were the consequences of the inflation process are among the subjects of the chapter which follows. First, however, we must discuss some features of Brazil's inflation which have not yet been adequately clarified.

The Magnitude of Brazil's Price Inflation

The testimony of contemporaries leaves little doubt that nineteenth-century Brazil experienced long-term inflation. And in reflection of a relatively high rate of monetary expansion, the country's exchange rate, which was free to float during most of this period, displayed a strong trend to depreciation. Between 1822 and 1913, the *mil-réis/* sterling parity depreciated at an annual trend rate of 1.4 percent. Similarly, price series which have been compiled for individual commodities, both in the expanding Southeast and in the depressed Northeast, also indicate long-term inflation. [1]

The material just cited relates to the rising price of individual products or of foreign exchange. There is some question, however, about the economy's *overall* pace of price increase. Two different price series are available to help us answer this question; each of these provides partial but complementary information. One series is a purchasing-power-parity index. That series, which we will call P_p, is derived and discussed in Appendix I of this chapter. By its nature, the P_p index primarily reflects changes in the prices of Brazil's internationally-traded goods: exports, imports, and their close substitutes.

The other price series available is an index of food prices in Rio de Janeiro.[2] Notwithstanding its limited product and geographical coverage, this series also yields information concerning broader price movements. At low levels of per capita income, some 50–60 percent of total consumption expenditure is typically allocated to food.[3] Consequently, the general price level might be expected to move together with food prices. This conclusion is reinforced if we recognize the fact that food was Brazil's major wage good, and hence a significant determinant of overall labor costs. Movements in this specific index of food prices in Rio de Janeiro are in fact highly correlated with movements in a broader sample of local prices.[4] Note further that Rio de Janeiro was Brazil's major market center, and hence the city's prices reflected inflation conditions over more than the immediate geographical vicinity. We will denote this price series, which was prepared by Professor Eulália Lobo and her associates, as P_E.

Annual changes in the P_E and P_p price series show some degree of association. The simple correlation between the yearly observations of the logarithms of the two series is .80. However, P_p and P_E do indicate a major difference in the magnitude of inflation in Brazil. Fitting logarithmic trends to each series in order to ascertain the annual rate of price increase, we observe the following results (*t*-ratios are in parentheses):

$$\ln P_p = .0096 \text{ trend} + .131 \tag{1}$$
$$\quad\quad (12.26) \quad\quad\quad (6.32)$$

$$R^2 = .63 \quad \text{D.W.} = 0.57$$

$$\ln P_E = .051 \text{ trend} + 7.086 \tag{2}$$
$$\quad\quad (42.25) \quad\quad (237.76)$$

$$R^2 = .96 \quad \text{D.W.} = 0.35$$

As these equations indicate, the P_p series rose at an annual long-term rate of approximately 1 percent per annum.[5] By contrast, between 1822 and 1913, the P_E series increased at an annual trend rate of 5.1 percent.

The very different rates of inflation which the two price series indicate raise obvious problems. Why are the estimates so far apart? Which rate of price increase did in fact characterize nineteenth-century Brazil? Why did the movements of the two price series not converge?

One way of dealing with these questions is to reject one or the other (or both) of the price series on grounds of unreliability. In the present instance, there are no grounds evident for taking that approach. The P_E series is not based on casual observations and interpolations, but rather on archival data collected by a group of professional historians.[6] Similarly, the P_p index is based largely on the data for Brazil's exchange rate, a series compiled by the country's Ministry of Finance and long subject to outside scrutiny. Consequently, it seems more fruitful not to reject the data out of hand, but to examine the two price indices in terms of the items they contain and the economic conditions which affected them.

As noted earlier, the two price indices have very different product coverage. The P_p series is basically an index of changes in the prices of Brazil's internationally-traded goods. The P_E index, by contrast, mirrors the changes in the market prices of domestically-produced foodstuffs. Thus manioc flour, beans, rice, and jerked beef (*charque*) account for 86.7 percent of the weighting in the P_E series.[7] In view of its composition, the P_E series is best interpreted as an index of the market prices of goods produced within the Southeast's domestic agricultural sector.

Once we recognize the different composition of the two indices, the disparate pace of price inflation which they indicate becomes readily understandable. Demand was expanding buoyantly both for internationally-traded goods and for domestically-marketed foodstuffs in nineteenth-century Brazil. There were, however, important differences in supply conditions between the two sectors. Because of more ample infrastructure and credit facilities, the supply of Brazil's traded goods was much more elastic with respect to price than was the supply of marketed domestic foodstuffs. Econometric evidence presented later in this chapter confirms this differential in supply elasticities between the external and the domestic agricultural sectors in Brazil.[8]

There is also a special reason why prices of marketed domestic foodstuffs in the Southeast should have risen at a relatively high rate during this period. During the nineteenth century, the population of Rio de Janeiro city grew rapidly. At the same time, agricultural resources within the Southeast shifted from subsistence to export-crop production.[9] Such a period in which the fraction of the population which is dependent on marketed food increases sharply is critical for price inflation in developing countries.[10] As the population which relies on purchased food increases from a small initial base, the demand for *marketed* output grows much more rapidly than does overall consumption of food products. This special pressure on supply means that food prices are likely to rise at a relatively high rate, as is in fact the case with the P_E price series.

So far we have discussed the disparity in sectoral rates of inflation in terms of movement along existing supply curves which had different degrees of elasticity. The long-term change in relative prices also reflected differences in the rate at which supply curves for diverse products shifted outward during the nineteenth century. International prices of Brazil's major imports fell with the productivity increases of the Industrial Revolution. Productivity gains of such magnitude certainly did not occur, however, in Brazil's domestic agricultural sector. Similarly, the rate at which international prices of Brazil's export products could increase was constrained by world-market competition. But imports of food to Brazil were small relative to the country's total food supply (see below); and internal transportation costs were too large for international trade to provide a comparable damper on domestic agricultural prices.

Both differential supply elasticities and differences in the pace with which supply curves in the two sectors shifted explain why prices of domestic foodstuffs rose at a much higher rate than prices of the country's traded goods. Note also that for reasons discussed in Appendix I, the P_p index is downward-biased, and understates the magnitude of inflation for Brazil's traded goods.[11] Further, because of factor-market imperfections and the country's high internal transportation costs, a low rate of price increase in the external sector would not do much to moderate inflationary pressures within the domestic agricultural sector.

To return to our earlier question, neither the P_E nor the P_p price index adequately measures inflation in the economy as a whole. The two series reflect price movements within two distinct sectors. For some purposes, however, it might be desirable to have an index that would indicate the pace of overall price inflation in Brazil during the nineteenth century. Apart from data problems, serious conceptual difficulties attend such an enterprise. Because of the sectoral and geographical fragmentation which characterized this economy, aggregation involves special problems in this case. For this reason, it is not clear what meaning to attach to a figure of aggregate price increase in nineteenth-century Brazil. Further, the most important part of the story here is not the magnitude of aggregate inflation, but the fact that: (1) going against world economic trends, Brazil experienced sustained price increases during the nineteenth century; (2) the pace of inflation varied greatly between the economy's major sectors.

Notwithstanding the cautions noted above, one may still want an overall view of price inflation in Brazil during the nineteenth century. The pressures to focus on the country as the unit of study in economic history and development are strong. Appendix II of this chapter presents an aggregate estimate, together with the steps followed in deriving it. This estimate can be regarded only as a likely order of magnitude rather than a precise figure. It suggests that the rate of long-term price inflation in Brazil between 1822 and 1913 was approximately 2.5 percent per annum.

Other Aspects of the Inflation

The pace of inflation in nineteenth-century Brazil was not constant, but rather varied significantly over time. Although most prices moved upward over the long term, they did so at different rates; and in some years, prices even fell. Table 6.1 presents illustrative data on this phenomenon, giving the price movements of three basic foods: rice, beans and maize. Between 1826 and 1875, prices of these commodities rose from a base of 100 to indices of 201, 259, and 496, respectively. Nevertheless, as Table 6.1 indicates, there was much intra-period variance in the rate of price increase for each of these products.

Similarly, the results of the trend equations (1) and (2) above also indicate considerable variation in the pace of price inflation. Although the t-ratios for the trend terms in those regressions are large, significant deviations above or below the trend line occurred in both equations. Moreover, the Durbin–Watson statistics of these trend regressions indicate considerable serial correlation, such that above-average (or below-average) price increases in one year were followed by a similar pattern in the subsequent year. Consequently, observing the pattern of residuals for these equations, we can demarcate relatively sustained periods in which the Brazilian inflation proceeded at a rate above or below its long-term trend value. This approach was followed with both

Table 6.1 *Short-Term Movements in the Prices of Rice, Beans, and Maize* (Milho) *in Rio de Janeiro, 1826–75*

Annual Percentage Rate of Price Change since Previous Observation:				Annual Percentage Rate of Price Change since Previous Observation:			
Year	Rice	Beans	Maize	Year	Rice	Beans	Maize
1826	—	—	—	1850	n.a.	−16.7	−4.8
1830	4.5	n.a.	n.a.	1853	4.1	11.4	11.9
1835	0.2	4.8	7.8	1862	0.6	−0.2	1.5
1838	14.5	15.3	4.0	1870	3.0	1.9	7.7
1842	−2.5	−2.4	−5.8	1875	−4.9	0	−3.7
1847	−1.4	6.3	7.2				

n.a. denotes no observation available.

Source: Computed from data in Mircea Buescu, *300 Anos de Inflacao* (Rio de Janeiro: APEC, 1973), pp. 133, 136, 164, 196. The underlying data are price quotations in Rio de Janeiro newspapers.

Table 6.2   Periods in Which Brazil's Inflation Was Above or Below the Long-Term Trend, 1822–1913

	Period of Above-Trend Inflation	Period of Below-Trend Inflation
I Deviations from P_p Trend Equation		
	1828–47	1822–26
	1854–60	1849–53
	1866–69	1874–89
	1892–1903	1904–12
II Deviations from P_E Trend Equation		
	1842–48	1822–36
	1853–61	·1883–91
	1866–79	1903–13
	1892–1900	

Source: For explanation, see the text.

the P_E and the P_p trend equations; and the years of significant deviations (i.e. differences between the actual price level and the value that would be expected on the basis of the long-term statistical trend) were noted. Considering the years with deviations of 5 percent or more in absolute value, we note the periods which are presented in Table 6.2.

Table 6.2 shows an inflationary process which is considerably more complex than the simplistic picture conveyed by our earlier trend equations. The data suggest a pattern of cycles in which inflation alternated at rates above and below long-term trend rates. Professor Mattoso's graphs of the price series for individual commodities in Bahia also show this cyclical phenomenon.[12] The presence of fluctuations in inflation (around a strong upward trend) is strikingly apparent in her graphs. In a later section, we will analyze these inflationary cycles in greater detail. One effect of this phenomenon is worth noting here, however. The variations which occurred in the rate of inflation introduced a special element of uncertainty in the lives of economic agents in nineteenth-century Brazil. This uncertainty was exacerbated by the differences in periodization which Table 6.2 shows as between the P_E and P_p price series.

It is also important to recognize that prices did not rise uniformly across sectors in this inflation. Our discussion of the different product coverage (and rates of price increase) of the P_E and P_p indices showed that prices in Brazil's domestic agricultural sector rose at a pace markedly higher than prices of the country's internationally-traded goods. Further, within the broad category of traded goods there were also disparate rates of price increase. The *mil-réis* prices of imported products rose over the period, as a consequence of Brazil's persistent

exchange-rate depreciation. The increase in import prices was mitigated, however, by the worldwide decline in the prices of manufactured
goods during most of the nineteenth century. By contrast, the prices of
many of Brazil's exports increased more rapidly than did the country's
import prices. As we saw in Chapter 5, the country's barter terms of
trade (p_x/p_m) were generally higher in the course of the century than at
its beginning.

Available data enable us to make a first approximation at measuring
these variables.[13] Changes in the *mil-réis* price of Brazil's exports were
determined by movements in the country's exchange rate and in
the export-price index. The *mil-réis*/sterling exchange rate rose at a
trend rate of 1.4 percent per annum between 1822 and 1913. Brazil's
index of export prices (in sterling) increased at an annual trend rate of
0.1 percent. Hence, the country's export prices in *mil-réis* rose at an
annual rate of approximately 1.5 percent from 1822 to 1913.

An index of the sterling price of Brazil's imports during the nineteenth century is not available. However, we do have the index of
British export prices, and Britain was the major source of Brazilian
imports during much of the century. Using the British export-price
series as a rough indicator of the change in Brazil's import prices, we
observe that this index fell at a trend rate of 0.8 percent per annum
between 1822 and 1913. Taken together with the 1.4 percent rate of
exchange depreciation, this index would imply that Brazil's import
prices rose at an annual trend rate of 0.6 percent between 1822 and
1913. In reality, however, the British export-price index understates
the fall in Brazil's import prices. First, the British index does not
reflect the lower prices which Brazilians paid as cheaper producers
replaced Britain in supplying imported products later in the century.[14]
Second, the nineteenth century saw a major decline in international
shipping costs.[15] Because of this decline in transportation costs, Brazilian import prices could fall by more than the decline in British export
prices.

As a result of the import and export-price movements just discussed,
Brazil's external terms of trade improved during the nineteenth century. The data cited above indicate that the barter terms of trade,
P_x/P_m, rose at an annual trend rate of 0.9 percent per annum. And that
improvement is without taking into account the conditions which make
our data understate the true fall in import prices. Thus, Brazil's international terms of trade were not a source of long-term inflationary
pressure. Also, as we saw in our discussion of the P_p and P_E price
indices, prices of traded goods in Brazil rose at a rate well below the
prices of goods that originated in the country's domestic sector. These
empirical observations lead us to an important analytical conclusion:
Brazil's external sector does not seem to have had a major causal role
in the country's inflation during the nineteenth century.[16]

Proximate Causes of the Inflation

Inflation in nineteenth-century Brazil was closely related to the growth of the country's stock of money (M).[17] Data on the Brazilian money supply are available beginning in 1839.[18] As might be expected, all of our measures of price inflation are highly correlated with the pace of monetary expansion. Thus, in the period 1840–1913 annual changes in Brazil's external parity were tightly linked with lagged changes in the domestic money supply.[19] Similarly, for the years 1839–1913 the simple correlation between annual observations of the logarithm of the money supply and the logarithm of P_p is a highly significant .78. The correlation between log M and log P_E is even higher, .98. Of greater analytical interest, however, are the pertinent elasticities. These show the extent to which a given percentage change in the country's money supply was associated with a percentage change in the price level.

In order to compute these elasticities, separate regression equations were estimated. Annual observations of each price series were specified as the dependent variable, and annual observations of the money supply as the independent variable. To clarify the direction of causality and to mitigate problems of simultaneous-equations bias, the money supply variable was lagged one year. The equations were specified in double-logarithmic form. This specification reduces possible heteroscedasticity; it also permits ready interpretation of the parameter estimate on the log M_{-1} term as an elasticity. As a first step, the equations were estimated for the entire period 1840–1913. (Equations for sub-periods are reported later in this chapter.) Preliminary estimates indicated the presence of strong positive serial correlation in the residuals. Accordingly the regressions were re-estimated using the Cochrane–Orcutt transformation.[20] Thus the equations also provide information on the magnitude of the serial correlation parameter, ρ. The results, with absolute values of the t-ratios in parentheses, are:

$$\ln P_p = -.973 + .221 \ln M_{-1} \tag{3}$$
$$(4.17)(5.30)$$

$$\rho = .69 \ (8.24) \quad R^2 = .81$$

$$\ln P_E = 5.494 + .454 \ln M_{-1} \tag{4}$$
$$(6.81)(3.60)$$

$$\rho = .94 \ (23.19) \quad R^2 = .98$$

The good statistical fit of equations (3) and (4) stems partly from the presence of strong trends in the price and monetary series. However, the Cochrane–Orcutt transformation which was utilized avoids the possibility of such inefficient estimation.[21] The size of the t-ratios on the lagged money supply term in both equations indicates the basic importance of monetary conditions as a proximate cause of Brazil's inflation during the nineteenth century. For the log P_E series, the regression accounts for .98 of the variance in the country's annual price inflation. For the log P_p series, which is basically the country's annual exchange rate, the R^2 is lower, .81. The poorer statistical fit for this equation presumably reflects the importance of omitted variables (e.g. capital movements and international price movements) in explaining annual changes of Brazil's external parity.

Equations (3) and (4) also show large magnitudes and a high level of statistical significance for ρ, the serial correlation parameter. These estimates indicate the strongly autoregressive nature of the Brazilian inflation, and may reflect the importance of expectational factors in maintaining price movements.[22] Thus prolonged experience with continuing price increases (which had begun in the country well before the period under consideration) may have dissipated money illusion among economic agents in nineteenth-century Brazil. Because of the high degree of autocorrelation, inflation assumed an internal momentum and became correspondingly more difficult to control.

Finally, a special interest attaches to the parameter estimates for the money-supply term in equations (3) and (4). Because aggregate output was growing and velocity was falling in the Brazilian economy during the nineteenth century, one would expect the elasticity of prices with respect to increases in the money supply to be well below unity. In fact, the short-term elasticities for the P_p and P_E terms with respect to annual changes in the lagged money supply are .22 and .45, respectively. The greater size of the coefficient in the P_E equation corroborates our earlier suggestion that supply was much less elastic with respect to price in Brazil's domestic agricultural sector. Consequently, monetary expansion of the same amount led to price increases which were much greater in that sector than in the activities which provided the country's internationally-traded goods. Because output in Brazil's domestic agriculture was relatively price-inelastic, the sector added appreciably to the country's overall rate of price inflation during the nineteenth century.

The parameter estimates of equations (3) and (4) show only the short-run elasticities of Brazilian prices with respect to changes in the country's money supply. However, it seems likely that the adjustment of actual cash balances to desired money holdings (and hence actual inflation to the long-run equilibrium level) occurred over a period longer than one year. This consideration suggests the need to estimate a partial-adjustment model of the response of Brazilian prices to changes in the stock of money.[23] Presentation of such a model is straightforward. Let us denote long-run equilibrium values with asterisks, and omit (for the sake of expositional simplicity) the lag on the log M term in equations (3) and (4). With the equilibrium price level a function, *inter alia*, of desired cash balances, we have:

$$\ln P^* = a + b \ln M \qquad (5)$$

Under a partial-adjustment process, the rate at which the equilibrium price level is attained is proportionate to the difference between the actual and the equilibrium levels. Accordingly,

$$\ln P - \ln P_{-1} = \lambda(\ln P^* - \ln P_{-1}) \quad 0 \leq \lambda \leq 1 \qquad (6)$$

where λ measures the speed of adjustment from actual to equilibrium values. It then follows that

$$\ln P = \lambda \ln P^* + (1 - \lambda) \ln P_{-1} \qquad (7)$$

Substituting equation (5) into (7), and specifying an error term, u, yields an estimating equation:

$$\ln P = a\lambda + b\lambda \ln M + (1 - \lambda) \ln P_{-1} + u \qquad (8)$$

With the data available, we can estimate the parameters of equation (8). We can thus obtain information on the empirical magnitude of λ, the adjustment coefficient; and we can then calculate the mean adjustment lag, $(1 - \lambda)/\lambda$. These measures indicate the speed of the adjustment process in nineteenth-century Brazil. Finally, we can compute the empirical magnitude of b, the long-run elasticity of prices with respect to changes in the money supply.

Before proceeding to such estimation and computations, note a potential pitfall. As Zvi Griliches has emphasized, researchers must be careful to avoid *imposing* the hypothesis of a partial-adjustment model on observations which are actually characterized by a purely autoregressive process.[24] Griliches proposed a statistical test to distinguish between these two possibilities.[25] Applying this test to the observations for P_p and P_E over the years 1840–1913 indicates that the true underlying model for the P_p series is indeed a purely autoregressive rather than a partial-adjustment process. The Griliches test does show, however, that the P_E series is characterized by a partial-adjustment process. Proceeding therefore to estimate equation (8) for log P_E, we observe the following behavioral parameters (t-statistics are in parentheses):

$$\ln P_E = 1.265 + .379 \ln M_{-1} + .570 \ln P_{E-1} \qquad (9)$$
$$(4.47) \quad (4.29) \qquad\quad (6.05)$$

$$\rho = .376 \ (3.46) \quad R^2 = .98$$

$$\lambda = .430 \quad \frac{(1-\lambda)}{\lambda} = 1.33 \quad b = .88$$

The parameter estimates for equation (9) indicate a relatively swift adjustment process in nineteenth-century Brazil. The estimate for λ indicates that 43 percent of the difference between actual and long-run equilibrium inflation levels was eliminated in one year. By the same token, the mean lag of adjustment was brief, 1.3 years. Most importantly, the long-run elasticity of prices with respect to changes in the money supply was high, 0.88. Similar results were obtained when, as a check against statistical bias, equation (8) was estimated with the technique of instrumental variables.[26] Those estimates indicated a long-run inflation elasticity with respect to monetary expansion of .91. These estimates point to an important finding which should not be lost in the discussion of how we obtained it. An inflation elasticity of 0.9 means that the long-run response of *output* changes in the money supply was relatively low in nineteenth-century Brazil.

The general picture which emerges from these results, then, is of an economy which, within the framework of its constraints, adjusted relatively quickly to macroeconomic changes. However, the constraints were such that in the relevant range, expanding aggregate output usually involved higher prices. Two sets of conditions, in turn, underlay Brazil's inelastic supply with respect to price. First, within individual production units, rigidities and inelastic factor supplies may have hampered the expansion of output. Those conditions affected pure production elasticities. Perhaps more important, however, were the circumstances which influenced the elasticity of supply in broader terms. These involved geography and transportation costs.

Nineteenth-century Brazil was predominantly an agricultural economy, both in terms of the products demanded and in terms of the goods produced. An obvious (but nonetheless important) feature of agriculture is that its production is closely connected to land. And because of land's peculiarly spatial nature, considerations of distance and transportation become of crucial significance in determining the cost conditions under which increments to marketed output are supplied. As discussed in Chapter 2, Brazil's infrastructure facilities during most of the nineteenth century were poor, and involved relatively high freight charges.[27] For this reason, agricultural supplies were available at constant prices only within a very limited geographical locale; thereafter, the gradient relating price to distance rose steeply. These conditions applied with special severity to the bulky, low-value foodstuffs produced within the domestic agricultural sector. And because of food's strategic importance as a wage good, Brazil's adverse geographical/transportation conditions led to the existence of relatively inelastic aggregate supply conditions in this economy.

As this discussion indicates, the econometric results presented earlier which showed the importance of monetary expansion for price inflation in nineteenth-century Brazil tell only part of the story. Growth of the money stock was only one blade of the scissors which determined Brazil's long-term inflation between 1840 and 1913. The other blade was the set of conditions which made for a relatively inelastic supply of goods, especially in the domestic agricultural sector. Thus, inflation in nineteenth-century Brazil seems to have reflected a standard situation in which the supply of money increased more rapidly than did the demand for cash balances. Expenditure of these excess balances, in turn, generated additional demand for goods. What was of special importance, however, was that these pressures encountered internal supply conditions which were relatively inelastic with respect to price. The result was chronic inflation. Later, we will discuss other aspects of domestic supply inelasticity, particularly its change over time. Let us consider here the determinants of the growth in Brazil's stock of money.

Determinants of the Growth of the Money Supply

The Brazilian authorities in the nineteenth century rarely followed a policy in which the growth of the domestic money stock was dictated by gold standard considerations.[28] Other conditions, however, did determine the pace of the country's monetary expansion. Brazil experienced steady long-term population increase and growth of aggregate output during the nineteenth century. Consequently, one would expect that trend would 'explain' most of the increase in the country's stock of money. Additional influences on the growth of the nominal money, however, might come from two special sources, the external sector and the government deficit. Budget deficits would increase the money supply to the extent that the government financed its operations by increasing the monetary base.[29] And conditions in the foreign-trade sector might also affect the country's money supply. For example, an excess of exports over imports might in principle lead to an expansion of the domestic stock of money. Foreign capital movements influencing Brazil's money supply would also be reflected in the country's international accounts.

In order to examine the empirical relevance of these considerations, a regression equation was estimated for the years 1840–1913. The annual money stock was taken as the dependent variable. (This is because Brazil's money supply and monetary base moved closely together during this period, and for our purposes little is gained if we distinguish between the behavior of the two series.[30]) The government's budget deficit (D) and country's trade balance (TB) were specified as the independent variables. The TB variable was utilized because the only balance-of-payments data available relate to the value of commodity imports and exports. In order to permit interpretation of the parameter estimates as elasticities, the equation was estimated in logarithmic form. And because the trade balance and the budget deficit sometimes assumed negative values, these variables were specified in ratio form. The TB variable was specified as the ratio of the value of commodity exports to commodity imports; and the D variable was specified as the ratio of central government expenditures to receipts. Because prior knowledge of the true specification was lacking, the right-hand side variables were specified both in current and in lagged form.

Preliminary estimation indicated the presence of strong serial correlation in the error terms. Accordingly, the regression was re-estimated using the Cochrane–Orcutt transformation. Estimation of the serial correlation parameter, which is central to this procedure, is tantamount to specifying a trend term, and provides an indication of the importance of trend in the long-term expansion of Brazil's money supply. The regression equation for the years 1840–1913, with t-ratios in parentheses, is:

$$\ln M = 7.561 + .043 \ln D + .126 \ln D_{-1} - .153 \ln TB + .024 \ln TB_{-1} \quad (10)$$
$$\quad (11.65) \quad (0.52) \quad (1.52) \quad (1.18) \quad (0.18)$$

$$\rho = .982 \ (44.65) \quad R^2 = .99$$

The t-ratios for all of the coefficients (except the constant term) in equation (10) are low. This result suggests that the good statistical fit of the regression is due mainly to the trend effects which are captured in the ρ term. Further, equation (10) shows no statistically significant relation between the current budget deficit and changes in the money supply. However, with a one-tailed test, as is appropriate in the present context, the lagged deficit term is statistically significant at the 5 percent level. By contrast, the parameter estimates for the trade-balance terms are not significantly different from zero at conventional confidence levels. Hence, at least in the form specified by equation (10), there is no indication that foreign trade and international capital conditions had a significant influence in the determination of Brazil's nominal money supply. Similar results were observed in other regressions, which were specified differently: in natural numbers, without the Cochrane–Orcutt transform (and the ensuing specification of ρ); and for a two-period division of the years 1840–1913. These regressions are reported in a note.[31] What is most noteworthy in this context is that the TB and D variables in those regressions accounted for virtually

Table 6.3   *Parameter Estimates and Summary Statistics for Regression Equations with the Logarithm of the Nominal Brazilian Money Supply as the Dependent Variable*

	Parameter Estimate for:						R^2	D.W.
Period	Trend	ln D	ln D_{-1}	ln TB	ln TB_{-1}	Constant		
1840–73	.052	−.219	.566	.128	−.018	4.333	.94	.42
	(11.90)	(0.96)	(2.48)	(0.37)	(0.05)	(120.36)		
1874–1913	.054	.281	.305	−.267	−.326	6.276	.87	.38
	(14.05)	(1.03)	(1.17)	(0.75)	(0.81)	(54.15)		
1840–1913	.052	.144	.327	−.081	−.185	5.326	.97	.34
	(28.27)	(0.89)	(2.04)	(0.32)	(0.69)	(132.76)		

Note: For explanation of the notation, see the text. Absolute values of the *t*-ratios are in parentheses.

none of the variance in the annual percentage growth of Brazil's money stock.

We can gain further perspective on the determinants of Brazilian monetary expansion if we explicitly specify a logarithmic trend in addition to the variables of equation (10). In this specification, the parameter estimates for the D and TB terms have a special meaning. The coefficients show whether budget-deficit and trade-balance variables can at least account for the annual deviations of the money supply from its long-term trend. Regressions with this specification were estimated both for the period as a whole and for two sub-periods, divided at 1873. The estimates are presented in Table 6.3.

Table 6.3 indicates that in the earlier period, the lagged budget deficit was a statistically significant determinant of the Brazilian money supply's annual deviations from the long-term trend. In the post-1873 years, however, the D terms are not statistically different from zero. Further, this disaggregated analysis also shows no measurable influence of the trade balance on domestic monetary expansion or contraction. Finally, Table 6.3 confirms the importance of trend in 'explaining' the long-term growth of the Brazilian money supply. The magnitude of the trend term in the earlier period, 1840–73, 5.2 percent per annum, is also noteworthy. This rate is almost as large as the 5.4 percent figure observed for the later years, a period which is sometimes considered to have been characterized by exceptionally rapid monetary expansion.

It is not surprising that a trend term accounts statistically for most of the long-term growth of the Brazilian money supply during the nineteenth century. Throughout this period, there were constant requests from the private sector for government measures to enlarge the domestic money supply. Similarly, the Brazilian state was also concerned to increase liquidity. This practice was especially attractive in cases where the government viewed expansion of fiat money as being little more than the issuance of non-interest-bearing debt. Finally, once inflation began, it acquired a self-sustained momentum. By eroding the real value of cash balances, long-term inflation itself intensified the pressures to increase the money supply at a relatively high rate.

What is noteworthy is not the statistical significance of long-term trend in accounting for the growth of Brazil's nominal money supply, but rather the quantitative magnitude of the trend term. The 5.2 percent annual rate at which the Brazilian authorities expanded the money supply (see Table 6.3) was sufficiently in excess of the growth of demand for cash balances that the country experienced persistent inflation. Indeed, the importance of the trend term in these equations reflects the height of the Brazilian authorities' monetary heterodoxy: the fact that the inflationary magnitude of monetary expansion came not as the result of occasional budget deficits, but rather as part of the normal practice of monetary policy.

Inflation and Macroeconomic Cycles

As noted earlier, the residuals of the trend equations for P_p and P_E indicate cycles in which inflation alternated at rates above or below its long-term trend values (see Table 6.2 above).[32] Inspection of the residuals of the trend regressions for other key macroeconomic series in Brazil also revealed a similar pattern. Moreover, the residuals of these individual macroeconomic series are highly intercorrelated. This observation suggests the existence in nineteenth-century Brazil of short-term macroeconomic cycles which involved interaction between inflation, foreign trade, and government expenditure.

In order to clarify the nature of this cycle the following procedure was followed. First, each of the time series in question was detrended: each variable was expressed in annual deviations from its logarithmic trend for the years 1839–1913. The deviations of the respective variables are denoted with lower case letters. Because simultaneous-equations bias is a real possibility in many of the relations, each equation reported below was estimated using two-stage least squares (TSLS), with the lagged exogenous variables specified as instruments. Since R^2 is not relevant in TSLS, that statistic is not presented; and we focus on the t-statistics (which are presented in parentheses) as indicators of statistically significant relationships.

Because the model was estimated in deviations, which are likely to contain considerable statistical 'noise', two further points are relevant. To the extent that the deviations of the dependent and independent variables include errors in measurement which are uncorrelated, the parameter estimates of the individual equations are biased toward zero. Second, because the variables specified may contain a relatively high ratio of noise to information, applying conventional levels of statistical significance involves a very stringent test. Further, such procedures can also be misleading in this context, for they may lead to Type I error – rejecting hypotheses which are in fact valid. One possible way of avoiding that pitfall is the following: as long as a parameter estimate is larger than its standard error (i.e. the *t*-ratio exceeds unity), accept it as providing positive support for the relation posited.[33]

The first equation in this short-term macro model considers the possibility that deviations in the money supply, current or lagged, led directly to a deviation of nominal imports from trend.

$$imp = -.307 \, m + .983 \, m_{-1} \qquad (11)$$
$$(0.51) \quad (1.83)$$

Equation (11) confirms this relation: unusually high growth in the domestic money supply spilled over, with a one-year lag, to unusually high growth in Brazil's imports. The same relation also prevailed on the down side, of course, as below-trend growth in the money supply led to below-trend demand for imports. Note, moreover, that the elasticity in equation (11) is close to unity.

Deviations of imports from trend, in turn, had two effects on Brazil's exchange rate. Increased demand for foreign exchange raised the *mil-réis*/sterling exchange rate; a relative-price effect reduced pressure on the country's parity. The net result was a rise in the *mil-réis*/sterling exchange rate.

$$er = -1.385 \, imp + 1.979 \, imp_{-1} \qquad (12)$$
$$(2.21) \quad (3.43)$$

Exchange-rate depreciation had a positive short-term effect on the *mil-réis* value of exports.

$$x = 1.130 \, er - .463 \, er_{-1} \qquad (13)$$
$$(2.90) \quad (1.26)$$

Further, because public-sector finances in Brazil were highly dependent on foreign-trade taxes, a deviation in imports and/or exports from trend might be expected to have a corresponding impact on government expenditures. Equation (14) shows that such a connection did indeed exist, at least in the case of imports.[34]

$$g = 1.009 \, imp - .808 \, imp_{-1} - .160 \, x + .509 \, x_{-1} \qquad (14)$$
$$(1.56) \quad (1.54) \quad (0.16) \quad (0.71)$$

Finally, to close the circuit, a deviation of government expenditure from trend in nineteenth-century Brazil led to a change in the growth of the money supply.

$$m = 1.617 \; g - .502 \; g_{-1} \qquad \qquad (15)$$
$$ (3.00) \quad\;\; (1.26)$$

Similarly, a deviation in the money supply would have a short-term impact on domestic prices.

$$p_E = .055 \; m + .675 \; m_{-1} \qquad \qquad (16)$$
$$ (0.09) \quad\;\; (1.20)$$

Equations (11) – (16) depict a system with strong feedback effects in the inflation/foreign trade/government sector nexus. Thus a random or exogenous positive deviation of the country's money supply, foreign trade, or government expenditures from their trend values would lead to a cumulative increase in those variables. And because of the links in the system, such a process would be self-perpetuating unless the government, reacting to intolerably high rates of price inflation, intervened to control it with contractionary monetary and/or fiscal measures. A negative deviation in the trend rate of monetary expansion would of course propel the whole system into a downward phase in the cycle around the inflationary trend. This model can obviously be refined and extended. It is presented here as a first approach at elucidating some key short-term macroeconomic relationships in Brazil's economy during the nineteenth century.

Some Effects of the Inflation

The Brazilian government's practice of expanding the stock of money at rates which involved persistent price inflation also had consequences for the country's long-term development.[35] Because of the differential supply elasticities which we noted in our discussion of P_E and P_P, inflation in Brazil could have relative-price effects and hence an impact which transcended the purely monetary sphere. In addition, inflation influenced the country's financial development; and distributional effects were also present.

The government's capacity to issue money in inflationary magnitudes may have increased the public-sector's share in Brazilian output. As is well known, inflation can be considered a tax levied on holders of cash balances. The possibilities for appropriating resources through inflationary rates of long-term monetary expansion (rather than simply with sporadic budget deficits) must have been especially welcome to Brazil's policy-makers. As discussed elsewhere,[36] the Brazilian state had a relatively weak capacity for collecting taxes during most of the nineteenth century.[37] The impact of the inflation tax on public-sector resources during the period as a whole should not be exaggerated, however. The government's revenue gains as a percentage of national income in such a case are equal to the rate of monetary growth divided by the income velocity.[38] Given the long-term rate of growth of the (total) money supply of 5 percent, and the probable magnitudes of velocity, the government's revenue gains in Brazil were usually very small.

During the last decades of the nineteenth-century, the Brazilian state seems to have had a relatively high marginal propensity to allocate its resources for developmental purposes.[39] To that extent, inflationary public finance may have had positive effects on economic welfare. But in view of the likely magnitude of some relevant parameters (the government's revenue gains, the relevant capital–output ratios, and the difference between public- and private-sector propensities to invest), the net welfare effect was probably of negligible proportions.

Inflationary public finance may also have had some adverse effects on Brazil's economic development. By raising the cost of holding money, inflation led to a situation in which economic agents rationally maintained cash balances smaller than would otherwise have been the case. Especially in production activities, the welfare cost of the liquidity services lost seems to have been relatively high. Endemic inflation with its associated instabilities also added to economic uncertainty. The uncertainty must have been especially severe because, as we have seen, inflation involved differential (and changing) rates of price increase for diverse commodities. Both of these conditions – increased uncertainty and reduced liquidity – probably led to a lower level of investment than would otherwise have prevailed. Further, persistent inflation may have inhibited Brazil's financial development. Financial intermediaries in nineteenth-century Brazil were often criticized for their high interest rates and for their focus on short-term lending. Persistent and uncertain inflation would help account for both of these phenomena. Deficient financial intermediation, in turn, would have had negative effects both on the volume and on the efficiency of capital formation.[40]

More generally, inflationary rates of monetary expansion clearly did not lead to rapid economic growth or development in nineteenth-century Brazil. The long-term conjunction of sustained inflation with slow structural change and modest growth of per capita income until the end of the century directly contradicts any such supposition.[41] A relatively high rate of increase in the money stock did ensure that insufficient aggregate demand was rarely the constraint on the pace of the country's economic expansion. However, the problems for economic development in this economy were usually on the supply side. More specifically, as noted earlier, the supply of output was less elastic in the domestic agricultural sector than in Brazil's traded-goods sector. Consequently, spurts in monetary expansion led to a shift in the internal terms of trade against the country's traded-goods sector (exports, imports, and import-competing activities like manufacturing). Acceleration in the growth of the money supply could thus provoke a sharp movement in relative prices ('*crise de subsistência*') which hurt urban consumers and the country's export sector. Higher food prices also reduced profits, investment, and the pace of expansion in the traded-goods activities (see below). Such an adverse relative-price shift was usually also accompanied by higher rates of aggregate inflation until the cycle was reversed by government policy, a financial panic, or external developments.[42]

In order to analyze this movement, it would be helpful to verify directly the shift of domestic agricultural prices relative to traded-good prices in response to a given amount of monetary expansion. Making use of the data which are available to consider this relative-price elasticity, a regression equation was fitted with log (P_E/P_p) as the dependent variable and log M_{-1} as the independent variable. Estimated with the Cochrane–Orcutt transform and with observations for the years 1840–1913, the equation is:

$$\ln (P_E/P_p) = 3.947 + .643 \ln M_{-1} \qquad (17)$$
$$(13.35) \quad (12.11)$$

$$\rho = .633 \ (6.99) \quad R^2 = .95$$

As equation (17) indicates, increases in the money supply were indeed followed by a rise in the prices of domestic foodstuffs relative to prices of Brazil's traded goods. The estimated short-term elasticity for internal relative prices with respect to log M_{-1} is .64.[43] The P_E index may possibly overstate the magnitude of the movement, but the direction of the relative-price effect is clear. Moreover, the adjustment was swift. Estimation of a partial-adjustment specification of equation (17) showed a two-year mean adjustment period, with a long-run elasticity of .67.

The cyclical shift in the internal terms of trade had important consequences. First, it enabled agricultural producers outside of the export activities to share, at least partly, in the gains of the country's expanding modern sector. Because of internal transportation costs, the gains of the domestic agricultural sector were not commensurate with the rise of relative prices as measured in the market centers (see below). Nevertheless, the relative-price movement probably did involve benefits for the small-scale farmers who produced foodstuffs (e.g.

manioc, beans, *milho*) in the domestic agricultural sector. The other side of the coin, however, was an increase in the relative price of domestically-produced food supply to the export sector. During this period, most of Brazil's food came from internal sources – food accounted for only 21 percent of the country's total imports in 1839–44, and 20 percent in 1870–75.[44] Consequently, the shift in the internal terms of trade raised the cost of wage goods and lowered profits in the export activities. The ensuing constraints on internal cash flow limited the export sector's capacity for investment and expansion of output.[45] This led to lower rates of aggregate productivity increase and structural change; for export growth was a major source of those developments in nineteenth-century Brazil.

Thus, because of the domestic agricultural sector's inelastic supply conditions, rapid increase in the stock of money did not lead to generalized economic development. High rates of monetary expansion reduced profits in the export sector and imposed constraints on its growth. The same underlying conditions also limited the impact of the 'advanced' sector's growth sector on development in the rest of the economy. As noted, expanding incomes and demand for food in the traded-good activities were partly dissipated in price inflation rather than in rising real output within the agricultural sector. Also, Brazil's heavy internal transportation costs made for large differences between the prices of agricultural goods in the market centers and the prices which producers received ex-farm. Under these price and output conditions, a rising relative price for food in the urban centers was not synonymous with a prosperous agricultural sector.

High internal freight charges also conditioned the impact of the shift in the internal terms of trade on Brazil's industrial development. Transportation costs influenced the relative prices and the consumption possibilities which people in the domestic agricultural sector faced. The principal effect of high shipping costs was to raise the on-farm relative price of urban industrial products, and to lower the relative price of food and leisure. It is therefore not surprising that the consumption pattern in Brazil's domestic agricultural sector was heavily weighted to the latter two goods, and generated relatively little demand for manufactures. And by the same token, the shift in the internal terms of trade which came with excessive rates of monetary expansion did not greatly increase the demand for manufactured goods within the domestic agricultural sector.[46] Finally, in the traded-good activities, the rising relative price for food also reduced the size of the market for industrial products. In such circumstances, a large internal market for manufactures did not emerge in nineteenth-century Brazil despite several decades of inflationary monetary growth.

Structural Change in the Relation between Monetary Expansion and Price Inflation

Increases in a country's money supply lead, in differing degrees, to price inflation, to changes in velocity (monetization), and/or to higher output levels.[47] The extent of each outcome will vary with specific conditions, including the pace of economic development. One of these relations, the quantitative connection between monetary expansion and price inflation, can be captured in a regression of prices on the lagged money supply, as in equations (3) and (4) above. In the course of time, however, the coefficient in such an equation may change in a manner which is statistically significant. Such a change in the parameter which relates price inflation to monetary expansion reflects a change in economic structure.

Consider, for example, the case where the parameter estimate for the money-supply term in equations (3) and (4) declines significantly over time. Such a change indicates that a given increase in the money supply is now associated with less price inflation and, instead, with greater output growth and monetization. A structural shift of this nature would signal an important break with the past, and a significant movement toward economic development. This is because inelastic supply conditions are a major feature of economic underdevelopment. So, too, is a situation in which the monetized sector is small relative to the rest of the economy, and barter transactions predominate. In this perspective, a significant shift toward accelerated monetization and increased elasticity in aggregate supply would constitute an important change in Brazil's economic history. A straightforward statistical tool is available which enables us to consider the possibility of such a structural change in the context of nineteenth-century Brazil. This is the special F-test developed by Gregory Chow.[48] By applying this test to the parameter estimates of equations (3) and (4), we can answer two important questions. Over the years 1840–1913, did statistically significant change occur in the coefficient which related price inflation to changes in the lagged money supply? If so, when did the structural shift take place?

The following procedure was followed in order to answer these questions. Our earlier equations [$\ln P_i = f(\ln M_{-1})$] were re-estimated for alternative sub-periods, which were divided at five-year intervals between 1840 and 1913. For each set of equations, the relevant F-statistic was computed in order to determine the statistical significance of the difference in the parameter estimates between the earlier and later periods. These estimates indicated that a change in structure had indeed occurred; and that the shift had taken place *circa* 1890. In order to ascertain the timing more precisely, the equations were then re-estimated for periods divided at one-year intervals for the years adjacent to 1890. For both the P_E and the P_p series, the relevant F-statistic reached its maximum with 1888 as the dividing year. For the P_E series, the F-statistic is 7.48, and for the P_p series, 7.82. Each of these F-statistics is significant above the 1 percent level. Before discussing the implications of 1888 as a structural turning point in Brazil's economic history, let us consider the parameter estimates of the equations for the two distinct periods.[49]

For the P_E series, the coefficient on the ln M_{-1} variable in the period 1840–88 is .940. Thus an increase of, say, 10 percent in the money supply during those earlier years was associated with a short-run increase of approximately 9.4 percent in the P_E price series. As this coefficient indicates, in the earlier period monetary expansion led to very little expansion of real output or monetization among the producers whose products are included in the P_E price index. By contrast, for the period 1889–1913 the parameter estimates on the log M_{-1} term is .616. Hence a 10 percent rise in the money supply was now associated with a smaller price rise than in the earlier years, and a larger increase in output and in monetization. This significant change in parameter values implies a major improvement in the capacity for economic development in Brazil's large Southeast region (the area to which the data of P_E directly apply).

The reasons why this structural economic change occurred *circa* 1888 are not self-evident. One might be tempted to attribute the shift to the abolition of slavery, which also came in 1888. That interpretation is not plausible, however. By the time emancipation came to Brazil, slaves accounted for only a small fraction of the labor force; and abolition seems to have had little effect on the overall pattern of Brazilian economic development (see Chapter 4). Similarly, the 1888 structural shift cannot be ascribed to changes which came with the accelerated inflation of the *encilhamento*. The rapid monetary expansion of the *encilhamento* began only in 1890; and the F-statistics associated with using that year as a dividing point were well below those for 1888. Rather, the change we have observed in the money–inflation relationship for the P_E series may have come from the post-1888 expansion of the railroads in the Southeast. As will be discussed in Chapter 7, growth of the railways seems to have led to an increase in the elasticity of supply from the domestic agricultural sector. In addition, the extension of low-cost transportation promoted an expansion of the market economy, and hence monetization.

Perhaps coincidentally, 1888 was also the year of a structural shift in the money–inflation coefficient for the P_p series.[50] The change here, however, is different in character. For the period 1840–88, the parameter estimate for the lagged money-supply term is .127. For the period 1889–1913, the coefficient is considerably higher – .511. In order to understand the nature of this change, note that the P_p price series is basically an index of Brazil's exchange rate (see Appendix I of this chapter). Accordingly, movements in the P_p series were closely related to changes in the demand and supply of internationally-traded goods (and assets) in Brazil. Hence the rise in the magnitude of the coefficient on the money-supply variable probably reflects the expansion of the external sector relative to the rest of the economy in the late nineteenth century.[51] As exports, imports, and their close substitutes grew to account for a larger share of GNP, changes in the supply of money which affected the demand and supply of such goods inevitably had a greater impact on Brazil's exchange rate.

The structural shifts that we have noted had important consequences for Brazilian economic development. Most importantly, they meant that monetary expansion and its stimulus to aggregate demand now had different economic effects than earlier. To see these differences, consider the economic consequences which followed from two episodes during the nineteenth century when Brazil experienced especially high rates of monetary expansion: the Paraguayan War of the 1860s, and the *encilhamento* of 1890–91.[52] Table 6.4 presents information on monetary and price conditions during these two episodes. Row (1) of the table shows the percentage increases in the money supply. Rows (2) and (4) show the percentage rise of P_E and P_p, respectively. Finally, rows (3) and (5) present the elasticities of P_E and P_p with respect to the money-supply increase of each episode.

Reading horizontally along row (1), we see that Brazil's money supply expanded much more rapidly in the *encilhamento* of the 1890s than during the Paraguayan War. Nevertheless, as row (2) indicates, the increase in domestic prices was smaller in the later period. What had happened in the interim, apparently, was the structural change which we have noted in the money–inflation coefficient. Row (3) documents this shift by comparing the elasticity of P_E with respect to changes in the money supply during the two episodes. The data show a dramatic decline in the percentage impact of monetary expansion on domestic prices. By implication, increases in the money supply and in aggregate demand now had a much greater promotional effect on Brazil's economic development.

Table 6.4 *Increases in the Money Supply and in Brazilian Prices during the Paraguayan War and during the Encilhamento* (in percent)

		Paraguayan War	Encilhamento
(1)	Increase in Money Supply, $\triangle \dot{M}$	133	200
(2)	Increase in P_E, $\triangle \dot{P_E}$	85	54
(3)	$\triangle \dot{P_E} / \triangle \dot{M}$	64	27
(4)	Increase in P_p, $\triangle \dot{P_p}$	12	77
(5)	$\triangle \dot{P_p} / \triangle \dot{M}$	9	39

Note: For explanation, see the preceding text.

The effects of the structural change on inflation in the country's traded-goods sector, however, went in the opposite direction. Row (4) shows the increase in the prices of internationally-traded goods during these two inflationary episodes. As row (5) indicates, the elasticity of P_p with respect to increases in the money supply had risen sharply by the 1890s. The external sector was thus much more exposed to the effects of increases in the domestic money stock. Hence, the structural shifts we have noted involved a twofold change for the Brazilian economy. Monetary expansion now had a much larger impact on the country's external imbalance; at the same time, it also provided a greater spur to internal economic development.

One cannot place much emphasis on the specific magnitudes of the money–inflation elasticities in the two cases just discussed. These episodes are cited here only for illustrative purposes, for each was affected by special circumstances and transitory elements.[53] Far more important than those particular episodes were the long-run consequences for Brazilian development which came with the year-by-year effects of these structural shifts. Each of the changes – increased capacity for internal development and heightened exposure to external disequilibrium – was important in itself. Each was to be a prominent feature of the Brazilian economy in future decades. But coming on the historical scene together, they involved a certain tension. Their conjunction helps to explain some of the problems which the Brazilian economy was to face in the twentieth century.

Conclusions

The domestic money stock was expanded in nineteenth-century Brazil at rates that were high relative to the elasticity with which real output was supplied. As a result, the country experienced chronic inflation. This is hardly a novel explanation, and it is borne out clearly by the econometric evidence we have presented.

Some special points are, however, noteworthy in this experience. First, the Brazilian authorities persisted with inflationary rates of money-supply increase despite the price increases which usually resulted. Second, the excess demand pressures which generated chronic domestic inflation and exchange depreciation were usually not large in magnitude. Thus the rate of long-term monetary expansion was not particularly high (5 percent per annum between 1839 and 1913). Also, the monetary expansion occurred in the context of conditions which greatly enlarged the demand for cash balances, and hence mitigated the inflationary impact of given increases in the money supply: population, aggregate output, and monetization were all growing in Brazil during this period. Despite these offsetting conditions, the outcome was endemic inflation. This result highlights the importance of price-inelastic aggregate supply as a structural feature of the nineteenth-century Brazilian economy.

Output was particularly inelastic in the country's domestic agricultural sector. Movements along existing supply curves, as well as the long-term rates at which supply curves in the different activities shifted outward over time, produced a situation in which the prices of domestically-produced foodstuffs rose at a higher rate than did the prices of the country's traded goods. Because of the relatively inelastic supply conditions in Brazil's domestic agriculture, that sector was a major source of the country's overall inflation. The other proximate cause of Brazil's inflation was, as we have seen, the country's excessive rate of monetary expansion. In addition, our econometric results showed that the growth of Brazil's money supply was dictated largely by domestic conditions. These considerations suggest that the causes of Brazil's inflation during the nineteenth century must in general be sought internally rather than in the country's external sector.[54]

Chronic inflation did not promote generalized economic development in nineteenth-century Brazil. As noted, high rates of monetary expansion raised the relative price of food rather than stimulated a parallel increase in the output of the domestic agricultural sector. And the ensuing shift in the internal terms of trade increased costs and lowered profits in the export sector, thus slowing the pace of expansion in the country's major growth activity.[55] Another consequence was that inflation led to a special cyclical pattern involving the money supply, prices, foreign trade, and the government sector. This cycle was a feature of Brazil's economy during the nineteenth century. The country's prolonged inflation also had an important long-term effect. The experience of chronic inflation led economic agents and financial institutions in Brazil to persistent inflationary expectations and special behavioral patterns. These were to help make inflation a continuing theme in Brazil's economic experience during the twentieth century.

Finally, we have repeatedly noted the inelasticity of supply in Brazil during the nineteenth century. Land and labor for expanding real output were available in elastic supply; capital, however, was not.[56] Further, the supply of food was necessarily linked to land, and therefore involved a spatial dimension. For this reason, Brazil's high transportation costs during the pre-railroad era were of critical importance in the country's inelastic supply conditions. We have also noted evidence that the elasticity of domestic supply rose significantly in the Southeast toward the end of the century. Chapter 7 discusses these conditions in the context of Brazil's overall economic retardation and development during the nineteenth century.

Appendix I: Derivation of a Purchasing-Power-Parity Price Index for Brazil, 1822–1913

The purchasing-power-parity (PPP) doctrine was originally developed to explain the movement of a country's exchange rate over time.[57] The doctrine posits that because international trade acts to equalize prices of the same goods in different countries, countries' exchange rates may be expected to move parallel with the prices of their traded goods. Consequently, information on the pace of price inflation in an individual country and in its major trading partners can be utilized to predict the movement of a country's exchange rate.[58]

Here we reverse the focus. We will use data on changes in Brazil's *mil-réis*/sterling exchange rate and prices in Great Britain in order to draw conclusions concerning the long-term change in Brazilian prices between 1822 and 1913. Clearly this approach can be applied only to the prices of internationally-traded goods. The PPP approach has other limitations as well. But in the absence of better information concerning price changes in Brazil during the nineteenth century, it may be helpful to see what a PPP index shows. We can then consider the direction in which the PPP assumptions were violated in nineteenth-century Brazil, and hence the bias which a PPP price index imparts to an estimate of price inflation in Brazil's traded-good activities.

We begin with the 'relative-movement' version of the PPP hypothesis. Thus, changes in the ratio of *mil-réis* prices to prices in the United Kingdom, Brazil's principal foreign supplier, would be approximately equal to changes in the *mil-réis*/sterling parity. Using dots to denote percentage rates of change over time and writing ER for the *mil-réis*/sterling exchange rate, we have

$$\dot{ER} \cong (\dot{P_{Brazil}/P_{UK}}) \cong \dot{P}_{Brazil} - \dot{P}_{UK} \qquad (18)$$

Rearranging terms, we have

$$\dot{P}_{Brazil} \cong \dot{ER} + \dot{P}_{UK} \qquad (19)$$

That is, changes in the Brazilian price level would be roughly equal to the change in the *mil-réis*/sterling exchange rate, plus the change in UK prices. Following this reasoning, a Brazilian PPP price series was constructed by forming the product of the annual *mil-réis*/sterling exchange rate and the British wholesale price index.[59] We will denote this price index P_p. Between 1822 and 1913, it rose at a trend rate of 1.0 percent per annum.

There are, however, reasons to believe that the P_p index understates the rate of price inflation in Brazil's external sector during this period. The ratio of Brazil's exchange rate to the PPP ratio would change over time if the demand and supply curves for foreign exchange shifted outward at different rates. During the nineteenth century, this condition probably prevailed in Brazil; for it is likely that exports and foreign exchange receipts grew more rapidly than did income in the economy as a whole. Because of the export orientation of the economy's expansion path, then, Brazil's exchange rate may not have depreciated fully in accordance with the movement of relative prices as between Brazil and the United Kingdom. A trend toward real exchange-rate appreciation during the nineteenth century is also likely because Brazil's barter terms of trade improved during the period.[60] The measured rate of improvement was approximately 0.9 percent per annum, and for reasons discussed in Chapter 5, this rate is understated.[61]

Accordingly, expressions (18) and (19) should be rewritten to include the partial offset of this appreciation term, $\dot{A}$, on the change in the *mil-réis*/sterling parity:

$$\dot{E}R = \dot{P}_{\text{Brazil}} - \dot{P}_{\text{UK}} - \dot{A} \tag{20}$$

$$\dot{P}_{\text{Brazil}} = \dot{E}R + \dot{P}_{\text{UK}} + \dot{A} \tag{21}$$

With $\dot{A}$ positive because of the terms-of-trade effect, inflation in Brazil would exceed the rate which is implied by a model in which the PPP assumptions are strictly satisfied. For all of these reasons, then, the P_{p} index probably understates the pace at which prices rose in Brazil's traded-good activities during the nineteenth century.

Appendix II: **Derivation of an Estimate of the Aggregate Rate of Price Inflation in Brazil, 1822–1913**

As noted in this chapter, the very notion of 'the' rate of price inflation in Brazil as a whole during the nineteenth century raises conceptual problems which are serious and perhaps insurmountable. This economy was fragmented along regional, sectoral, and class lines, such that aggregation is not very meaningful. However, the focus on the country as the unit of study is strong; and that perspective may impel one to seek an aggregate figure. Putting aside the conceptual difficulties, construction of an estimate of the country's overall rate of inflation would proceed as follows.

Brazil's aggregate rate of inflation would depend on the sectoral rates of price increase, and on the shares of the traded-good and domestic agricultural sectors in total output. From the P_{E} and P_{p} price indices, we have available estimates of the sectoral rates of price inflation. These estimates for the period 1822–1913 are 5.1 percent and 1.0 percent, respectively, for the domestic agricultural and traded-good sectors. We now require estimates of the shares of these sectors in aggregate output. These shares determine the weights which must be applied to the sectoral rates of price increase in order to compute the country's overall rate of inflation.

During the nineteenth century, exports and imports accounted for approximately one-third of aggregate output in Brazil.[62] For present purposes, however, we must also include in the traded-good sector related activities (e.g. import-competing activities) whose prices were also sensitive to movements in P_{p}. Making a rough allowance for such activities, we may raise the share of the external sector, broadly defined, to 0.45. The rest of the economy would of course account for the remaining 0.55. In addition, we must take account of another consideration, regional disaggregation of the domestic sector of the economy.

It is unlikely that the prices of marketed food in the Northeast rose as rapidly as in the expanding Southeast. Income was growing at a higher rate in the latter region, and consequently, the demand pressures on food prices were more intense. At the same time, nineteenth-century Brazil's high transportation costs precluded large-scale shipment of high-bulk/low-value foodstuffs from the Northeast to the Southeast. Hence, prices in the domestic sector of the two regions could rise at a different pace. Katia de Queirós Mattoso's study of Bahia, a major city and market center in the Northeast, is helpful in this context of seeking information concerning price conditions in that region. Her annual price observations for manioc flour (the principal food staple at this time) provide an indication of the pace of price inflation in the Northeast's domestic sector. Inspection of Mattoso's graph for this series suggests that the price of this key product rose at a long-term rate of approximately 2.5 percent per annum.[63]

Information is available concerning the geographical distribution of Brazil's population *circa* 1822.[64] Regional estimates of the free population suggest that the size of the domestic sector in the Northeast and in the rest of Brazil was, in rough terms, approximately the same. We will therefore divide the domestic sector's 55 percent share of aggregate output equally between the two regions. Hence our weights for Brazil's traded-goods sector, the Northeast's domestic sector, and the Southeast's domestic sector, respectively, are: .45, .275, and .275.

Applying these weights to the sectoral rates of inflation (1.0 percent, 5.1 percent, and 2.5 percent, respectively), we obtain a rough estimate of the annual rate of long-term price inflation in Brazil between 1822 and 1913. The figure is 2.5 percent per annum.[65]

Notes

1   For the Southeast, see the observations which Mircea Buescu has compiled from Rio de Janeiro newspapers and presented in his *300 Anos de Inflação* (Rio de Janeiro: APEC, 1973) *passim*. Those observations relate mainly to individual benchmark years between 1826 and 1887, with interpolation to form annual series. For the important Northeast market of Bahia, see the graphs presented by Katia M. de Queirós Mattoso, *Bahia: A Cidade do Salvador e Seu Mercado no Século XIX* (São Paulo: HUCITEC, 1978), pp. 303–8. For Pernambuco, another major Northeast province, Peter L. Eisenberg has compiled price information for the years 1852–1903. This is presented in his book *The Sugar Industry of Pernambuco: Modernization without Change, 1840–1910* (Berkeley, and Los Angeles: University of California Press, 1974), Table 26. Oliver Ónody's *A Inflação Brasileira, 1820–1958* (Rio de Janeiro, 1960) also discusses aspects of the country's inflation.

2   Eulália Lobo *et al.*, 'Evolução dos Preços e do Padrão de Vida no Rio de Janeiro, 1820–1930,' *Revista Brasileira de Economia*, vol. 25, no. 4 (October 1971), pp. 260–3. The series used here is the one with 1856 weights; for as the authors emphasize there (pp. 250–1), that series reflects the consumption pattern which is most representative for the mass of the Brazilian population during the nineteenth century. The price series is based on annual price quotations for eight products. The specific products, with their respective weights in parentheses, are: manioc flour (37.6 percent); beans (20.9 percent); jerked beef (16.8 percent); rice (11.8 percent); wheat flour (5.7 percent); coffee (3.4 percent); cod-fish (2.3 percent); and sugar (2.0 percent). Note that the Buescu and Mattoso price series cited in the previous note could not be used as general price indices because their data are not weighted to reflect the differing importance of individual commodities in overall expenditure.

3 Bruce Johnston and John Mellor, 'The Role of Agriculture in Economic Development,' *American Economic Review* (September 1961), p. 573.

4 Buescu's price index (see n. 1) is based on an (unweighted) list of products which is much more extensive than those of the Eulália Lobo series discussed here. Nevertheless, the simple correlation between the logarithms of annual observations of the two series is very high, .97.

5 The Durbin–Watson statistics of equations (1) and (2) indicate the presence of strong serial correlation. This does not bias the parameter estimates for the trend terms, but does lead to an understatement of the standard errors. The t-statistics in both of these equations are sufficiently large, however, that the efficiency of estimation is safely within conventional confidence limits.

6 The comments here apply to the price data compiled by Eulália Lobo *et al.* in 'Evolução dos Preços,' op. cit. Some problems may attend the wage data which that article also presents. Notice also that data may sometimes be rejected as 'unreliable' simply because they do not conform to *a priori* notions. The empirical basis for the latter, however, may be weaker than the rejected data.

7 Eulália Lobo *et al.* 'Evolução dos Preços,' op. cit., p. 263; and n. 2, above.

8 See pp. 115–16, below.

9 Although the coffee plantations' self-sufficiency in food was of more than negligible proportions at the end of the period, it had apparently declined significantly as compared with the beginning of the nineteenth century. Estimates of the population of Rio de Janeiro, the city whose demand was most relevant for the P_E series, are contained in Richard Graham, *Britain and The Onset of Modernization in Brazil* (Cambridge University Press, 1968), p. 32; and in Mary Karasch, 'From Porterage to Proprietorship: African Occupations in Rio de Janeiro, 1808–1850,' in Stanley L. Engerman and Eugene D. Genovese (eds), *Race and Slavery in the Western Hemisphere: Quantitative Studies* (Princeton University Press, 1975), pp. 370, 373. Those estimates indicate a population of some 86,300 in 1821 and one of approximately 746,750 in 1900. The annual geometric rate of increase implicit in these numbers is 2.7 percent per annum.

10 See Bruce Johnston and Soren Nielsen, 'Agricultural and Structural Transformation in a Developing Economy,' *Economic Development and Cultural Change*, vol. 14 (April 1966), pp. 282–3. I am grateful to Paul Mandell for bringing this article to my attention.

11 See pp. 122–3, below.

12 Mattoso, *Bahia*, op. cit., pp. 303–20. Note that the commodities in question included both traded goods and goods produced within the domestic agricultural sector.

13 The next three paragraphs draw on data and computations which are discussed in Chapter 5, pp. 81–3.

14 D. C. M. Platt, *Latin America and British Trade, 1806–1914* (New York: Harper and Row, 1973), Chapters 7 and 8.

15 See Chapter 5, n. 12.

16 For a different view, see André Gunder Frank, 'The Capitalist Development of Underdevelopment in Brazil,' in his *Capitalism and Underdevelopment in Latin America: Historical Studies of Chile and Brazil* (New York: Monthly Review Press, 1967), p. 165. We return to this question in n. 54, below, after further relevant material is introduced in this chapter.

17 This connection has been noted before. See Dorival Teixeira Vieira, *O Problema Monetário Brasileiro* (São Paulo, 1952), p. 57, as cited in Mattoso, *Bahia,* op. cit., p. 273.

18 These data on the annual stock of money (M_1) are from Carlos Manuel Peláez and Wilson Suzigan, *História Monetária do Brasil* (Rio de Janeiro: IPEA, 1976), Table A.3.

19 The following regression equation shows the close association between changes in

Brazil's money supply and subsequent short-term changes in the *mil-réis*/sterling parity. (Other aspects of this equation's form and notation are explained in the text below.)

$$\ln ER = -.671 + .359 \ln M_{-1} + .408 \ln ER_{-1}$$
$$(1.21) \quad (4.69) \qquad\qquad (4.35)$$

$$\rho = .954 \; (27.32) \quad R^2 = .96$$

Note that this equation was estimated using the Cochrane–Orcutt transformation to correct for serial correlation of the residuals. Hence the high correlation between the lagged money supply and the country's exchange rate is not due to the presence of strong trends in the series for both variables.

20   D. Cochrane and G. H. Orcutt, 'Application of Least Squares Regressions to Relationships Containing Autocorrelated Error Terms,' *Journal of The American Statistical Association*, vol. 44 (January 1949), pp. 32–61.

21   Similar results were obtained in a regression (reported below) in which the independent and dependent variables were the deviations of log M and log P_E from their trend values.

22   The strongly autoregressive nature of Brazil's inflation is brought out graphically if we regress observations of the logarithm of the annual price level against the logarithm of the previous year's price level. The estimated equations are:

$$\ln P_p = .883 \ln P_{p,-1} + .032 \quad R^2 = .77$$
$$(15.51) \qquad\qquad (1.61)$$

$$\log P_E = .983 \log P_{E,-1} + .166 \quad R^2 = .98$$
$$(58.91) \qquad\qquad (1.31)$$

23   For detailed discussion of the economics and econometrics of partial-adjustment models like the one which follows, see, for example, Marc Nerlove, *The Dynamics of Supply Estimation of Farmers' Response to Price* (Baltimore; Johns Hopkins University Press, 1958).

24   Zvi Griliches, 'Distributed Lags: A Survey,' *Econometrica*, vol. 35 (January 1967), pp. 15–49.

25   Griliches' test involves including in the regression a lagged value of the independent variable. If the parameter estimate for this variable is approximately equal to the product of the coefficients of the current independent and lagged dependent variables, with reversed sign, then the true underlying model is likely to be one of serial correlation of the residuals rather than of partial adjustment.

26   Concerning the use of instrumental variables, the error process in (9) is characterized by serial correlation, and Cochrane–Orcutt adjustment may involve bias because of the presence of the lagged endogenous variable. Hence, it is comforting to obtain a very similar parameter estimate when we use instrumental variables. More generally, note that the estimate of ρ in these equations also plays an important substantive role. This term may proxy for the growth of population and output between 1840 and 1913. Hence, the parameter estimates for the other terms focus on the relation between monetary expansion and price inflation.

27   See pp. 15–18 in Chapter 2, above.

28   For a discussion of the institutional and doctrinal context of changes in the Brazilian money supply during the nineteenth century, see Peláez and Suzigan, *História Monetária*, op. cit.

29   For the view that government budget deficits were a major factor in the growth of the country's money supply, see Celso Furtado, *Formação Econômica do Brasil*, 5th edn (Rio de Janeiro, 1963), Chapter 29, esp. pp. 199–200.

30   Peláez and Suzigan, *História Monetária*, op. cit., pp. 81, 89, 136, and 176.
31   The notation in the following table is the same as in the text. All variables were
     specified in natural numbers; and *t*-ratios are in parentheses.

*Parameter Estimates and Summary Statistics for Regressions with the
Annual Percentage Change in the Brazilian Money Stock, M/M_{-1}, as the
Dependent Variable*

Period	Parameter Estimate for:					R^2	F	D.W.
	TB	TB_{-1}	D	D_{-1}	Constant			
1840–1913	−.159	.142	.035	.021	1.007	.03	0.50	1.23
	(1.19)	(1.07)	(0.42)	(0.25)	(7.69)			
1840–73	.031	.014	.076	.011	.905	.13	1.13	1.07
	(0.17)	(0.07)	(0.86)	(0.12)	(9.26)			
1874–1913	−.228	.079	−.082	.057	1.401	.05	0.45	1.36
	(1.17)	(0.37)	(0.52)	(0.38)	(3.44)			

As the low R^2 and *F*-ratios for these equations show, by themselves and without the
implicit specification of a trend term, the *D* and *TB* variables did not account for
much of the annual percentage change in Brazil's money supply.
32   See pp. 101–2, above.
33   None of the constant terms in the equations which follow was significantly different
     from zero by any standard; and accordingly, those terms are not reported.
34   The statistical non-significance of the export terms in equation (14) probably
     reflects a high degree of multicollinearity between the import and export variables.
     Further econometric material on the close relation between Brazilian foreign trade
     and annual government expenditures is presented in Nathaniel H. Leff, *Under-
     development and Development in Brazil, Vol. II: Reassessing the Obstacles to
     Economic Development* (London: Allen & Unwin, 1982), Chapter 5.
35   Some models of monetary expansion and economic growth lead to the neutrality of
     money on long-term equilibrium. However, as Harry G. Johnson points out in
     'Money in a Neo-Classical One Sector Growth Model,' in *Essays in Monetary Econ-
     omics* (London: Allen & Unwin, 1967), those models are predicated on very limiting
     assumptions. Many of these assumptions do not appear to fit the Brazilian case: for
     example, saving and investment behavior which are independent of the returns to
     capital; omission of the impact of liquidity on the elasticity of output supply; and,
     most importantly in the present context, the failure to disaggregate by sector and
     consider the effects of differential supply inelasticities.
36   Leff, *Reassessing the Obstacles*, op. cit., Chapter 5.
37   The constraints on the Brazilian state's capacity to raise tax revenues are discussed
     in Leff, *Reassessing the Obstacles*, op. cit., Chapter 5. Inflationary rates of long-
     term monetary expansion cannot, however, be attributed entirely to a weak public-
     finance structure. Thus even as large a fiscal shock as the Paraguayan War was
     financed in part by measures other than the issuing of money. Peláez and Suzigan
     (*História Monetária*, op. cit., p. 142) cite a Brazilian Treasury study of the sources
     used to finance the special expenditures of the war. The percentages are the
     following: foreign borrowing, 8 percent; domestic borrowing of various kinds, 32
     percent; taxes, 43 percent; issue of money, 17 percent. Nevertheless, as noted
     below, the money supply did increase considerably during the war, in part because
     of monetization of government debt.
38   Milton Friedman, 'Government Revenue from Inflation,' *Journal of Political
     Economy*, vol. 79, no. 4 (July 1971), p. 851.
39   See Leff, *Reassessing the Obstacles*, op. cit., Chapter 5.

40   For a theoretical analysis of such effects in contemporary underdeveloped countries, see Edward S. Shaw, *Financial Deepening in Economic Development* (New York: Oxford University Press, 1973); and Ronald McKinnon, *Money and Capital in Economic Development* (Washington: The Brookings Institution, 1973). Note that financial development in Brazil may also have been hampered by another condition related to inflation. Under inflationary finance, the government's revenue gains are increased to the extent that the public has available few alternative financial assets other than those issued by the state. That is, acting as a monopolist, the government maximizes its gains when the substitution possibilities offered by a supply of competing assets are minimized. During much of the nineteenth century, the Brazilian government insisted on retaining the monopoly power to issue bank money. This policy, with its adverse consequences for the development of financial institutions, may in part be explained by the state's desire to enlarge its gains from inflationary public finance.

41   By the same token, the presence of persistent inflation was not a sufficient condition to prevent the onset of sustained economic development in Brazil toward the end of the century.

42   For a formal analysis of the impact of an adverse terms-of-trade shift in a two-sectoral growth model, see Harry G. Johnson, *International Trade and Economic Growth* (Cambridge, Mass.: Harvard University Press, 1958), pp. 96 ff. The phenomena discussed in the text would imply that export growth in nineteenth-century Brazil proceeded in cycles around the long-term trend. Some econometric evidence for this pattern is presented in Table 3.1 of Leff, *Reassessing The Obstacles,* op. cit. That table shows the statistical results for supply-response equations which were estimated for several of Brazil's export commodities. The dependent variable in each equation is the annual deviation from trend in the quantity for each export product. Despite detrending, the equations show clear evidence of positive serial correlation in the residuals, and hence the existence of cycles around the trend in the various export commodities.

43   Because of differences in the serial-correlation coefficient ρ, the parameter estimates of equation (17) are not identical with those derived from equations (3) and (4). Both sets of equations, however, indicate the same general pattern: monetary expansion led to a sharp increase in P_E relative to P_p. The discussion here puts no great weight on the specific magnitude of the parameter estimates of (17), and focuses only on the direction of the relative-price movement.

44   Mircea Buescu, *Evolução Econômica do Brasil* (Rio de Janeiro: APEC, 1974), p. 133. The figures in the text refer to the share of food in Brazil's total import supply. The share of food imports in the total *food* supply was of course much lower.

45   Planters could (and did) react to a spurt in food prices by shifting resources from export to food production. Adjustment was not instantaneous, however. Moreover, such resource allocation also lowered the pace of expansion in the export sector as compared with the rate that would have been achieved with a more elastic supply of foodstuffs.

46   Following standard Engel's curve analysis, income levels are also relevant here. Per capita income levels in the domestic agricultural sector were probably lower than those of the people who generated demand for manufactures in the traded-goods sector; and income-elasticities of demand for manufactures, lower. Further, at low levels of per capita income, food accounts for a large share of total expenditure; and income elasticities of demand for food are relatively high. Consequently, the response to the higher income created by favorable prices in the domestic agricultural sector may have been an increase in on-farm consumption of food. Recall also that the data of the P_E price index refer to *marketed* output; that is, they are net of producers' own food consumption.

47   See pp. 30–1 in Chapter 3, above.

48   See Gregory C. Chow, 'Tests of Equality Between Subsets of Coefficients in

Two Linear Regressions,' *Econometrica*, vol. 28 (May 1960), pp. 591–605.
49 The Chow test is predicated on the assumption that the error terms in the regressions are normally distributed. In order to satisfy this condition in the present case, the equations described above were estimated using the Cochrane–Orcutt transformation. The regression results reported are from OLS equations, for as is well known, serial correlation in the residuals does not yield biased parameter estimates.
50 The fact that in the next year, 1889, significant changes occurred in Brazil's constitutional arrangements is probably also coincidental. Nevertheless, the sequence, in which a major political shift followed the changes in economic structure, raises interesting questions concerning the nature of the political changes. Some of these issues in Brazilian political history are discussed in Richard Graham, 'Government Expenditures and Political Change in Brazil, 1880–1899,' *Journal of Interamerican Studies and World Affairs*, vol. 19 (August 1977). The structural shifts we have noted occurred both in the domestic and in the traded-goods sectors of the economy. Also, as noted in Chapter 7, Brazil's domestic and external sectors had become much more integrated after the 1880s as compared with the earlier period. Taken together, these shifts imply some fairly complex economic changes. Correspondingly, the political changes occurring at this time and the political meaning of the new constitutional order may have been more complex than might be supposed *a priori*.
51 Table 5.1 presents decadal data on the value of Brazil's exports. The figures for the 1890s and 1900s show increases of a size which suggests that in the post-1888 years, the external sector reached a new scale within the Brazilian economy.
52 Some explanation is necessary concerning the dating of these episodes. Brazil's formal entry to the Paraguayan War came in 1865; but hostilities had begun in 1864, and so too had expansionary fiscal and monetary policy. Central-government expenditures rose 40 percent in the fiscal year 1864–65, and at the end of 1864 the money supply was 19 percent higher than at the end of 1863. Monetary expansion during the Paraguayan War proceeded at high rates through 1869; but in 1870 the money supply increased only 0.6 percent. Accordingly, money supply increases for the war which are cited below refer to the years 1864–1869. In the *encilhamento*, the money supply increased 99 percent in 1890, and 51 percent in 1891. The money supply fell by 11 percent in 1892; and thereafter increased at an average annual rate of 4 percent from 1893 to 1898. This episode's monetary expansion was thus limited to 1890–91. Following the specification of equations (3) and (4), I assume a one-year lag for the impact of monetary expansion on prices. Hence the price increases presented in Table 6.4 relate to the years 1865–1870 and 1891–1892.
53 For example, the rise in P_E during the Paraguayan War would probably have been even more pronounced if the war had not happened to follow the liquidity crisis which struck Brazil in September 1864. Because of this coincidence, increased demand for money to replenish cash balances reduced the inflationary impact of the monetary expansion. Similarly, exchange-rate depreciation and the rise in P_p during the war years were mitigated by exogenous supply and demand shifts which facilitated expansion of Brazil's exports. Those developments are discussed in Antônio Delfim Netto, *O Problema do Café no Brasil* (São Paulo: Faculdade de Ciências Econômicas, 1959), pp. 11–15.
54 Celso Furtado has proposed a different interpretation, in which the inflation was triggered by conditions in the external sector (see his *Formação Econômica*, op. cit., Chapter 27, pp. 185–6). His model seems to envision the following sequence: falling export prices lowered the availability of foreign exchange and led to balance-of-payments disequilibrium. Adjustment was achieved via exchange depreciation, which then provoked internal inflation. This model is examined critically, with historical data, in Carlos Peláez, 'Theory and Reality of the Hypotheses of Economic Imperialism and Neocolonial Dependence in the Coffee Economy of Nineteenth-Century Brazil,' *Economic History Review* (August 1976). Furtado's

interpretation also seems to neglect the effects of internal monetary expansion in putting pressure on the exchange rate. See, however, equation (11) above. The estimation form (two-stage least-squares, with the variables expressed as deviations from long-term trend), as well as the lagged specification of the right-hand-side variable, indicate that internal money growth led to exchange-rate depreciation in nineteenth-century Brazil. More generally, it is hard to see how falling export prices led to long-term inflation in Brazil; for the index of Brazil's export prices did not decline, and the country's terms of trade improved during the nineteenth century. On these points, see the data presented in Tables 5.2 and 5.4.

55 The shift in the internal terms of trade seems also to have involved an income distributional effect different from the one which Furtado envisaged. Furtado suggested that inflation and the associated exchange depreciation favored the export producers by transferring income to them from the consumers of imports (mainly urban groups) (*Formação Econômica*, op. cit., Chapter 28, pp. 193–4; Chapter 29, p. 196). However, the newly available data on the rise in the relative price of food indicate that the principal distributional transfer was from the traded-goods sector (including the exporters) to the domestic agricultural sector.

56 See pp. 131–7 in Chapter 7, below.

57 On the purchasing-power-parity doctrine, and particularly on the 'relative price movement' version which we will utilize here, see Bela Balassa, 'The Purchasing-Power-Parity Doctrine: A Reappraisal,' *Journal of Political Economy* (December 1964).

58 Available data for other countries do provide some support for the PPP theory's suggestion of a rough correspondence between long-term changes in prices and in exchange rates. See H. J. Gailliot, 'Purchasing Power Parity as an Explanation of Long-Term Changes in Exchange Rates,' *Journal of Money, Credit, and Banking*, vol. 2, no. 3 (August 1970); and Lawrence H. Officer, 'The Productivity Bias in Purchasing Power Parity: An Econometric Investigation,' *IMF Staff Papers* (November 1976).

59 Because the PPP hypothesis has usually been formulated in terms of the ratios of general price levels, the British wholesale price index was utilized for these computations. The series used was the Rousseaux index, available in B. R. Mitchell and Phyllis Deane, *Abstract of British Historical Statistics* (Cambridge University Press, 1962), pp. 472–3. The P_p price index is presented in the Statistical Appendix, below.

60 See pp. 81–3 in Chapter 5.

61 Because of data constraints, the measured rate does not reflect the significant fall in international shipping costs that occurred during the nineteenth century. It also fails to include the lower import prices that Brazil faced in the last quarter of the century as lower-cost producers replaced Great Britain as Brazil's major foreign supplier.

62 See pp. 90–1 in Chapter 5.

63 This graph is available in Mattoso, *Bahia*, op. cit., p. 311. The figure there is hard to read, however, and I have therefore utilized the more legible graph presented in Katia de Queirós Mattoso, 'Os Preços Na Bahia de 1750 à 1930,' in Colloques Internationaux du Centre National de Recherche Scientifique, *L'Histoire Quantitative du Brésil de 1800 à 1930* (Paris: CNRS, 1975), p. 174.

64 These population estimates for 1823 are presented in Stanley J. Stein, *Vassouras* (Cambridge, Mass.; Harvard University Press, 1957), p. 296.

65 This figure is computed as a weighted average, by applying the sectoral weights to the estimate of each sector's annual rate of price inflation. Thus:

$$.45 \times 1.0\% + .275 \times 2.5\% + .275 \times 5.1\% = .45\% + .69\% + 1.40\% = 2.5\%$$

7
Economic Retardation and Development

Introduction

Our study thus far has discussed key aspects of Brazil's economic structure and its change in the nineteenth century. Drawing on that material, we can now focus on the two central features of Brazil's economic experience during the nineteenth century: the slow pace of economic development during most of the century, and its significant acceleration toward the end of the period (see Chapter 3). These two states may of course have been governed by the same underlying model. Thus changes in the conditions which had earlier constrained the country's economic progress may help explain the subsequent shift to sustained development.

Brazil's secular inflation during the nineteenth century provides an important starting point for our analysis. Chronic price inflation suggests that aggregate demand was usually more than sufficient to permit sustained expansion of per capita output, and that the growth problems of this economy stemmed largely from the supply side. Accordingly, we will focus on the supply conditions – capital formation and technical progress – which might have enabled Brazilian output (and income) to grow much more rapidly than the increase in population. Rising *wage* levels, however, depended also on changes in the functional distribution of income; and we will therefore discuss that question, too, in the context of nineteenth-century Brazil. Finally, the development of low-cost transportation was of particular importance in this economy of abundant land and vast distances. By increasing the elasticity of supply, improved transportation facilities would have helped transform rising aggregate demand into higher real output rather than price inflation. For this reason, we will devote special attention to the pace of railway expansion in nineteenth-century Brazil.

Capital Formation

Until the end of the century, the country's overall rate of capital formation seems to have been low. Investment data for these years are not available, but statistics on the composition of Brazilian imports from the United Kingdom in 1835 do not give the impression of a high rate of fixed investment. Imports of iron and hardware were necessary as an input to bringing new land under cultivation, particularly since Brazil lacked a domestic iron industry. Nevertheless, the value of iron and hardware imported from the United Kingdom in 1835 amounted to only £153,000.[1] Apart from its low absolute level, this figure was less than 6 percent of the value of Brazilian imports from the United Kingdom. The small percentage of iron and hardware in Brazil's imports from the United Kingdom is especially noteworthy for two reasons. The United Kingdom was the major supplier of imported investment goods to Brazil during this period. And the share of total imports in aggregate Brazilian income was itself not unusually high at this time.[2]

In the course of the century, the share of investment goods in Brazil's total imports rose. But as Table 7.1 shows, in 1870–75 investment goods still accounted for less than 12 percent of total imports. The data available on Brazil's imports of capital goods from Great Britain tell a similar story. Table 7.2 shows that the value and the share of these imports showed a steady upward trend. However, Table 7.2 also indicates that Brazil's capital-goods imports from Great Britain began from a low initial base. Hence, despite the rising trend, the level of capital goods imports from Great Britain remained low in absolute terms through the century. As late as the 1880s, when Great Britain was still the predominant supplier of capital goods to the Brazilian market, Brazil's imports of these products from Great Britain still amounted to less than £1.8 million per annum (see Table 7.2). Moreover, part of the increase in imported capital goods reflects the substitution of imports for domestically-produced investment goods, for example, railways for traditional means of conveyance. Consequently, aggregate Brazilian investment probably did not rise at the same rate as did the country's imports of capital goods.

We can gain additional perspective on the pace of capital formation in nineteenth-century Brazil if we consider the magnitude of capital good imports from Britain relative to the size of Brazil's growing

Table 7.1 *Shares of Selected Products in Total Brazilian Imports, 1839–44 and 1870–75* (in percent)

Products	1839–44	1870–75
1 Iron, Steel, Copper, and Hardware	4.8	8.8
2 Machines and Parts	0.2	2.9
3 Coal	1.0	3.5
4 Cloth and Clothing	51.6	46.4
5 Food	21.0	19.6

Source: Computed from data in Mircea Buescu, *Evolução Econômica do Brasil* (Rio de Janeiro: APEC, 1974), p. 133.

Table 7.2 *Brazilian Imports of Capital Goods From Great Britain, 1850–1899*

Period	Average Annual Value of Capital Goods Imported from Britain (Thousands of £)	Capital Goods as a Percentage of Total Imports from Britain (%)
1850–54	460	14
1855–59	660	18
1860–64	680	15
1865–69	790	16
1870–74	1,790	26
1875–79	1,530	24
1880–84	1,800	27
1885–89	1,690	28
1890–94	2,900	37
1895–99	2,400	39

Note: Capital goods include metals, hardware, coal, chemicals, cement, and machinery.
Source: Computed from data of the British Board of Trade which are presented in Richard Graham, *Britain and the Onset of Modernization in Brazil, 1850–1914* (Cambridge University Press, 1968), pp. 330–2.

population. Two tabulations are relevant here. First, we can express the value data of Table 7.2 on a per capita basis. Second, since British export prices fell during the nineteenth century, it would be helpful to compute the per capita import series in constant-price terms. A price series which is specific to British capital good exports is not available. Use of the overall British export-price series, however, should help give a clearer idea of the growth of 'real' capital-good imports per person in Brazil.

Table 7.3 confirms the picture of a rising value for Brazilian capital-good imports. The data show sharp jumps for the years 1870–74 and 1890–94, with a threefold increase in the constant-price series from the 1850s to the 1890s. Apart from the trend, however, what is most striking is the low absolute value of the per capita imports. Thus the current-price series indicates that in 1850–54, Brazil's imports of capital goods from Great Britain amounted to approximately 30 US cents on a per capita basis. As late as 1890–94, the figure was still below one dollar. Of course Britain supplied only a fraction of all the capital goods used within Brazil. But even if this ratio was as low as 10 percent, Table 7.3 suggests that the level of annual investment per person in Brazil was not high during most of the nineteenth century.

Great Britain was also Brazil's major source of foreign investment in the nineteenth century; and the data on British financial investment in Brazil provide additional information on the pace of Brazilian capital formation during this period. This is because foreign investment was both a component of aggregate capital formation in Brazil and, by

Table 7.3 *Annual Per Capita Value of Brazil's Imports of Capital Goods from Great Britain, Current and Constant Prices, 1850–1899*

Period	Imports of British Capital Goods per Person in Brazil	
	Current Prices (£)	Constant (1880) Prices (£)
1850–54	.062	.060
1855–59	.082	.075
1860–64	.079	.065
1865–69	.084	.065
1870–74	.176	.140
1875–79	.138	.129
1880–84	.147	.153
1885–89	.126	.150
1890–94	.194	.231
1895–99	.143	.156

Source: Computed with data from the following sources. Data on the annual value of Brazil's capital-good imports from Britain are from Richard Graham, *Britain and the Onset of Modernization in Brazil* (Cambridge University Press, 1968), pp. 330–2. The British export-price deflator is from Albert Imlah, *Economic Elements in the Pax Britannica* (Cambridge, Mass.: Harvard University Press, 1958), pp. 94–8. Data on the population of Brazil are from the Statistical Appendix, below.

providing external economies, may also have stimulated domestic investment. Table 7.4 presents data on the stock of British investment in Brazil, in aggregate and in per capita terms.[3] Foreign loans to the Brazilian government were not always allocated to capital formation,

Table 7.4 *The Stock of Aggregate and Per Capita British Loans and Investments in Brazil, 1825–1913, Including and Excluding Brazilian Government Obligations*

Year	Stock of British Investment (millions of £)	British Capital Per Capita Brazil's Population (£)	British Capital Stock Excluding Brazilian Government Loans (millions of £)	British Capital Stock Excluding Brazilian Government Loans Per Capita Brazil's Population (£)
1825	4.0	0.8	0.3	0.06
1840	6.9	1.1	0.9	0.14
1865	20.3	2.2	7.3	0.82
1875	30.9	2.8	10.5	0.99
1885	47.6	3.7	24.4	1.89
1895	93.0	5.8	40.6	2.55
1905	124.4	6.2	41.1	2.06
1913	254.8	10.8	135.2	5.71

Source: Computed from data in Irving Stone, 'The Geographical Distribution of British Investment in Latin America, 1825–1913,' *Storia Contemporánea*, vol. 3 (1971), Table 3. See n. 3 at the end of this chapter for Stone's definitions.

however, particularly in the first half of the century. A separate tabulation therefore shows British investment net of loans to the Brazilian government. Table 7.4 also suggests that during most of the century, the capital stock remained small relative to the size of Brazil's population. And these figures, too, show a substantial increase in capital formation toward the end of the period.

Finally, if we attempt to take account of the capital formation that occurred in the form of newly cleared and planted land, a similar picture emerges. The most prosperous sector was coffee, where the quantum exported grew at an annual trend rate of 5.3 percent between 1822 and 1873, and at 3.7 percent per annum between 1874 and 1913. Assuming no significant technical progress or changes in factor proportions, the capital stock in coffee would have grown at a rate similar to the growth in the export quantum.[4] By all accounts, however, coffee was the most rapidly expanding part of the agricultural sector. Moreover, coffee did not account for an overwhelmingly large share of the country's overall agricultural output during most of the century. Hence, the growth of the capital stock in Brazilian agriculture as a whole was probably well below the rate in coffee. Finally, from the viewpoint of individual economic progress, the relevant variable is not capital formation *per se*, but rather the growth of the capital stock per capita. And the impact of nineteenth-century Brazil's accumulation on capital–labor ratios was much diluted by the elastic supply of labor which we discussed in Chapter 4.

Causes of a Low Rate of Capital Formation

Why aggregate rates of capital formation were low in Brazil during most of the nineteenth century is another question. Indeed, it might have been expected that in an inflationary economy, wealth-holders would hold a relatively large portion of their assets in real capital rather than in money. One possible explanation is that fixed investment was low because of the opportunities for accumulating wealth in alternative assets such as slaves or land rather than in physical capital. In an economy where saving and investment are undertaken for the sake of wealth accumulation (rather than, for example, for 'development'), land and physical capital are portfolio substitutes from the viewpoint of private investors. Hence, the rate of physical capital accumulation is adversely affected by the rate of appreciation of land values.[5] Such conditions do seem to have applied in nineteenth-century Brazil. Land values rose as population and aggregate production expanded steadily, while the availability of prime land was limited by the inelastic supply of infrastructure facilities. Similarly, slaves were another alternative asset for Brazilian capitalists during much of the century. The private returns available from ownership of slaves may well have been more attractive than the yields offered by many investments in physical capital accumulation (see Chapter 4).

Slavery (and its successor institutions) also led to lower fixed investment in another way. The elastic supply of low-cost labor which Brazilian capitalists faced through the nineteenth century reduced the incentive to investment aimed at raising capital–labor ratios. In addition, the country's long-term inflation and its uncertainties may well have stunted financial development and the associated capital accumulation.[6] Finally, the high interest costs noted in Chapter 4 meant that investment in projects which offered relatively low returns was not profitable.

More fundamentally, however, the attractiveness of the alternative assets we have noted reflected a situation in which the returns to investment in fixed capital formation were relatively low. In this perspective, the slow pace of capital accumulation in Brazil during most of the century may have derived from a situation in which the marginal rates of return to physical capital were too low to elicit a large annual flow of fixed investment. This suggestion may seem counter-intuitive for a capital-scarce economy like nineteenth-century Brazil; but when considered in a broader perspective, the interpretation is straightforward. Some investments which offer high returns to private capitalists are indeed available in an underdeveloped economy. But the volume of high-return private investments accessible each year ('absorptive capacity') is typically limited in such a country. The underlying cause is the relative absence of the external economies which in more advanced countries are provided by an ample stock of social-overhead capital. In the Brazilian case, the low level of human capital and the country's high transportation costs would have been of special importance in increasing the inelasticity of the country's marginal efficiency of investment schedule. Because of these conditions, private incremental rates of return may have been too low to stimulate a large flow of capital formation.

This interpretation which emphasizes relatively low returns to capital in explaining Brazil's slow pace of capital formation is supported by a comparative observation. In contrast with the United States, Brazil received a relatively small share of British foreign investment during the nineteenth century. Thus between 1865 and 1914, Brazil attracted approximately 4 percent of Britain's overseas investment. By contrast, the United States received some 21 percent of the total.[7] The disparity was even greater in earlier decades, for British capital had been actively involved in the United States economy during the preceding half century. As late as 1865, however, Brazil had only a small stock of British investment (see Table 7.4, above).

British investment was not directed toward the United States and away from Latin America because of distortions in the London capital market.[8] Moreover, nineteenth-century British investment in Brazil was not deterred by special risks associated with political conditions.[9] Unlike the Latin American countries which defaulted on their international loans in the 1820s and in the 1870s and 1880s, Brazil kept a good international credit rating.[10] In addition, information costs concerning new investments in Brazil were not prohibitive, for British commercial interests maintained a presence in the country throughout the nineteenth century.[11] Moreover, for reasons of portfolio diversification, foreign investors might have been willing to accept marginally lower returns in Brazil than were available elsewhere. Further, conditions on the demand side, too, might have been expected to attract a large flow of foreign investment to Brazil. Thus, the country had a large area and an elastic labor supply, small domestic savings, and, very importantly in this context, limited indigenous financial intermediation. All of these conditions might be expected to draw a large flow of foreign capital. Nevertheless, as we have seen, Brazil was able to attract only a relatively small share of British overseas investment. This experience suggests that through most of the nineteenth century the Brazilian economy did not offer potential investors private returns which, at the margin, were high enough to sustain a large volume of foreign investment. We were led to this discussion of British investment in nineteenth-century Brazil because of the light it might shed on the behavior of Brazilian capitalists. The limited availability of high profit opportunities would also help explain low rates of fixed capital accumulation by Brazilians.[12]

The behavior of British capitalists with regard to investment in Brazil carries with it an important implication concerning the norms which influenced Brazilian entrepreneurs. Low rates of saving and investment in Brazil as compared with the United States have sometimes been attributed to Brazilian culture and psychocultural conditions. These allegedly led to high rates of time preference for immediate consumption (*'imediatismo'*), and an aversion to investing in projects with long gestation periods and delayed gratification. In fact, however, in cases where high private returns were available, Brazilians did invest in projects which involved risk and long gestation periods.[13] This observation, too, suggests that an inelastic supply of high-return investment projects, perhaps due to an absence of social overhead capital and publicly supplied externalities, lay at the heart of Brazil's low aggregate rate of accumulation during most of the nineteenth century.

Technical Progress

Technical progress – raising the value of output relative to the cost of all factor inputs – might have been another source of economic development in nineteenth-century Brazil. All indications, however, are that the country's overall rate of productivity increase was low.

Exports seem to have been the most important source of increasing factor productivity, in value terms, in nineteenth-century Brazil. Access to the world market and its special demand and supply conditions permitted higher productivity due to factor reallocation and changes in the composition of output. A major problem with exports as a source of technical progress, however, was quantitative. As discussed in Chapter 5, nineteenth-century Brazil did not experience a rapid increase in the value of per capita exports during the nineteenth century.

A standard two-sector growth process, in which the rate of aggregate economic growth is augmented by a non-negligible rate of technical progress in the 'advanced' sector, seems also to have been limited in Brazil because of another reason. The rate of productivity increase *within* the modern sector of export agriculture and manufacturing was apparently low. New activities such as coffee, railroads, and manufacturing emerged, and permitted a rise in total factor productivity. But the productivity increase seems to have been limited mainly to a once-and-for-all shift, due to an intersectoral factor reallocation. Within the new activities, large and continuing productivity increases which might have been a major source of autonomous development do not seem to have occurred. This picture should not be overdrawn. Particularly in the second half of the century, there are reports of export producers who adopted more productive techniques.[14] The general rule, however, appears to have been relatively stagnant technology.[15]

Some evidence for this suggestion of meager productivity increase within Brazil's 'advanced' sector is available for the cotton textile industry. This was the largest single manufacturing activity in nineteenth-century Brazil. Table 7.5 presents data on the change in output per unit of input in this industry, and shows a rise in factor productivity between 1866 and 1885. But the data also indicate that efficiency did

Table 7.5 *Growth of Productivity in the Brazilian Cotton Textile Industry, 1866–1915*

		Physical Output Per:	
Year	Spindle	Loom	Worker
		(indices: 1866=100)	
1866	100	100	100
1885	121	94	144
1905	128	88	152
1915	122	88	127

Source: Computed from data in Stanley J. Stein, *The Brazilian Cotton Textile Manufacture* (Cambridge, Mass.: Harvard University Press, 1957), p. 191.

not increase substantially in this infant industry over the half century between 1866 and 1915.

The absence of high rates of productivity increase in the cotton textile industry is especially noteworthy for two reasons. First, substantial internal and external economies might have been expected in this activity because of the rapid growth of output and the large increase in the scale of the industry. Between 1866 and 1885 production rose at an annual cumulative rate of 9.4 percent; and between 1885 and 1915, at an 11 percent annual rate.[16] Second, the possibilities for technical progress were probably greater in manufacturing than in agriculture. Not only was there greater scope for learning-curve gains in manufacturing, but more productive technology developed in the advanced countries could also be readily imported in the form of equipment. In agriculture, by contrast, improved techniques suitable for tropical commodities had to be developed domestically or, at the least, adapted to local ecological conditions.

Causes of a Low Rate of Technical Progress

The general failure of producers in nineteenth-century Brazil to adopt more productive technology and achieve a higher rate of technical progress has often been attributed largely to the capitalists' elastic supply of low-cost labor and land. Such conditions are certainly relevant. Relative factor costs different from those of the United States can explain many instances in which Brazilians continued to use techniques which were elsewhere considered obsolete.[17] This is not a complete explanation, however. Although low-cost land and (unskilled) labor were readily available, some innovations might have been economically justified by saving scarce factors such as capital and skilled labor, or by reducing the absolute magnitude of all factor inputs. New techniques might also have resolved specific problems such as peak-load demand for labor in harvest periods.

The failure to adopt more productive techniques embodied in new equipment has also been ascribed to the prevalence of slavery, and the planters' fear of the sabotage which might occur if they placed costly capital goods in hostile hands. As the experience of the South in the ante-bellum United States indicates, however, slaveowners have found ways to deal with such problems. Finally, stagnant technology has sometimes been explained by referring to the often-cited special 'mentality' of many Brazilian producers – psychocultural attitudes which made for 'routinism' and rigidity toward acceptance of new techniques.[18]

Adoption of innovations obviously does require a stimulus to overcome inertia, and encourage investors to assume the costs and uncertainties associated with change. Hence, we can readily accept the view that rigidities impeded the adoption of improved technology in nine-teenth-century Brazil. That hardly ends the discussion, however, for the relevant question then becomes: why were the stimuli and incentives to overcoming such impediments to technical progress apparently so weak in this case? If we consider the conditions affecting the supply and demand for more productive techniques, the picture becomes clearer. The country's small human-capital stock raised the supply price of innovations in Brazil. Perhaps even more important quantitatively was the impact of the country's meager socioeconomic infra-structure on the rate of technological *diffusion*. Brazil's low literacy rates and poor communications increased the costs of disseminating information about improved techniques which were already available.[19]

Similarly, the demand for more productive technology cannot be discussed in isolation from the cost of capital and from profitability. Some new techniques which were used in other countries may not have been profitable in Brazil because external economies that were present elsewhere were not available here. In addition, special tradeoffs between risks and returns were sometimes involved. For example, some higher-yielding sugar strains were apparently also less resistant to plant disease.[20] Further, the high cost of capital facing many pro-ducers in Brazil would have led to heavy discounting of the (uncertain) future benefits to be expected from adoption of new technology. Finally, low marginal returns to capital in *existing* techniques were also pertinent in this context. Capital-market imperfections were common in Brazil during the nineteenth century; and as a result, current profits were a major source of finance for the purchase of new capital goods. For this reason, low marginal returns constrained the adoption of more productive technology which was embodied in new capital goods.

Our emphasis on the economic costs and incentives that were in-volved in accepting new techniques also helps explain the cases where innovations *were* adopted in nineteenth-century Brazil. In coffee, for example, agricultural yields and rates of return to capital were mich higher in São Paulo province than in the older coffee zones of Rio de Janeiro. And as might be expected from the preceding discussion, the planters of São Paulo did in fact invest more heavily in new technology than did the *fazendeiros* on the depleted lands of Rio de Janeiro. Similarly, in cotton the high profits of the 1860s cotton boom led to a shift from hand-roller gins to American saw gins.[21] And in Northeast sugar production, the wealthiest families of the region were able to overcome capital-market imperfections, and they were the ones who invested in new production techniques.[22] In the economy as a whole, however, rates of return and profits were apparently insufficient to overcome the costs and rigidities which discouraged the more universal acceptance of improved technology.

Finally, a high cost of capital and discount rates also affected the pace of technical progress in another way. Agricultural producers in nineteenth-century Brazil were prodigal in their use of land. Slash-and-burn techniques were common in the domestic agricultural sector; and even in the plantation sector, little effort was devoted to maintaining soil fertility. Such practices are readily understandable in the presence of high discount rates and abundant land. Over time, however, soil depletion led to both lower yields and a shift in production to new lands which were more distant from the market centers. Both of these consequences imply a falling value of output relative to inputs, and hence, declining productivity. The extension of the railway network in Brazil eventually lowered transportation costs. This new development opened possibilities for intraregional crop specialization and thus helped overcome the aggregate economic effects of soil depletion. During much of the century, however, declining soil fertility was a factor that made for a *negative* rate of technical progress in nineteenth-century Brazil.

Per Capita Output Growth, Wages, and Changes in the Distribution of Income

The preceding sections have discussed the pace of technical progress and capital formation not only because of their intrinsic interest, but also because of the light which they shed on the growth of per capita output and wages. Drawing on concepts from production theory and using asterisks to denote proportional rates of change over time, we can express the growth of per capita output as:

$$(Q^* - L^*) = (1-a)(K^* - L^*) \tag{1}$$

where Q denotes output; L denotes labor; K denotes capital *and* land, considered as a joint input; and $(1-a)$ is the share of capital and land in output. Technical progress (such as it was) enters the formula via the specification of the inputs. These are considered in 'augmented' form; that is, in terms of their effective contribution to output.[23]

The stock of land utilized in the Brazilian economy increased over the nineteenth century, and so too did inputs of capital. Overall, land and capital inputs may have grown at a pace which exceeded the 1.8 percent per annum rate of long-term population increase. This tentative conclusion is reinforced if we consider the factor bias of productivity increase. The main forms of technical progress in the nineteenth-century Brazilian economy were export growth and railroads. Both of these were land-augmenting. Thus even taking into account the effects of soil depletion, it is likely that the stock of land and capital measured in efficiency units grew at a higher rate than in natural units.

As equation (1) indicates, however, increases in output per worker depend on the difference between K^* and L^*. In the advanced sector of the Brazilian economy, this difference was kept small by the country's labor-market institutions. As discussed in Chapter 4, these provided a highly elastic supply of unskilled labor. Similarly, in the country's domestic agricultural sector it is unlikely that there was a large disparity between the rates of growth of Brazil's labor and capital–land inputs. Land was initially abundant relative to labor, and continued that way. There are also no indications that capital–labor ratios in domestic agricultural production rose significantly. Hence output in that sector probably expanded without major increases in land and capital per worker, the $(K^* - L^*)$ term of equation (1).

Equation (1) also shows that the impact of such factor-deepening as did take place in nineteenth-century Brazil was reduced by the $(1-a)$ term. This term, which reflects the share of capital and land in aggregate output, was a fraction less than unity and of non-negligible magnitude. Because of the $(1-a)$ term in (1), even though the stock of capital and land may have increased at a rate marginally higher than the labor force, the impact on per capita output growth was mitigated. (This effect is accentuated to the extent that institutional conditions and market imperfections enabled Brazilian landowners to appropriate a larger share than would have been determined under more competitive factor-market conditions.) Thus equation (1) suggests a situation in which per capita output rose at an annual long-term rate which was positive, but very small in magnitude. This conclusion is consistent with the results of the analysis in Chapter 3, which was based on monetary data.

In order to analyze the likely evolution of wages (rather than of per capita output), we must also take into account shifts in the distribution of income. This is because wages can increase at a pace higher or lower than per capita output, depending on changes in the share of capital and land in aggregate income.[24] We will first see the implications of a highly aggregated analysis based on neoclassical theory, and then consider the effects of some intersectoral and intrasectoral shifts.

Since capital and land were distributed very unequally in nineteenth-century Brazil, we can analyze long-term changes in income distribution in terms of movements of the share of capital and land in output. The proportional rate of change over time of the capital–land share can be written as:

$$(1 - \overset{*}{a}) = -\frac{1-\sigma}{\sigma} \, a \, (K^* - L^*) + \lambda^* \tag{2}$$

where σ is the elasticity of substitution; and a is labor's share in output. As noted earlier, however, wages were not always determined under competitive market conditions. Recognizing this fact, we also include a term λ^* in equation (2). This term denotes the change in the ratio of labor's marginal value product to actual wages. The percentage of slaves in Brazil's total labor force declined during the nineteenth century. Labor-market efficiency was also enhanced by the slow amelioration of transportation facilities and the ensuing increase in labor mobility. Consequently, λ^* can be taken as small but positive. (Equivalent improvement in the efficiency of Brazil's capital market probably did not occur during the nineteenth century.[25])

In order to evaluate equation (2), we require information on the magnitude of σ. Econometric estimates are not available for the economy-wide elasticity of substitution in nineteenth-century Brazil. However, other pertinent information does exist. The level of technological development was relatively low in this economy. Further, the array of techniques which was accessible to producers – many of whom were illiterate – was narrow. These conditions suggest that the elasticity of substitution in nineteenth-century Brazil was probably below unity.[26] A similar conclusion is suggested by the keen concern of Brazil's landowner-capitalists to maintain a highly elastic supply of labor (see Chapter 4). With $\sigma < 1$, high rates of labor-force growth were necessary to offset the negative impact of land and capital formation on the landowners' returns.[27] It is unlikely, however, that σ was so small as to make the term $(1-\sigma)/\sigma$ in equation (2) greater than unity. Furthermore, labor's share in output, a, was also less than unity. Taking these conditions into account, we see that equation (2) suggests that the share of capital and land in Brazilian output fell slightly, but by less than the increase in $(K^* - L^*)$. Such a shift in factor shares, in turn, implies that wages increased somewhat more than per capita output in nineteenth-century Brazil.

The conclusion that the distribution of income may have become slightly less unequal is reversed, however, if we disaggregate the analysis, and consider some important sectoral movements. Export growth enhanced the relative position of landowners within the individual regions of Brazil. This occurred because much of the increment to income from exports went to landowners, who earned quasi-rents on their lands as new areas were brought into production (see Chapter 5). And as economic rents and land values rose, the large landowners often expropriated squatters from the domestic agricultural sector. In addition, the nineteenth century saw the opening of a significant regional differential as between the Southeast and the large Northeast region in Brazil. These considerations suggest that inequality in the distribution of income probably increased somewhat during the nineteenth century.

Transportation Costs and Economic Retardation

Like most other studies of the nineteenth-century Brazilian economy, our discussion thus far has focused largely on the relatively small 'advanced' sector. Exports and industrial development understandably evoke a special interest. However, the main reason for Brazil's poor economic experience during the nineteenth century lay elsewhere – in the conditions of the domestic agricultural sector.[28]

Because a large portion of the country's labor force was employed in this sector, its modest rate of output growth, in per capita terms, weighed heavily on the pace of aggregate development. The low income levels which prevailed in the domestic agricultural sector also deprived Brazil's industrial producers of an internal market for manufactures which was large relative to the size of the economy.[29] Further, the country's price-inelastic supply of foodstuffs aggravated inflationary pressures, and hampered expansion in the economy's advanced sector. Inelastic supply conditions in the domestic agricultural sector meant high incremental costs for the economy's basic wage good, food. As a result, the marginal returns to capital were affected adversely, and so too was the pace of capital accumulation.[30] Thus conditions in the domestic agricultural sector posed serious problems for economic development in nineteenth-century Brazil.

Central to the domestic agricultural sector's retarding role were the high transportation costs which characterized this economy.[31] These costs diminished the net receipts which producers obtained from the sale of bulky, low-value foodstuffs to the market. As a result, income in the domestic agricultural sector was reduced – both because of the low value received for output, and because of the disincentive effect which unfavorable prices had on the quantities produced. The latter effect seems to have been especially pronounced in nineteenth-century Brazil. Depressed prices in the domestic agricultural sector were reflected in a small marginal-value product for labor; and relatedly, in widespread substitution of leisure for monetary income. Finally, high transport costs for bulky foodstuffs also had an important intersectoral effect. The country's steep price–distance gradients in regional markets limited the economy's capacity to draw on distant supplies in the face of buoyant demand conditions. Expanding aggregate demand therefore generated inflationary pressures. And under nineteenth-century Brazilian conditions, higher inflation reduced the returns to capital and the rate of expansion in the advanced sector, with little impact on higher real output levels in the economy's backward sector.

Railroads might have helped this situation by lowering transportation costs. This would have provided a necessary condition for linking part of the domestic agricultural sector with the rest of the economy, and permitting it to shift from subsistence to market-oriented production (for the domestic market or for exports), whether in family farms or in large-scale agriculture. Lower transportation costs would have provided producers with the stimulus of market demand and with the incentive of new, market-produced consumption goods. On the demand side, this might have affected the marginal rate of substitution between consumption and leisure, and led to higher output levels.[32] On the supply side, producers would have been able to reap the gains from specialization and local comparative advantage. Hence, even with unchanged physical productivity, lower transport costs would have raised the value of production in the domestic agricultural sector. Gains would have accrued both from increases in the quantities produced and, with new relative prices, from changes in the composition of output.[33]

Notwithstanding these potential benefits, large-scale railroad construction came relatively late in nineteenth-century Brazil. Table 7.6 presents data on the late start and the slow pace of the country's railway expansion. Thus despite its vast territorial expanse, as late as 1884, Brazil had only 6,240 kilometers of track. This amounted to approximately 0.7 kilometers of track for every 1000 square kilometers of Brazil's territory.[34] The great increase in railway construction reaching beyond the areas of export agriculture in Brazil began only in the 1890s; and the largest absolute increase in railway track occurred in the twenty years before 1914. To gain some comparative perspective, it is worth noting that in 1900 railway trackage in the United States was almost twenty times as great as in Brazil, and even after the large post-1900 increase in Brazil's railway construction, in 1914 the country had only 26,060 kilometers of track. This was a figure which the United States had surpassed by the 1850s.

Why were the railways built so late in nineteenth-century Brazil? The difficult terrain often led to high construction costs. However, these would not have been an insuperable obstacle if the net private returns to railway investment had been satisfactory. Some of the first railroads in the coffee region were built with local capital participation. In general, however, construction of Brazil's railways depended

Table 7.6   *Length of Railway Track in Brazil 1854–1914*

Year	Kilometers	Year	Kilometers
1854	14	1894	11,260
1864	470	1900	15,320
1874	1,280	1904	16,320
1876	2,080	1914	26,060
1884	6,240		

Source: Instituto Brasileiro de Geografia e Estatística, *Brazil – 1938* (Rio de Janeiro, 1939), p. 218.

heavily on foreign investment, which in the nineteenth century was largely British.[35] British investment was not directed to Brazil by non-market considerations such as imperial policy. And as noted earlier, the private rate of return on Brazilian railway investments was apparently not high enough to attract substantial British capital from its alternative opportunities during most of this period. Just as Brazil was unable to compete with the United States to attract much of the international flow of human capital during the nineteenth century, so too the country did not receive much of the limited flow of financial investment before the turn of the century.

Brazil's limited attractiveness to foreign investors, however, is not a complete explanation of the long delay before large-scale railway construction occurred. If private returns were insufficient but investment in low-cost transportation facilities was justified in terms of external economies and social returns, another approach might have been followed. In principle, the task of providing the country with an adequate transportation system might have been undertaken by government – central, provincial, or local. This was the course followed with many of the 'public improvements' that were supplied in the nineteenth-century United States. In fact, however, Brazil did not follow this approach until the end of the period. For reasons discussed elsewhere, during most of the century Brazilian governments failed to provide on a sufficient scale the external economies needed for the country's economic development.[36]

Railroads and the Domestic Agricultural Sector

Once the railway network was extended, development seems to have proceeded along the lines outlined earlier. Even with unchanged output levels, the higher ex-farm prices made possible by low-cost transportation would have raised producer incomes.[37] In addition, producers in the domestic agricultural sector appear to have responded to the new market opportunities opened by lower transport costs. Producers increased the volume of their output for the market, while the fall in transportation costs led to new patterns of intraregional specialization.[38] These changes, in turn, facilitated import substitution in food (see below).

Some numerical information on these developments is available for Minas Gerais. This large state had some 21 percent of Brazil's population in 1900. It is adjacent to São Paulo; but despite its geographical proximity to the country's largest regional market, Minas Gerais was not economically advanced. However, in the words of one historian, in the 1890s the state 'caught railroad fever'; half of Minas Gerais' pre-1899 trackage was laid in that decade.[39] Table 7.7 presents data on the subsequent increase in food shipments from Minas Gerais. As

Table 7.7 *The Growth of Food Shipments from Minas Gerais, 1900–1910*

Product	Annual Geometric Growth Rate (%)
Corn	10.5
Beans	17.4
Rice	40.0
Livestock[a]	10.4

[a] 1895–1905.

Source; Computed from data presented in John Wirth, *Minas Gerais in The Brazilian Federation, 1889–1937* (Stanford: Stanford University Press, 1977), pp. 44, 46.

these high rates of growth indicate, demand existed for the products of the domestic agricultural sector; and supply responded effectively once low-cost transportation was made available.[40]

The process through which the railroads promoted economic growth in Brazil's domestic agricultural sector had some special features. The railways helped domestic agricultural producers not only when the lines reached the distant frontier areas, but also when they were built in the zones of export production. Part of the country's food supply was produced in and around the plantation areas. Hence, food producers in those areas benefited directly from the new availability of cheap transportation to the regional market. In addition, the lines opened in the export zones also lowered the cost of shipments which originated in the far interior and proceeded, via the railhead, to the markets. Because of these connections, even railways that were built primarily to carry export commodities came to transport large volumes of products from the domestic agricultural sector.

Table 7.8 presents data on this phenomenon in the state of São Paulo. The data relate to three major railroads which were built mainly to transport coffee. The table shows that even on those railways non-coffee commodities came to account for a sizable share of total shipments. Much of the tonnage consisted of foodstuffs and industrial raw materials which were transported from the hinterland to the expanding regional market.

As Table 7.8 indicates, on the Sorocabana, one railroad for which data are presented, the proportion of goods other than coffee was very high at the outset.[41] On the other two railways, the share of non-coffee products rose steadily to dominate total shipments (see columns 1, 3, and 5).[42] Overall, the volume of domestic agricultural products shipped on these lines increased at a pace similar to that of coffee shipments – and this in the heyday of the São Paulo coffee boom. Between 1886–90 and 1911–15, the quantum of non-coffee products in Table 7.8 rose at an annual geometric rate of 9.5 percent. This compares with an annual growth rate of 7.2 percent for coffee shipments on these lines.[43]

Table 7.8   *The Growth of Non-Coffee Freight on Three 'Coffee' Railways, 1876–1915*

	Paulista Railway		Mogiana Railway		Sorocabana Railway	
	(1)	(2)	(3)	(4)	(5)	(6)
Period	Share of Non-Coffee tonnage (%)	All Freight Shipped (tons)	Share of Non-Coffee Shipments (%)	All Freight Shipped (tons)	Share of Non-Coffee Shipments (%)	All Freight Shipped (tons)
			(annual averages)			
1876–80	n.a.	n.a.	50	29,200	98	16,200
1881–85	37	132,000	36	57,300	n.a.	n.a.
1886–90	50	209,400	57	111,100	85	61,000
1891–95	63	520,100	63	215,900	85	139,700
1896–1900	57	728,400	58	395,700	82	248,100
1901–05	48	785,600	51	531,300	73	269,500
1906–10	48	1,018,800	56	720,600	76	412,600
1911–15	63	1,356,000	70	1,097,300	86	588,000

Note: n.a. indicates data are not available.

Source: Computed from data in Flávio Azevedo Marques de Saes, 'Expansão e Declínio das Ferrovias Paulistas: 1870–1940,' in Carlos Manuel Peláez and Mircea Buescu (eds), *A Moderna História Econômica* (Rio de Janeiro: APEC, 1976), p. 79.

The growth in shipments of domestic agricultural products was also facilitated by government tariff and rate-setting policies. Brazil experienced considerable price inflation in the decades before 1913. But in reflection of both normal regulatory lag and hostility to the foreign railway companies, the government rate-setting authorities resisted efforts to have transportation charges keep pace with the country's inflation.[44] Thus, not only did shipping costs fall when the railways were opened but, in addition, the price of railway transportation seems to have declined thereafter relative to the general price level. This rate-setting policy led to government subsidies for the railways and eventually to nationalization. What is important in the present context is that government regulations also operated to lower the real freight charges for producers in the domestic agricultural sector.

The structure of railway rates that was established also discriminated in favor of the domestic agricultural sector. Between 1874 and 1900, the rates charged for shipments of foodstuffs on the railways listed in Table 7.8 ranged between 26 and 49 percent of the rates charged for coffee.[45] For livestock and timber, the rates were even lower. Moreover, in 1899 the government implemented a general policy which obliged the railway companies to lower their charges on domestically-produced foodstuffs.[46] Thus the domestic agricultural sector drew special and disproportionate advantage from the fall in transport costs which the railroads made possible. For this reason, meaningful comparisons with shipping costs in the pre-railroad era, which might serve as a basis for welfare analysis, are hard to make. In the earlier period, freight charges for the domestic agricultural sector's high-weight/low-value commodities had often been so high that these products had not been shipped at all in many areas.

Finally, government policy with respect to import duties also helped promote the expansion of the domestic agricultural sector. At the turn of the century, Brazil imposed protective tariffs on many foodstuffs that were produced locally.[47] The fact that politicians from Minas Gerais took a prominent role in this policy initiative suggests that the new measures should not be viewed as determined randomly, or by a process that was completely exogenous. The advent of low-cost transportation had greatly increased the potential returns which protective tariffs offered to domestic food producers. Correspondingly, political returns also rose for the political entrepreneurs who would implement the necessary measures. In this perspective, the provision of the tariffs may be regarded almost as endogenous to the process.[48]

The consequences of the new import duties were clear-cut: reduced uncertainty, higher prices, and a larger market for the domestic agricultural sector. Moreover, the fact that part of the sector's market growth came at the expense of imports also helped avoid a potential pitfall. That would have been a situation in which sharp increases in domestic food supply pressed on static, price-inelastic demand, and thus reduced aggregate revenues for producers. Finally, the policy initiative also had broader economic effects. As noted, the new tariffs were implemented in conjunction with the heightened domestic supply response which low-cost transportation made possible. Under such conditions, the tariffs led to import substitution in many food products, and thus intensified intersectoral linkages within the Brazilian economy.

Railroads and the Onset of a More Generalized Pattern of Development

As in the ante-bellum United States economy, the main impact of the extended railway network seems to have been in lowering transportation costs for goods (and people) within individual regional markets.[49] The Northeast also benefited to some extent from a decline in transport costs. Thus in zones where railways were built, internal freight charges for sugar and cotton in the region appear to have fallen some 50 percent from their level in the pre-railroad era.[50] Mainly because of the region's poor export conditions, however, relatively little railroad construction took place in the Northeast.[51] As late as 1900, the entire region had only 1,048 kilometers of public track. Railways obviously could not promote economic development unless they were built; and that did not happen on a large scale in the Northeast. As a historian of the region described the situation: 'At the turn of the century, railroads had barely begun to penetrate the Northeast.'[52] Further, the Northeast's economic difficulties stemmed from conditions other than high-cost transportation. Particularly in the Southeast, however, extension of the railways seems to have opened a new period of more generalized economic development in Brazil.

Prior to the extension of the railways, a rising value of output per capita in Brazil had been limited mainly to the country's export sector. By lowering transport costs and increasing the size of the economically relevant markets, however, the railways permitted more rapid growth of income in the domestic agricultural sector. As noted earlier, income in the sector rose both because of higher output levels and because of improved price relations. In addition, the railways also led to other structural shifts and new intersectoral linkages in the Brazilian economy.

We have already noted the railways' role in linking diverse activities within the rural areas. Further, by their nature, the railways went in both directions. Hence the lines lowered transportation costs for producers (actual or potential) in Brazil's industrial sector as well as for the country's agricultural producers. As a result, urban manufacturers, too, gained access to new consumers in the country's distant and fragmented markets. Hence the railroads helped give some reality to the promise of large potential markets which was offered by the size of Brazil's population. Because of these developments, new sources of income growth were opened which permitted economic expansion more widely and at a faster rate. Further, the railroad's impact on transportation costs also meant that the sources of food supply were now considerably broadened. Consequently, not only did the supply curve of domestic agricultural products shift downward; but its elasticity also increased. The new capacity to draw on more distant and diverse producers probably contributed to the post-1888 rise in Brazil's domestic supply elasticity which we noted in Chapter 6.[53]

Coming together with import substitution in food production, these changes transformed the structural relations which linked domestic agriculture, manufacturing, and the foreign-trade sector in the Southeast. Income growth in agriculture and the advent of cheaper transportation to the hinterland shifted demand constraints on the expansion of Brazilian manufacturing. At the same time, the higher domestic supply elasticity reduced the inflationary impact of a given rise in autonomous expenditures. Finally, the new market linkages intensified intersectoral integration. Production increases in one activity now had a greater multiplier effect on output levels elsewhere in the economy; and economic expansions in the various sectors were increasingly mutually supporting. These structural changes permitted the onset of a more generalized pattern of economic development in Brazil.

The timing is hard to pinpoint, for the changes proceeded piece-meal, and long-term shifts were often overshadowed by the short-term inflation–deflation cycles which occurred between 1880 and 1906. Nevertheless, as we saw in Chapter 3, the Brazilian economy's long-term development experience was markedly better after 1900 than in the preceding century. For the reasons discussed, the extension of the railways seems to have played a key role in that transformation.[54]

Further Discussion

It may appear old-fashioned to attribute an important place to rail-roads in the onset of a more generalized pattern of development in Brazil. Revisionist research has greatly qualified some of the claims which had earlier been made for the role of railways in the economic development of the United States during the nineteenth century.[55] As noted above, however, the extension of the railways was important in Brazil mainly because of its effects on *intra*regional trade. By contrast, much of the revisionist discussion concerning the impact of the rail-ways in the United States has focused on their *inter*regional effects.

Further, the social returns to railways were probably much larger in Brazil than in the United States. This is because the alternative trans-portation modes which are relevant for calculating the 'social savings' of railways in Brazil are generally not improved rivers or canals (as in the United States), but mule trains over very poor roads, or small boats on difficult rivers. Each of the latter modes involved relatively high unit transport costs. Similarly, the social savings and social returns attributable to the railroads in Brazil were also higher because of another major difference with the United States. Brazil's individual railway lines did not connect easily to form a single national or regional system. Nevertheless, intraregional transportation costs fell sharply, with gains which were proportionately greater than in the United States. This is because Brazil's interior lacked the interconnecting river–lake and canal *networks* which had lowered intraregional ship-ping costs in the pre-railroad United States.

Finally, it is helpful to broaden our comparative perspective, and consider the effects of the railroad in some historical cases other than the United States. The experience of Mexico and Siberia, two other underdeveloped, land-abundant countries in the late nineteenth century, is especially relevant. Those countries shared Brazil's features of high transportation costs in the pre-railroad era. And in those countries, too, the fall in transport costs which followed railway con-struction was a major factor in the onset of sustained economic development.[56]

Contemporaries seem to have taken the key role of the railroads in Brazil's economic development as self-evident. However, the railways' importance has been obscured in some later writings, which have approached the subject of the railroads with different concerns. For example, Brazil's railroads have sometimes been discussed in terms of the merits or demerits of foreign investment, or of public versus private ownership.[57] The fact that most railways were built primarily to transport export staples to the ports has also influenced subsequent perspectives. These have often viewed the railroads as a mere adjunct of the export economy. Accordingly, many studies have focused on the impact of the railroads on Brazil's exports rather than on the country's internal trade. Analysis has sometimes also been hampered by a failure to distinguish between the subjective, *ex ante* intentions of the railway companies and the objective, *ex post* effects of the railroads on the Brazilian economy. The companies' export orientation is understandable in terms of their immediate economic prospects (and the rate structure noted earlier). But the companies' emphasis on exports should not divert attention from the possibility that the railroads may also have promoted internal trade and development within the domestic sector of the Brazilian economy.

Similarly, Brazil's railroads have often been assessed in terms of their accounting losses and the ensuing call for government subsidies. The picture as regards private profitability was in fact mixed. Some early railroads showed poor financial results, while others yielded respectable returns.[58] Subsequent deterioration in many lines owed much to the government rate-setting practices in an inflationary environment rather than to intrinsic economic deficiencies of the railways *per se*. Further, subsidies to many of Brazil's railroads may well have been justified on standard welfare criteria; for it is likely that at the time, many of the country's lines operated under conditions of decreasing average costs. Note also that because of the discriminatory rate structure, a railway's private returns could well worsen, the greater was its service to the domestic agricultural sector. Hence, low private returns and the need for government subsidies hardly constitute *prima facie* evidence that the railroads were not desirable from the viewpoint of Brazilian welfare. In any case, the pertinent issue in the context of economic development is social rates of return. These include the impact of intersectoral effects and external economies. Because of the social benefit and cost conditions which we have discussed, social returns probably exceeded private returns for many Brazilian railways.[59]

Finally, some discussions have focused on the high costs of some Brazilian railroads; or on the greater advantages offered by the highway-truck system which emerged in the second third of the twentieth century.[60] These are interesting and important issues. But in the present context, the relevant question is the economic development experience of nineteenth-century Brazil with railroads or without them. And for the reasons discussed, the advent of the railroads seems to have had a major effect.

Before concluding this discussion, however, we should note briefly some alternative explanations for the onset of sustained development in Brazil after the 1890s. It might appear plausible to consider the upsurge in growth as a 'long swing' induced by a spurt in demand due to European immigration.[61] In view of the country's chronic inflation during the nineteenth century , however, deficient aggregate demand does not seem to have been a key problem for long-term economic development in Brazil. Rather, changes on the supply side seem to have been necessary for this economy's development. The importance of supply conditions in constraining Brazil's economic development in the pre-railroad period is suggested by events during the Paraguayan War of the 1860s. Government expenditure and the aggregate money supply rose sharply. But coming before the railways and the associated shift toward more elastic domestic supply conditions, the spurt in demand led to accelerated inflation rather than to sustained economic development.

It also appears unlikely that the *encilhamento* of the 1890s can be credited with a major role in the onset of a more generalized pattern of development in Brazil. This burst of monetary expansion and company promotions may have helped spur industrial development, but Brazil was still overwhelmingly an agrarian economy in the 1890s. Consequently, broad economic development necessarily required the participation of the agricultural sector. Finally, other interpretations have stressed the importance of exports and of industrialization for Brazil's economic development. Notwithstanding the importance of these activities, however, the advanced sector was too small to lead the entire economy forward. Because of its large size in the economy, the domestic agricultural sector had to achieve higher growth if Brazil was to experience a more generalized pattern of economic progress.

Conclusions

This chapter has noted the low overall rates of saving and investment which appear to have prevailed in Brazil until the end of the nineteenth century. As we have seen, the slow pace of accumulation in this economy seems to have reflected a situation of low marginal returns to capital. We have also considered the supply and demand conditions which limited the rate of technological innovation and diffusion. Brazil's technical progress and capital formation appear particularly moderate when they are compared with the country's rate of long-term population increase – approximately 1.8 percent per annum. Under these conditions, it is not surprising that Brazil achieved only modest progress in per capita income and economic development during the nineteenth century.

The considerations just discussed apply, in varying degrees, both to Brazil's 'advanced' sector and to the country's 'backward' sector of domestic agriculture. Conditions in the domestic agricultural sector were of special importance, however, for the country's economic retardation and development. Both because of its large weight within the economy as a whole and because of its impact on the advanced activities, the domestic agricultural sector played a central role in nineteenth-century Brazil's economic experience. As we have seen, this sector required investment in low-cost transportation facilities in order to enlarge its market opportunities and promote its development. Unfortunately, large-scale railway construction within Brazil's interior did not take place until the two decades before 1913.

With the extension of the railways, a new era of more generalized development seems to have begun in Brazil. With its bulky, low-value commodities, the domestic agricultural sector drew special cost advantages from the opening of the new transportation mode. And the sector also benefited substantially from railways which were built primarily to serve areas of export production. Consequently, domestic agriculture could now participate more effectively in the country's economic development – both directly, with higher rates of income growth, and indirectly, with intensified output and income linkages among exports, domestic agriculture, and manufacturing in the Southeast. Thus the extension of the railway network, with its associated structural changes, seems to have been a key condition in the onset of sustained Brazilian development toward the turn of the century. This experience is also consistent with interpreting the country's earlier stagnation as stemming largely from an absence of the external economies which railways would have provided. Because of the country's factor endowment and geographical features, the availability of low-cost transportation was of special importance for the economic development of nineteenth-century Brazil.

At this point, our study branches analytically in two different directions. The preceding chapters have left unanswered important questions concerning the underlying causes of Brazil's economic experience during the nineteenth century. In analyzing any complex social process, however, it helps to separate the proximate from the more ultimate causes. That was part of our task in the preceding chapters. Moreover, in view of the uncertainty concerning the structure and dynamics of Brazil's economy in the nineteenth century, it was necessary first to clarify those topics. The companion volume to this study considers the underlying obstacles to Brazil's economic development in the nineteenth century.[62]

Another set of questions involves the economic changes which occurred in Brazil once the country was launched on a path of accelerated economic development. The next two chapters discuss key features of Brazil's economic development in the decades after 1900.

Notes

1 These data are from Alan K. Manchester, *British Preeminence in Brazil: Brazil: Its Rise and Decline* (Durham, NC: Duke University Press, 1933), p. 314, n. 8.

2 On the latter point, see pp. 90-1 in Chapter 5, above. We might also consider the pace of capital accumulation in the first half of the century from another vantage point. Slaves were an important 'capital good' in nineteenth-century Brazil. Consequently, one might attempt to form an impression of trends in capital formation by considering trends in the number of slaves per capita of the total population, or per capita of the total population minus slaves. The results of such calculations are presented in the accompanying table.

Slaves Per Capita of Brazil's Total and Non-Slave Population

Year	Estimated Slave Population (Thousands)	Slaves Relative to Total Population	Slaves Relative to the Non-Slave Population
1800	1,960	.54	1.18
1810	1,930	.48	0.93
1819	1,107	.25	0.33
1823	1,148	.24	0.32
1850	2,500	.35	0.53

Source: The estimates for the stock of slaves are from Roberto Simonsen, *História Econômica do Brasil*, 4th edn (São Paulo: Companhia Editora Nacional, 1962), p. 271, n.; and from Stanley Stein, *Vassouras: A Brazilian Coffee County, 1850–1900* (Cambridge, Mass: Harvard University Press, 1957), p. 294. In cases of conflicting estimates, the ones utilized were those which could be corroborated by another source, or which presented data sufficiently detailed as to lend credence to the overall figure.

As the table indicates, the number of slaves per capita fell in the first two decades of the century, and then rose (to a level lower than the 1800 figure) by 1850. This picture is consistent with other impressions of the Brazilian economy between 1800 and 1850. However, the underlying data may be too unreliable to justify excessive focus on these computations.

3 The data on British investment which are presented in Table 7.4 were compiled by Irving Stone and the late Matthew Simon. They computed the value of government obligations and company debentures at face value, and the value of company shares on the basis of paid-in capital. Investments not in the form of publicly issued securities were not included. Because of this omission (which relates to direct investments by individuals in industry and land), D. C. M. Platt considers the Stone–Simon estimates a lower limit on total British investments in Brazil. See his *Latin America and British Trade, 1806–1914* (New York: Harper and Row, 1973), pp. 286–8. In the present context, the effect of this omission would be to raise the total investment figures observed, particularly toward the end of the century. Most

of the data underlying Table 7.4 are also available in Irving Stone, 'British Direct and Portfolio Investment in Latin America before 1914,' *Journal of Economic History*, vol. 37 (September 1977).

4 The capital stock in some coffee regions sometimes grew at rates higher than the 4–5 percent annual rates suggested in the text. Thus Thomas Holloway's estimates of the stock of coffee trees in western São Paulo imply a 5.8 annual growth rate in the boom period between 1886 and 1913. (See his paper 'Creating The Reserve Army? The Immigration Program of São Paulo, 1886–1930' in *International Migration Review*, vol. 12 (June 1977), Table 1.) The effect of this growth on *aggregate* capital formation, however, was partially offset by low (or negative) rates of investment in the older, depleted coffee areas. See Stein, *Vassouras*, op. cit., Chapter 9.

5 See D. A. Nichols, 'Land and Economic Growth,' *American Economic Review*, vol. 60 (June 1970), pp. 332–40.

6 See Chapter 6, pp. 113–4, and the references cited there.

7 Matthew Simon, 'The Pattern of New British Portfolio Foreign Investment 1865–1914,' in John Adler (ed.), *Capital Movements and Economic Development* (New York: St. Martin's Press, 1967), pp. 40–3. More detailed information on Brazil's share in British foreign investment is presented on pp. 76–7 in Nathaniel H. Leff, *Underdevelopment and Development in Brazil, Vol. II: Reassessing the Obstacles to Economic Development* (Allen & Unwin, London, 1982), Chapter 4.

8 See Michael Edelstein, 'The Determinants of U.K. Investment Abroad, 1870–1913: The U.S. Case,' *Journal of Economic History*, vol. 34 (December 1974), p. 982, n. 5, p. 1006.

9 See D. C. M. Platt, *Finance, Trade, and Politics in British Foreign Policy, 1815–1914* (London: Oxford University Press, 1968), pp. 20, 308–52, for a discussion of the political context in which British capital exports took place during the nineteenth century.

10 Irving Stone, 'British Long-Term Investment in Latin America, 1865–1913,' *Business History Review*, vol. 42 (Autumn 1968), pp. 312–16.

11 Platt, *Latin America and British Trade*, op. cit., Chapters 3, 6, and 9.

12 Pedro Carvalho de Mello has presented data showing that in the latter part of the century (1870–88), the mean annual return to investment in a sample of Brazilian equities transacted on the London stock exchange was 9.4 percent. See his 'The Economics of Labor in Brazilian Coffee Plantations, 1850–1888,' (PhD dissertation, University of Chicago, 1977), p. 142, Table 36. As Mello recognizes, however, these returns were not representative for the Brazilian economy as a whole. Moreover, these data refer to average returns; the issue in the present context is whether marginal returns were sufficiently high to sustain a large annual volume of investment in Brazil.

13 See pp. 53–5 in Leff, *Reassessing the Obstacles,* op. cit.

14 For example, there are reports of individual producers introducing new mechanized techniques in the processing of coffee beans for export. See, for example, Pierre Monbeig, *Pionniers et Planteurs de São Paulo* (Paris: Armand Colin, 1952), pp. 87–8. Refugees from the American Confederacy introduced the plough into São Paulo agriculture. See Viotti da Costa, *Da Senzala a Colonia* (São Paulo, 1966), pp. 183–5. In the late 1880s, sugar planters in Brazil's Northeast apparently began to use the plough more widely. See Peter Eisenberg, *The Sugar Industry of Pernambuco: Modernization Without Change, 1840–1910* (Berkeley and Los Angeles: University of California Press, 1974), p. 34. Adoption was slow, however, and primitive hoes apparently persisted well into the twentieth century. See Robert Levine, *Pernambuco in The Brazilian Federation, 1889–1937* (Stanford: Stanford University Press, 1978), p. 25. Paul Mandell has informed me in a personal communication that towards the end of the century, barbed-wire fencing and zebu cattle were introduced in livestock raising.

15 For example, on conditions in coffee, see Stein, *Vassouras*, op. cit., pp. 48–9, 214–15.

16 See pp. 170–1, below. The data of Table 7.5 understate somewhat the rate of productivity increase in the cotton textile industry, for during this period the composition of its output shifted toward finer grade, higher value products (Stanley J. Stein, *The Brazilian Textile Manufacture: Textile Enterprise in An Under-developed Area, 1850–1950* (Cambridge, Mass.: Harvard University Press, 1957), p. 100.

17 For example, David Denslow has presented estimates showing that in the 1850s, relative factor costs in Brazil's Northeast did not justify shifting from water mills to steam power in sugar processing. These estimates are given in his 'Sugar Production in Cuba and Northeast Brazil, 1850–1914' (mimeographed, 1972), Chapter 3.

18 Stein, *Vassouras*, op. cit., pp. 48–9, 214–15; Eisenberg, *The Sugar Industry*, op. cit., pp. 42–3; José Arthur Rios, 'Coffee and Agricultural Labor,' in Carlos Manuel Peláez (ed.), *Essays on Coffee and Economic Development* (Rio de Janeiro: Instituto Brasileiro do Café, 1973), p. 8.

19 For example, in 1816 a sugar planter published a manual on new production techniques which urged the use of bagasse as a fuel in sugar mills. (See Caio Prado, Jr, *The Colonial Background of Modern Brazil* trans. by Suzette Macedo (Berkeley and Los Angeles: University of California Press, 1967), p. 455, n. 6.) Diffusion of this innovation was slow, however. Decades later, the sugar planters generally did not use bagasse as a fuel, even though it was also not used for fertilizer. See Eisenberg, *The Sugar Industry*, op. cit., pp. 36–9. In Leff, *Reassessing the Obstacles*, op. cit., Chapter 3 (pp. 54–8, we return briefly to the question of sociocultural conditions as an impediment to technical progress in nineteenth-century Brazil.

20 Levine, *Pernambuco*, op. cit., pp. 25–6, 164.

21 Stein, *The Brazilian Cotton Textile Manufacture*, op. cit., p. 48. David Denslow has proposed another explanation which also emphasizes the microeconomic rationality in Brazil's delayed adoption of saw gins in cotton production. Brazilian cotton was the long-staple variety, which commanded a premium of some 25–35 percent in British markets until the mid-1850s. Use of saw gins, however, severely damaged the fiber of the long-staple cotton. When new spinning techniques in Great Britain eroded the superiority and price premium of long-staple cotton, Brazilian producers abandoned the use of roller gins in favor of saw gins, which were now more economic. This discussion is contained in pp. 22–4 of David Denslow, 'The Origins of Regional Economic Inequality in Brazil,' (University of Florida, mimeo., 1978). This explanation which focuses on rates of return to adoption of new techniques can be considered complementary to the one mentioned in the text.

22 Eisenberg, *The Sugar Industry*, op. cit., pp. 48–9. However, as discussed in Leff, *Reassessing the Obstacles*, op. cit., Chapter 2, low profits caused by macroeconomic conditions in the Northeast constrained the possibilities for most sugar producers to invest in more productive technologies which were available.

23 For an exposition of the concepts used here, see J. E. Meade, *The Growing Economy* (London: Allen & Unwin, 1968), esp. Chapters 3–7. A simplified presentation is available in P. A. Neher, *Economic Growth and Development: A Mathematical Introduction* (New York: John Wiley, 1971), Chapters 5–7. Note that in equation (1) of our text the term $(1-a)$ is given only at a point in time. Also, technical progress enters the model through the manner in which the inputs are specified. Hence equation (1) is not restricted to the case of a Cobb–Douglas production function.

24 Meade, *The Growing Economy*, op. cit., pp. 63–74.

25 Such improvements in capital-market institutions as did occur were partially offset by the decline of the market in slaves. That pervasive institution had in the earlier period provided an effective mechanism for capital-market arbitrage across activities and regions in nineteenth-century Brazil.

26　Nineteenth-century Brazil was of course largely an agrarian economy, so the estimates of σ which are most relevant are those in agriculture. On the basis of his extensive experience in the agricultural sector of underdeveloped countries, Vernon Ruttan has written to me that a value of $\sigma<1$ is probably most likely for nineteenth-century Brazil. For empirical evidence of $\sigma<1$ even in a case of a technologically-advanced agricultural sector in a contemporary developing country, see G. Fishelson, 'Relative Shares of Labor and Capital in Agriculture: The Case of Israel,' *The Review of Economics and Statistics*, vol. 56 (August 1974), pp. 348–52.

27　The importance of $\sigma<1$ in this context is apparent when we consider the equation for changes over time in the rate of return to capital and land (r^*). If capital-augmenting technical progress was of fairly small quantitative proportions, we have: $r^*=a/\sigma\,(K^*-L^*)$.

28　Information on the size and nature of Brazil's domestic agricultural sector is presented in Chapter 2, pp. 20–2, above.

29　The pattern of a very small percentage of demand for manufactured goods in aggregate demand at low levels of per capita income is summarized in Engel's Law. The size of the market for manufactures in Brazil is discussed in Chapter 4 of Leff, *Reassessing the Obstacles*, op. cit.

30　See pp. 114–16 in Chapter 6, above.

31　On the high transportation costs in Brazil during the nineteenth century, see Chapter 2, pp. 15–18.

32　See J. R. Miller, 'A Reformulation of A. V. Chayanov's Theory of the Peasant Economy,' *Economic Development and Cultural Change* (18 January 1970), p. 225.

33　A formal model analyzing the impact of lower transportation costs on agricultural development is presented in Martin T. Katzman, 'The Von Thuenen Paradigm, The Industrial–Urban Hypothesis, and the Spatial Structure of Agriculture,' *American Journal of Agricultural Economics* (November 1974), esp. pp. 683–6. Note that in addition to raising the ex-farm prices of all agricultural products, cheaper transportation also changes the relative prices which producers face at different locations. This differential price impact of freight charges on diverse products provides a basis for intraregional specialization and trade even under homogenous production conditions. In general, producers who are more distant from the major consumption center will find that their comparative advantage lies in crops which are cheaper to transport, while producers closer to the market will specialize in products on which transportation costs weigh more heavily. The gains due to relative-price effects and compositional change are additional to those which stem from increase in market production *per se*.

34　It may be suggested that much of Brazil's territory is uninhabitable. Note, however, that transportation conditions and the associated economic opportunities also help determine whether a specific locality can attract population and hence is 'inhabitable'. Similarly, to limit consideration (and international comparison) of Brazil's railway trackage to the zones of export production is to miss much of the story: the long delay in building railways to areas in which the domestic agricultural sector predominated.

35　The more than doubling of Brazil's railway trackage between 1894 and 1914 (see Table 7.6) was accompanied by a roughly proportionate increase in British-held Brazilian railway investment. See Stone, 'British Long-Term Investment in Latin America,' op. cit., p. 329.

36　The reasons for the Brazilian state's failure to fill an entrepreneurial role on a sufficient scale during the nineteenth century (and the reasons for the major shift here toward the end of the period) are discussed in Leff, *Reassessing the Obstacles*, op. cit., Chapter 5. The qualifying phrase 'on a sufficient scale' is important. By 1913, the government's railway-promoting activities had extended to the point where a sizable share of the country's trackage was state-owned or subsidized.

37 On the magnitude of this output-valuation effect in underdeveloped economies, see Dan Usher, *The Price Mechanism and the Meaning of National Income Statistics* (London: Oxford University Press, 1968), especially Part II.

38 See J. Pandiá Calogéras, *A Política Monetária do Brasil* (translated by Thomas Newlands Neto from the 1910 edition of *La Politique Monetaire du Brésil* (São Paulo: Companhia Editora Nacional, 1961), pp. 433–4. As noted in n. 33, above, lower freight charges promoted intraregional comparative advantage via their differential impact on relative commodity prices at different locations. In addition, local differences in soil and climate provided a basis for specialization and internal trade once transportation costs declined. The process of providing lower transport costs to integrate the domestic agricultural sector with the rest of the Brazilian economy was not completed in 1913. Indeed, the process was not completed by the Second World War. On the great impact of road construction in the twentieth century, see Gordon W. Smith, 'Agricultural Marketing and Economic Development: A Brazilian Case Study' (PhD dissertation, Harvard University, 1966); and Paul I. Mandell, 'The Development of the Southern Goias-Brasilia Region: Agricultural Development in a Land-Rich Economy' (PhD dissertation, Columbia University, 1969).

39 John Wirth, *Minas Gerais in the Brazilian Federation, 1889–1937* (Stanford: Stanford University Press, 1977), p. 58. A map which shows the timing of railway construction in the Minas region is presented on p. 417 of Kempton Webb, 'Origins and Development of a Food Economy in Central Minas Gerais,' *Annals of The Association of American Geographers*, vol. 49 (December 1959). Valuable material on the railroads in São Paulo is presented in Fernando de Azevedo, *Um Trem Corre para O Oeste* (São Paulo, 1950), and in Odilon Nogueira de Mattos, *Café e Ferrovias* (São Paulo, 1974).

40 The data of Table 7.7 show exceptionally high growth for shipments of rice. These must be viewed within the broader context of Brazil's successful effort at import substitution in rice. Information on that process is presented in Paul Mandell, 'The Rise of the Modern Brazilian Rice Economy,' *Food Research Institute Studies*, vol. 10 (June 1971), pp. 167–8, 201–4, 217–19.

41 The extent to which the Sorocabana was originally built as a coffee railroad is not certain. But regardless of original intentions, as with the other companies whose data are presented in Table 7.8, the process described in the text operated to give the Sorocabana a large amount of non-coffee freight. If we omit the Sorocabana from consideration because of questions concerning the initial objectives of its promoters, the points in the text are amply supported by the data for the two other (much larger) lines.

42 Since coffee was shipped in only one direction within Brazil, it may seem unreasonable to expect that coffee would account for more than 50 percent of total shipments on any of these lines. However, a common expectation concerning railroads that were built to transport export staples to the port in underdeveloped countries is that the companies will in fact return many boxcars empty to the production areas, and cover their expenses from the lucrative export trade.

43 If we take 1906–10 as the terminal period for the computation, to avoid the years of the First World War, we observe an 8.9 percent annual growth rate for non-coffee shipments, and a 9.2 percent annual rate for coffee. Again, the growth rates for the two classes of goods are similar.

44 See Flávio Azevedo Marques de Saes, 'Expansão e Declínio das Ferrovias Paulistas: 1870–1940,' in Carlos Manuel Peláez and Mircea Buescu (eds), *A Moderna História Econômica* (Rio de Janeiro: APEC, 1976), esp. pp. 80–1; Wirth, *Minas Gerais*, op. cit., pp. 44, 50, 180; Levine, *Pernambuco*, op. cit., pp. 40–1.

45 Marques de Saes 'Expansão,' op. cit., pp. 80–1.

46 Calógeras, *Política Monetária*, op. cit., p. 434.

47 Nícia Villela Luz, *A Luta pela Industrialização do Brasil* (São Paulo: Difusão

Européia do Livro, 1961), pp. 119, 126, 130; Wirth, *Minas Gerais*, op. cit., pp. 47, 180; Mandell, 'Brazilian Rice Economy,' loc. cit.

48 See Vernon Ruttan, 'Induced Institutional Change,' in Hans Binswanger and Vernon Ruttan *et al.*, *Induced Innovation* (Baltimore: Johns Hopkins University Press, 1978), esp. pp. 348–52.

49 See Albert Fishlow, *American Railroads and the Transformation of the Ante-Bellum Economy* (Cambridge, Mass.: Harvard University Press, 1965), esp. Chapter V.

50 On sugar, see Eisenberg, *The Sugar Industry*, op. cit., pp. 53 ff. On cotton, see the figures cited by Stein, *The Brazilian Textile Manufacture,* op. cit., p. 221, n. 3, and p. 222, n. 5. Cf. Levine's summary statement (*Pernambuco*, op. cit., p. 40): 'The impact of the expansion of the [region's major railway] system was tremendous.'

51 The Northeast's economic experience during the nineteenth century is discussed in Leff, *Reassessing the Obstacles*, op. cit., Chapter 2. Because of the region's very low rate of export growth (and poor export prospects), the region was in a poor position to attract large-scale railroad investment from any of the likely sources: foreign investors, domestic investors, Brazil's central government, or (with public finance heavily dependent on foreign trade taxes) the region's provincial governments.

52 Levine, *Pernambuco*, op. cit., p. 32. That page is also the source for the kilometer figure cited earlier in the text.

53 See pp. 117–20, above. Note that increased price elasticity of supply is consistent with higher rates of inflation if the growth of the money supply also accelerates. This was in fact the case in Brazil during the 1890s. But as noted in Table 6.4, given the rate of monetary expansion, price inflation was much lower than would have occurred with the earlier conditions of less elastic domestic supply.

54 The onset of more generalized economic development did not mean that an idyllic period had begun in Brazil. For a discussion of some of the changes which did occur, see Chapters 8 and 9, below.

55 See, for example, the chapters by Robert Fogel and Albert Fishlow which deal with railroads in Robert Fogel and Stanley Engerman (eds), *The Reinterpretation of American Economic History* (New York: Harper and Row, 1971).

56 Siberia's experience, in which the advent of the railroad led to rapid agricultural development, is analyzed by Daniel Kazmer in 'The Agricultural Development of Siberia, 1890–1917,' (PhD Dissertation, MIT, 1973). On Mexico, see John H. Coatsworth, *The Mexican Economy, 1800–1910* (mimeo, University of Chicago, 1978), Chapter 9. In Mexico, too, railroads that were constructed as part of a strategy focusing on export expansion turned out to have major stimulating effects on production of goods for the internal market. Data for two important Mexican trunk lines indicate that between 1885–87 and 1907–08, the volume of goods transported for the domestic market rose at annual rates of 9–11 percent. These figures were computed from data which are presented in John Coatsworth, *El Impacto de Los Ferrocarriles en el Porfiariato* (Mexico City: Sepsetentas, 1976), Vol. 2, p. 15. In 1907, after an immense growth of export shipments, goods for the domestic market (including import substitution in food), accounted for some 47 percent of ton-miles on Mexico's railroads (ibid., p. 19). A study accessible to English language readers is John H. Coatsworth, *Growth against Development: The Economic Impact of Railroads in Porfirian Mexico* (DeKalb, Ill.: Northern University Press, 1981).

57 See, for example, Julian Duncan, *Public and Private Operation of Railways in Brazil* (New York: Columbia University Press, 1932).

58 On railroad failures (in the Northeast) see Graham, *Britain and The Onset*, op. cit., pp. 69–70. Pedro Carvalho de Mello has estimated real rates of return for the equities of a sample of ten Brazilian railroads transacted on the London Exchange. Between 1870 and 1888, real returns averaged 9.3 percent. Mello has also computed real returns for a sample of nine railroads transacted on the Rio do Janeiro stock exchange. For 1877, 1878, and 1882, real returns averaged −3.5 percent, 10.3

percent, and −4.3 percent, respectively. These estimates are presented in Mello, 'Economics of Labor,' op. cit., pp. 136, 142. It is worth noting that in Australia, the railroads did not yield positive (private) returns for decades. See Noel Butlin, 'Colonial Socialism in Australia, 1860–1900,' in H. G. J. Aitken (ed.), *The State and Economic Growth* (New York: Social Science Research Council, 1959), p. 71. On some special conditions which were to worsen the position of railroads in Brazil during later years, see the next note.

59   As suggested in the text, the connection between a railway's deteriorating financial position (in private terms) and its social impact (in terms of freight transported for the domestic agricultural sector) could often be causal. The government's rate-setting policies may well have been justified by standard welfare criteria (decreasing average costs, and the externality which cheap transportation for the domestic agricultural sector generated to Brazil's economic development). However, a socially-optimal pricing policy would also have contained another component: subsidies sufficient to enable the railways to maintain their capital stock and avoid undue deterioration in the quality of service provided. It is not apparent that this second half of a consistent optimizing policy was in fact implemented. Both the public-finance difficulties of Brazilian governments and hostility to the foreign-owned companies played a role here. In subsequent decades, the deterioration of the railways' service and the attraction of a highway-truck system weakened the ability of the railways to evoke a high priority in Brazilian elite opinion.

60   See, for example, Wirth, *Minas Gerais*, op. cit., pp. 59–60.

61   Allen C. Kelley, 'Demographic Cycles and Economic Growth: The Long Swing Reconsidered,' *The Journal of Economic History*, vol. 29 (December 1969).

62   Leff, *Reassessing the Obstacles*, op. cit.

Part II

The Acceleration of Development, 1900–1947

8

Industrialization and Development, 1900–1947

Toward the end of the nineteenth century, the pace of economic growth in Brazil accelerated sharply. This acceleration involved important structural shifts in the Brazilian economy. The present chapter analyzes some of the key changes which occurred as Brazil embarked on a path of sustained economic development. We will focus mainly on the four decades following 1900, but with some qualifications. Consideration of some topics requires that we begin the discussion before 1900, in order to view conditions within their broader historical context. Second, because Brazil's official national income accounts start in 1947, many of the statistical materials presented here will also terminate in that year. This procedure enables our study to provide a bridge between Brazil's more remote economic history and analyses of the country's economic development which begin in the period following the Second World War. Topically, we will focus on Brazil's industrial development. This is a form of economic growth and structural change which has been of special interest to students of the development process. We defer to the next chapter an extended discussion of macroeconomic conditions, and of the place of government policy and the external sector in the country's development during these years.

Some Central Features

Sustained, rapid growth of aggregate output seems to have begun in Brazil toward the end of the nineteenth century. The rate of per capita income growth in the country as a whole was relatively modest during the nineteenth century.[1] By contrast, the estimates available from 1900 show aggregate output increasing steadily, and at a rapid pace after 1900. As Table 8.1 indicates, Brazil experienced relatively high rates of real output growth in each decade of the first half of the twentieth century. Between 1900 and 1947, Brazilian Real Output (an index whose movements approximate those of real gross domestic product) rose at a trend rate of 4.4 per annum.[2]

Brazil's population increased at an annual rate of 2.1 percent

Table 8.1   *Annual Trend Rates of Growth of Aggregate Real Output,
Industrial Production, and Agricultural Output in Brazil, 1900–1947*

Period	Real Output (percent)	Industrial Production (percent)	Agricultural Output (percent)
1900–09	4.2	5.6	3.5
1900–19	3.0	5.4	2.4
1920–29	5.2	5.4	3.8
1930–39	5.8	8.7	3.8
1940–47	7.1	8.6	2.4
1900–47	4.4	5.9	3.1

Note: Real Output is an index comprising output in agriculture, industry, commerce, transport and communications, and government.

Source: The annual trend rates of growth were computed by regressions fitted to Divisia indices which are presented in Claudio Haddad, *Growth of Brazilian Real Output, 1900–1947* (PhD dissertation, University of Chicago, 1974), Table 1.

between 1900 and 1947. Consequently, the country's output *per capita* rose at rates much lower than those shown in Table 8.1. Also, as a consequence of the economy's poor overall performance during the nineteenth century, Brazil in 1900 was still very much an underdeveloped country in terms of the *level* of per capita income and general development. However, our focus here is on the *rate* of economic growth in Brazil between 1900 and 1947. It is likely that Brazilian GDP rose at a pace similar to that of the Real Output index. This would mean that in the first half of the twentieth century, Brazil achieved a rate of economic growth which was very high in terms of international comparisons. Subtracting the rate of population increase in Brazil from the 1900–47 rate of Real Output growth, we obtain 2.3 percent per annum as the country's long-term rate of growth of per capita Real Output. This pace of economic progress exceeds the rate at which per capita GDP increased in the United States and in the countries of Western Europe at the onset of their modern economic development.[3]

The data of Table 8.1 show that both the agricultural and the industrial sectors participated in Brazil's economic expansion during these decades. Agricultural output increased at a rate greater than the pace of population growth, and that sector's growth was essential for the Brazilian economy's overall development. As late as 1920, some 68 percent of the country's labor force was engaged in agriculture.[4] Expansion of agricultural output was of course also important to help feed the country's growing population.

The agricultural index utilized in Table 8.1 includes output of export crops such as coffee. For the years after 1921, however, disaggregated production series are available for food products which were staples of domestic consumption. Brazil did not export these commodities on a regular basis, and the domestic income elasticity of demand for such

Table 8.2 *Annual Trend Rates of the Growth of the Quantum of Food Crops and of Staple Food Production in Brazil, 1921–1940* (in percent)

Period	Staple Foods	Food Crops
1921–30	1.6	2.0
1930–40	1.9	1.9
1921–40	1.8	2.5

Note: The index for staple foods comprises the following products: rice, beans, corn, manioc, potatoes, sugar cane, and wheat. The index of food crops also includes bananas and oranges.

Source: Computed from Paasche indices which were kindly made available by Paul Mandell from his study 'The Growth of Brazilian Agricultural Production, 1920–1970: An Intersectoral Analysis Based on Index Number Bias' (typescript, Spring 1974).

products (mainly cereals and carbohydrates) was well below unity.[5] Consequently, one would expect output of these products for the domestic market to increase at lower rates than total agricultural production. The data of Table 8.2 show that this was indeed the case. However, the rate of growth of food crop production between 1921 and 1940, 2.5 percent per annum, was far from negligible. Further, taken together with information on the country's net imports of food, the data on domestic agricultural production can be used to form an idea of the long-term trend in per capita consumption of rice and beans (two foods of mass consumption in Brazil), and of the total per capita intake of six major carbohydrate staples. These data are presented in Table 8.3. They show a perceptible long-term increase in consumption and nutritional standards, but an increase which began from very low initial levels.[6]

Finally, rising output and income in Brazilian agriculture were also essential for the third major feature apparent in Table 8.1 – the high rates of industrial growth. Coming together with income-elastic demand for manufactured products and with domestic import

Table 8.3 *Growth of Per Capita Consumption of Rice and Beans, and of Caloric Intake from Six Major Carbohydrate Products in Brazil, 1900 to 1948–50*

Year	Daily Consumption		Daily Caloric Intake from Six Food Staples[a]
	Rice	Beans	
	(kg/person)		(calories/person)
1900	.030	.040	1364
1910	.039	.045	1478
1920	.070	.070	1663
1935–39	.093	.059	1680
1948–50	.147	.065	1794

[a] Rice, beans, corn, wheat flour, manioc flour, and sugar.

Source: Claudio Haddad, *Growth of Brazilian Real Output, 1900–1947* (PhD dissertation, University of Chicago, 1974), p. 25.

Table 8.4 *The Share of Industrial Value-Added in Total Value-Added by Agriculture, Industry, Transport and Communications, and Government in the Brazilian Economy, 1908–1947*

Period	Share of the Industrial Sector (%)	Period	Share of the Industrial Sector (%)
1908–14	19.4	1930–34	24.0
1915–19	26.6	1935–39	29.9
1920–24	23.7	1940–44	36.1
1925–29	23.9	1945–47	37.6

Note: Choice of periods and of sectors was dictated by the availability of data in Haddad. The underlying estimates on sectoral value-added are in current prices.
Source: Computed from data in Claudio Haddad, *Growth of Brazilian Real Output, 1900– 1947* (PhD dissertation, University of Chicago, 1974), pp. 186–7, Table 75.

substitution, growing income in the agricultural sector helped provide the market for Brazil's accelerating industrialization. Further, as industrial production grew at rates higher than output in the rest of the economy, the structure of the economy changed. Value-added in the industrial sector came to constitute a larger percentage of Brazilian national product. Table 8.4 shows this process of increasing industrialization, with the rise of net value-added in industry relative to net value-added in four important sectors of the economy: agriculture, industry, transport and communications, and government. By 1939, income originating in the industrial sector accounted for some 22 percent of Brazilian GDP.[7]

The Timing of Brazilian Industrialization

The data of Table 8.4 show the rising share of industrial output in the Brazilian economy during the first half of the twentieth century. The table also indicates that even in the years 1908–14, value-added in Brazil's industrial sector was of more than negligible proportions. This early industrial development may seem surprising; for some writers have viewed Brazilian industrialization as beginning essentially with the interruption of the country's normal international trade relations during the First World War.[8] Information from Brazil's 1920 census, however, enables us to consider more carefully the timing of Brazil's industrialization. This subject is important not only for its historical interest, but also for the light it sheds on the nature of the industrialization process in Brazil.

The 1920 industrial census contains information on the output, the capital stock, and the labor force of Brazil's industrial sector. Moreover, the data are grouped according to the dates in which the firms surveyed were founded. Consequently, we can use these data on the industrial firms which survived until 1920 in order to determine a time

Table 8.5 *Periods in which Brazilian Industrial Firms Were Founded and Their Share in the 1920 Industrial Sector*

Firms Founded in the Period:	Share (in percent) in the 1920 Industrial Sector's:		
	Value of Output	Capital Stock	Labor Force
1915–19	26.5	24.2	23.2
1910–14	21.6	18.5	19.6
1900–09	19.9	18.4	19.4
1890–99	14.0	16.8	16.6
before 1889	18.6	22.1	21.2

Source: Computed from data in Directoria Geral de Estatística, *Recenseamento Do Brazil . . . 1920*, Vol. V (Rio de Janeiro, 1927), p. lxix.

profile of Brazil's pre-1920 industrial development. Table 8.5 presents this information for the firms which comprised the country's 1920 industrial sector.

Table 8.5 shows that approximately 25 percent of the 1920 industrial sector's output, capital, and labor force was attributable to firms that had been founded in the years 1915–19. But the general pattern indicated is of an industrialization process which had begun before 1889, and had accelerated in subsequent years. Thus, firms founded in the five years between 1910 and 1914, which had survived until 1920, accounted for some 20 percent of the 1920 industrial sector. This reflected a rise in the pace of industrial expansion as compared with the years 1900–1909,when it took twice as long to achieve a similar proportion (see Table 8.5). The 1900–1909 firms, in turn, made a larger contribution to 1920 industrial output than did enterprises which dated from the last decade of the nineteenth century. Making allowance for differential rates of attrition over time, these data suggest a pattern of evolution in which Brazil's industrial sector expanded at an accelerating rate.

Such exponential growth might in principle have reflected a process of 'learning-by-doing' at the enterprise level. In such a process, the cumulative output produced in earlier years raises productivity and thereby stimulates industrial expansion at a rising rate. Overall, however, Table 8.5 does not indicate the presence of significant learning-by-doing effects at the enterprise level in Brazil. On the contrary, the data suggest that productivity in the firms established after 1900 was marginally higher than in the enterprises founded earlier. This is indicated by the fact that the share of the post-1900 firms in industrial output was larger than their share in the sector's capital and labor inputs. Presumably, the younger firms' equipment was more modern than that of the older firms, an advantage that offset any special gains to experience which may have accrued to the pre-1900 firms.

In reality, however, the accelerating growth of Brazil's industrial sector may indeed reflect a form of learning-by-doing, albeit of a special kind. At the national level, the experience gained in the country's earlier industrial development was important, in two ways, for hastening subsequent expansion. Earlier achievements helped attract an ever larger flow of new entrepreneurs to manufacturing industry. In addition, the first decades of industrial development aided in laying the sector's political foundations. As discussed below, government policy support was important in facilitating the sector's expansion and the emergence of new industrial enterprises.

Three further points emerge from the data of Table 8.5. First, Brazilian industrialization had clearly begun well before the First World War. In fact these figures understate the extent of prewar industrial activity. This is because the table does not include the data for manufacturing firms which contributed to industrial output in earlier years, but did not survive until 1920. Second, Table 8.5 does not indicate that the 1890s, a period that included years of rapid inflation and stock exchange boom (the *encilhamento*), were of special importance in the launching of Brazilian industrialization.[9] A similar perspective concerning any unusual long-term impact of the *encilhamento* on Brazil's economic modernization comes from another source: a tabulation of the founding dates of the firms whose shares were transacted on the Rio de Janeiro stock exchange in 1922.[10] Companies founded between 1890 and 1900 accounted for 15 percent of the total. This compared with a figure of 14 percent for companies established between 1880 and 1890, and 13 percent for companies founded between 1840 and 1880. Finally, Table 8.5 suggests that the beginnings of Brazil's pre-First World War industrial development date even further back than might have been imagined. As the data indicate, firms established before 1889 accounted for some 20 percent of the 1920 Brazilian industrial sector.

This picture is corroborated by the more detailed information which is available for the country's largest single industry, cotton textiles. The data pertaining to that industry show rapid growth, both before the First World War and prior to the 1890s. Investment in the cotton textile industry seems to have expanded at especially high rates in the early 1870s and 1880s.[11] And, as the figures of Table 8.6 indicate, between 1866 and 1885 output increased at an annual geometric rate of 9.4 percent. From 1885 to 1915, even after the earlier rapid growth from a minimal base, output in the industry grew at an annual cumulative rate of 11.0 percent.[12]

Further, cotton textiles was by no means the only industry to have emerged in this early period. Food processing and other consumer-good production had also developed rapidly. Thus, in the industrial survey of 1907, cotton textile workers constituted some 27 percent of the industrial work force.[13] And in 1920, all textiles accounted for approximately 24 percent of value-added in Brazilian industry.[14] The

Table 8.6   *Growth of the Brazilian Cotton Textile Industry, 1866–1915*

	Annual Geometric Growth Rate (in %) of:		
Period	Output	Workers	Looms
1866–85	9.4	7.6	10.0
1885–1905	13.1	13.4	13.5
1905–10	n.a.	7.1	5.7
1905–15	6.9	7.7	6.9
1885–1915	11.0	11.4	11.2

Source: Computed from data in Stanley J. Stein, *The Brazilian Cotton Manufacture* (Cambridge, Mass.: Harvard University Press, 1957), p. 191.

textile industry was one of the earliest to develop in Brazil. Hence the fact that other industries had achieved this relative position *vis-à-vis* the textile industry indicates that they must have experienced similar high rates of growth during the preceding decades.

Finally, Table 8.7 presents data on the growth of electricity consumption, an indicator of industrialization and economic modernization. These statistics, too, confirm the impression of rapid industrial and urban development in Brazil in the decades before the First World War.

Table 8.7   *Growth of Electricity Consumption in Brazil, 1883–1940*

Period	Annual Rate of Increase (%)
1883–89	110.0
1890–1900	11.3
1900–10	29.4
1919–20	8.9
1920–30	9.2
1930–40	3.1

Note: Part of the increase in electricity consumption, of course, reflects substitution for other sources of energy. Hence, total energy consumption did not increase at the rates indicated in this table.
Source: Computed from data in Jean-Marie Martin, *Processus d'Industrialisation et Developpement Energetique du Brésil* (Paris, 1966), p. 29.

Effects of Brazil's Early Industrial Development

The importance of this early industrial development in Brazil has sometimes been dismissed. Thus some writers have proposed a distinction between 'an era of industrial growth', such as the pre-First World War decades, and 'a period of industrialization'.[15] The latter supposedly occurred in Brazil only in the 1930s, when industry became the 'leading sector of the economy'. It is certainly legitimate to distinguish between the level and the pace of Brazil's industrial development in different periods. This distinction, however, does not negate the importance of the country's earlier industrialization. For without the industrial development that occurred during the earlier period, Brazil's manufacturing sector would not have become large enough for its subsequent growth to have much impact on the economy's overall expansion. The greater scale of Brazil's industrial development in later decades required an increase in the manufacturing sector's share of aggregate output. That condition had perforce to be satisfied through earlier industrial growth.

Similarly, other writers have suggested that: 'Before 1945, there was no process of continuous, large-scale industrialization in Brazil. What there was were industrial spurts.'[16] That picture, however, is not consistent with the strong statistical trends observed for Brazil's industrial output in each of the decades before 1947. All of the trend coefficients presented in Table 8.1 above are associated with low standard errors, and with a very high degree of statistical significance. Further, when industrial growth was interrupted during the earlier decades, it was, as we shall see, because of occasional episodes of import stringency or slow growth in the country's real money supply. These were the very same conditions that were to lead to periodic interruptions in Brazil's industrial development during the post-1945 years of 'continuous industrialization'. Consequently, it is hard to see a major difference in the process of Brazilian industrialization between the earlier and the later periods.

The importance of Brazil's early industrial development has also been discounted because of the composition of its output.[17] Industrial production consisted largely of 'traditional consumer goods', and there was relatively little domestic production of intermediate products and capital goods. Thus food, beverages, and tobacco accounted for 42 percent of industrial value-added in 1920; and textiles and clothing, another 32 percent. By contrast, intermediate products and capital goods amounted to only 18 percent of total value-added in Brazilian industry.[18]

These numbers, from Brazil's Industrial Census, understate somewhat the magnitude of the country's production of metallurgical products and capital goods in 1920.[19] But even accepting the figures at face value, it should hardly be surprising that Brazilian industrial development concentrated first on production of food and textile products. These were the products ('basic needs') for which local demand was greatest, given the relatively low levels of per capita income which prevailed in Brazil at the time. Moreover, the composition of Brazil's early industrial production output does not seem to have been an anomaly in terms of comparisons with patterns of industrial output in other very low-income countries.[20] Further, the economic consequences of concentrating early industrial expansion on the textile and food industries were beneficial. Since the raw materials for these activities were mainly supplied by the local agricultural sector, Brazil intensified the backward linkages of its initial industrialization. Finally, the early emphasis on food and textiles did not create rigidities which hindered later development of investment-goods production. Any such suggestion is belied by the actual course of subsequent events in Brazil. When economic conditions changed, in the 1920s and subsequent decades, the country proceeded with rapid expansion of output in capital goods and intermediate products.[21]

In reality, the early industrialization we have noted was important both because of its immediate economic effects and because it facilitated subsequent industrial development. Labor and management skills as well as industrial capital which were formed in the earlier period were utilized for manufacturing growth (both horizontal and vertical) in later decades.[22] In some cases, this industrial expansion and diversification took place within the same enterprises that were established in the earlier period. All of the large multi-activity 'economic groups' which were prominent in Brazil's industrial sector during the post-Second World War period – Matarrazzo, Votorontim, Jafet, Klabin, and Lundgren – began their operations before 1914. In addition, the successes of the first entrepreneurs in Brazil's manufacturing sector provided a signal which helped attract subsequent industrial investors. Finally, early industrial growth helped create the political infrastructure which led to future government support for Brazilian industrialization. By 1919, industrial interests had eclipsed the coffee planters in the political control of São Paulo, the dominant state in Brazilian national politics. The entire congressional delegation of São Paulo state voted against export groups who had attempted to lower the country's high import tariffs.[23]

Brazil's early industrial development also had more immediate effects on factor allocation and productivity in the economy. By 1920, there were approximately 374,000 industrial workers in Brazil.[24] These amounted to some 4 percent of the country's total labor force. Equally important, industrialization had created a sector with a relatively high level of productivity in the Brazilian economy. In 1920, value-added per worker in Brazil's industrial sector was approximately 2.7 times greater than in the economy as a whole.[25] Finally, the extent of import substitution provides another index of Brazil's early industrialization. This measure shows the degree to which local producers supplied the total domestic market for manufactured products. Thus it indicates the size of domestic manufacturing output relative to the opportunities offered by demand for manufactures within Brazil. In 1919, local industry supplied approximately 60 per cent of the industrial value-added that was consumed in Brazil.[26]

The 1920 Industrial Census also provides pertinent information on other features of Brazil's early industrial development. The census surveyed a total of 13,336 industrial firms. The average size of these enterprises was small, with only twenty-one workers per establishment. This situation partly reflected a dualistic pattern, in which large firms coexisted with a multitude of small enterprises. Craft and home producers, whose output and workers were not included in the Industrial Census, competed with modern factories in the production of some goods.[27] There were also many little, unincorporated firms that were included in the Census, but which accounted for only a small fraction of industrial output.[28] This dualistic pattern also had another side. Even in 1920, the firms which provided most of the country's industrial output and employed most of its industrial labor force were not small. Of the total labor force enumerated in the 1920 Industrial Census, almost half of all workers (48 percent) were in firms which employed more than 200 workers. Almost a third of this labor force (32 percent) was in firms which employed more than 500 workers.

Proprietors comprised 6 percent of the labor force surveyed by the Industrial Census. Engineers, administrators, and technical personnel accounted for 2 percent of this work force; other white collar workers, 4 percent; and factory workers (operários), 88 percent. Most of this work force was male (67 percent), and more than 14 years of age (91 percent). The fact that Brazilian industrialization was not based on the labor of women and children may have affected the wage scales that were adopted in the industrial sector relative to the rest of the economy.[29] The absolute level of wages, however, reflected the low level of capitalization and worker productivity. Horsepower per factory worker averaged only 1.1 in 1920.

The Role of The Tariff in Brazilian Industrial Development

The industrial growth which we have noted for Brazil in the pre-1929 and pre-1913 years should not be surprising. Throughout this earlier period, Brazilian industry had substantial tariff protection. Although the pre-1929 Brazilian tariff has sometimes been described as being only of modest proportions, the rates were in fact high.[30]

Until 1844, external treaties restricted Brazil's capacity to impose protective tariffs.[31] In 1844, however, the Brazilian government imposed a 30 percent *ad valorem* duty on most of the country's imports. Thereafter, the tariffs on many products – and especially those that were of interest to local producers – were often increased. Thus in 1869 the duties on a sample of common cotton cloth averaged approximately 47 percent.[32] The rates on these textiles rose steadily after the 1870s, and by 1913 had tripled. More generally, the tariff imposed on many imported products in 1874 was approximately 40 percent; and in 1879, 50 percent. Subsequently, there were numerous legislative and administrative changes in the country's tariffs, and in 1900 a major upward revision. Tariffs were raised again in 1905. In

1913, for some products with a relatively large domestic market – shoes, rough cottons, and printed cotton textiles – the tariff rates were, respectively, 115, 154, and 127 percent.[33]

Tariff legislation does not, however, give a complete picture of the protection which shielded Brazilian producers from import competition. This is because changes also occurred in the administrative procedures which determined the valuation of imports for tariff purposes. Moreover, political pressures could affect the classification of particular imports and the rates at which their duties were levied.[34] Exemptions from tariffs were also available under certain conditions.[35] Finally, in the 1930s the importation of certain goods was prohibited outright, in order to restrict competition with locally-made manufactures. These conditions – and particularly changes in the manner with which the country's import legislation was implemented – were important in determining the actual protective effect of Brazil's tariffs. Consequently, it would be helpful to have an index other than the tariff code to measure the extent to which tariffs raised the prices of Brazil's imports above world-market levels.

The value of the import duties paid relative to the value of Brazil's imports can provide a rough measure of this protective effect. As is well known, this ratio does not indicate accurately the complete height of a country's protective measures. This is because goods which face a prohibitive tariff or complete prohibition are not imported; hence they do not enter the ratio's denominator, the value of imports. Consequently, this measure *understates* the magnitude of a country's protection against imports. Bearing in mind the direction of this bias, then, we note that import duties amounted to 36 percent of the value of Brazil's imports in the 1870s, and 39 percent in the first half of the 1880s.[36] The figures for later quinquennia are presented in Table 8.8.

Table 8.8 shows that tariff duties added appreciably to the price of imports which reached the Brazilian market. Moreover, the protective effects on local production were much greater than these average

Table 8.8 *Import Duties as a Percentage of the Value of Brazilian Imports, 1890–1939*

Period	Annual Average (%)	Period	Annual Average (%)
1890–94	26.3	1915–19	21.7
1895–99	28.1	1920–24	20.6
1900–04	39.6	1925–29	25.3
1905–09	47.8	1930–34	32.9
1910–14	39.7	1935–39	22.4

Source: Computed from data in Annibal Villela and Wilson Suzigan, *Política do Governo e Crescimento da Economia Brasileira, 1889–1945* (Rio de Janeiro, IPEA, 1973), pp. 418–19, 439–40.

figures indicate. This is because the tariffs were not uniform, but rather were especially high on the products (such as consumer goods) which were manufactured within Brazil.[37] Furthermore, when exchange-rate movements reduced the magnitude of the protection provided by duties which had been set in specific terms, the government raised the tariff rates.[38]

The exact amount of the protection which the tariff conferred on Brazilian industry is hard to ascertain. In an effort to stimulate agricultural import substitution and to increase the backward linkages of industrialization, the government also levied high import duties on some primary products and raw materials.[39] These tariffs on inputs to the industrial sector meant that the effective rates of protection for Brazilian manufacturers were often lower than the nominal rates.[40] Also, in some products the internal market grew to a size sufficiently large to permit entry by many local producers. Competition between these firms prevented them from setting their prices on the basis of the world market price plus the tariff.[41]

Regardless of its exact magnitude, the impact of the tariff on Brazilian industrialization is clear. Protective tariffs provided early Brazilian industrialists with the assurance that they would be able to compete with imports in supplying the domestic market for manufactured products. And by changing relative prices and the internal terms of trade within Brazil, the tariff shifted intersectoral rates of return, and thus enabled the industrial sector to attract factors of production from elsewhere in the economy. The effects of the tariff were additional to the protection which came from another source: the high transportation costs which stemmed from Brazil's great distance from the major industrialized countries in the world economy.[42] But the central place which the tariff issue took in policy debates over Brazilian industrialization makes it clear that the natural protection afforded by international transportation costs was not enough. Protective policy measures were also needed to enhance the capacity of local producers to compete with imports in the local market for manufactures. Without the protective tariff, it is inconceivable that Brazilian industrialization would have been launched and proceeded at the rapid pace we have noted.

Determinants of Brazilian Industrial Growth

Favorable relative prices *vis-à-vis* competition from imports were a necessary condition for Brazilian industrialization. However, the small share of the manufacturing sector in the output and labor force of the aggregate Brazilian economy in the nineteenth and early twentieth centuries indicates that high tariffs were not sufficient to assure large-scale industrial development. Another essential condition for Brazilian industrialization was the existence of a domestic market for manufactured products.[43] The problem was that during much of the nineteenth century, income levels in Brazil were too low to provide much demand for industrial goods.[44]

As the internal market for manufactured products increased in Brazil, industrial output could, with the aid of the tariff, expand rapidly. Starting from its small initial base, the industrial sector came to supply a substantial fraction of Brazil's consumption of manufactures, and achieved a correspondingly large scale of output. Favorable conditions in the product market generated high potential returns for local producers. Under these conditions, the supply of factors to Brazil's industrial sector was readily forthcoming. Entrepreneurs appeared both from Brazil's native-born elite and from the country's immigrant population.[45] Importers constituted a relatively large proportion of the country's first industrialists, presumably because they were familiar with local product markets. Skilled labor came from a diversity of sources – expatriates, immigrants, and, increasingly, from native-born Brazilians.

In addition, capital was supplied with sufficient elasticity to permit the high rates of output growth which we have noted earlier (see Tables 8.1 and 8.6). It is worth noting that investment in machinery did not account for an overwhelmingly large portion of the capital used in the industrial sector. The 1920 Industrial Census tabulated the components of the sector's overall capital structure under three headings: land and buildings; machinery; inventories and work-in-progress. The respective shares were: 33, 31, and 36 percent.[46] The last of these figures indicates the importance of working capital for Brazil's industrial sector. The need for circulating capital, in turn, made the sector's expansion highly dependent on government monetary policy and increases in the availability of credit. Another feature of this industrialization process is also noteworthy. Brazil's early industrial development does not seem to have been characterized by a high rate of total factor productivity increase and technical progress. Thus Table 8.5 shows that output in the cotton textile industry increased at a long-term rate similar to the growth of the industry's capital and labor inputs. The table gives little indication of an unexplained 'residual' and technical progress.

Nevertheless, once Brazil's industrialization had been launched by favorable demand conditions, its natural state seems to have been steady growth at a relatively high rate. Deviations from trend might occur, however, due to either of two causes. First, there were occasional deflationary episodes in which the growth of the economy's real (constant-price) money supply was curtailed. Industrial expansion slackened in those years, both because of the slower growth of demand and for lack of credit to provide the working capital which, as noted above, was an important feature of the industrial sector's capital structure. Second, Brazil's industrial sector utilized some imported inputs of complementary raw materials and intermediate products. Consequently, the rate of aggregate industrial growth seems to have fluctuated directly with the country's supply of imports.

In order to test this interpretation rigorously, we would need a complete econometric model of Brazilian industrial development. Estimating the supply side of such a model would be very difficult, however, for lack of annual data on the industrial sector's capital stock and labor force. Notwithstanding these difficulties, we may achieve some analytical progress in this area by using a heuristic, reduced-form approach.

Let us estimate a regression equation in which we take as our dependent variable the annual observations of Brazilian industrial output *(IND)*. These are regressed against a trend variable, which is specified as a proxy for the increasing size of the domestic market as well as the growth of the capital stock and the labor force in the industrial sector. In addition, to investigate the existence of special effects due to changes in the real money supply (M_1) and in the quantum of Brazilian imports *(IMP)*, we also specify those terms on the right-hand side of our equation. Given Brazil's usual state of inflation and excess aggregate demand, changes in these variables can be interpreted as reflecting shifts on the supply side. Since a trend variable is specified, this equation is equivalent to regressing the annual deviations of manufacturing output from its trend against the annual deviations of the real money supply and of imports from their trend values.[47] Thus the signs and statistical significance of the M_1 and *IMP* terms indicate whether unusually high or low growth of real liquidity and import supply were in fact associated with exceptionally high or low growth in industrial output.

In order to permit interpretation of the parameter estimates for the *IMP* and M_1 terms as elasticities, the annual observations of those variables are specified in logarithms. Further, the regression is specified without lags in order to ascertain the impact values of the variables on the right-hand side of the equation. A price index for deflating the money supply is available from 1908, and the *IMP* index that was utilized ends in 1945.[48] Hence the sample period is 1908–45. The estimated equation, with t-ratios in parentheses, is:

$$\ln IND = 5.213 + .049 \text{ trend} + .103 \ln IMP + .129 \ln M_1 \qquad (1)$$
$$(12.26) \quad (9.04) \qquad (2.91) \qquad (1.43)$$

$$R^2 = .99 \quad D.W. = 0.71$$

As might be expected, the overall fit of the equation is good, and the trend term is highly significant. Of greater analytic interest, however, is the fact that the coefficients on the log M_1 and log *IMP* terms are positive. And using a one-tailed test, since we have definite *a priori* expectations concerning the signs of these parameters, both coefficients are statistically significant above the .90 level. Note, moreover, that the coefficient on the import term is biased downward. The index of Brazil's import quantum which is specified in equation (1) was computed using fixed weights as between complementary goods and imports which competed with domestic industrial output. In fact, however, the share of competitive goods in Brazil's total import supply declined over this period.

The parameter estimates of equation (1) indicate that deviations of import supply or of real liquidity growth from their trend values were indeed associated with above-average increases or decreases in the pace of Brazilian industrial growth. This formulation, however, reflects a multi-factor explanation of Brazil's industrial expansion; each of the variables specified operates only in *ceteris paribus* terms. Thus, if import supply increased but real liquidity growth slackened, industrial output might expand at a relatively low rate. As discussed below, the historical values were such that a conjuncture of this sort seems to have occurred in Brazil during the 1920s. Similarly, equation (1) implies that increases in real liquidity might help offset a decline in import supply. This would occur as credit expansion in real terms facilitated domestic production of industrial inputs which had previously been imported. Such conditions, we will see, help explain the acceleration of Brazil's industrial development in the thirties.

The preceding analysis also has important implications for understanding the broader development pattern ('model') which Brazil followed in its historical experience. Foreign trade and domestic industrialization appear to have been mutually supporting rather than competitive patterns of development in Brazil during these decades. Expanding international trade stimulated Brazil's industrial development in three ways. First, as just mentioned, imports supplied complementary inputs which permitted an acceleration in the pace of industrial growth. Second, export expansion provided the resources for Brazil's infrastructure, such as railroads, which promoted industrial development.[49] Third, the growth of income in Brazil's export sector helped create the domestic market on which the country's industrialization was based. A pattern of complementarity seems also to have prevailed in Brazil during the last half of the nineteenth century. As noted below, Brazil's initial industrial development occurred at the same time and in the same place (Rio de Janeiro and São Paulo) as the coffee export boom. Because of the forward and backward linkage effects that were present in this case, far from being 'alternative' patterns of development, as has sometimes been suggested, export expansion and industrial development were mutually supporting in Brazil.[50]

Reflecting the promotional effects of expanding foreign trade on domestic industrial development, an important geographical shift occurred in the locus of Brazilian industrialization during the first decades of the twentieth century. The country's first industrial development had been concentrated in Rio de Janeiro, the initial center of the country's coffee production. This early industrialization conferred significant external economies, for example, in the formation of a pool of skilled labor and technical personnel, which facilitated further industrial development within the same conurbation. Consequently, it might have been expected that Brazil's subsequent industrial development would also be concentrated in Rio de Janeiro. Nevertheless, as the center of Brazil's coffee exports moved from Rio de Janeiro to São Paulo state, so too did the center of Brazil's industrialization.

The Intensified Industrial Development of the 1930s

By all accounts, the 1930s constituted a period of intensified industrial development in Brazil.[51] The composition of industrial output deepened to include many new intermediate products and capital goods. The pace of industrial expansion also increased markedly. Industrial output growth accelerated from an annual trend rate of growth of 5.4 percent in the years 1920–29 to an annual trend rate of 8.7 percent in the years 1930–39.[52] This intensification of the industrialization process can readily be understood within the perspective of our earlier discussion.

Diversification of industrial output was facilitated by government measures which provided an elastic supply of protection, and facilitated domestic production of new products which had previously been imported.[53] Also, in reflection both of international and of domestic conditions, relative prices shifted to favor industry *vis-à-vis* the country's agricultural sector. Between 1930 and 1939, industrial prices in Brazil rose relative to agricultural prices at an annual trend rate of 2.3 percent.[54] By contrast, industrial prices had *fallen* relative to agricultural prices at an annual rate of 1.8 during the 1920s. Under conditions of improved access to the internal market (see below) this shift in the internal terms of trade helped provide Brazil's industrialists with incentives and profits for more rapid capital accumulation and output expansion in the 1930s.

Our earlier analysis also emphasized the importance for Brazil's industrial development of a growing domestic market for the country's manufactured goods. During the 1930s, aggregate Brazilian output and (income) grew more rapidly than in the earlier decade. Thus

Haddad's Real Output series rose at a rate 12 percent higher in the thirties as compared with the twenties. More importantly, there were major shifts within the Brazilian economy which led to a higher rate of industrial expansion per unit of domestic income growth. These changes were in some ways similar to those that accelerated the pace of development in Brazil toward the end of the nineteenth century.[55] In particular, the domestic agricultural sector seems to have played a key role in the intensified industrialization which occurred in Brazil during the 1930s.

In the 1920s, Brazil's export agricultural sector, notably coffee, had experienced rapid income growth which had helped provide the market for the manufacturing sector. In the 1930s, however, this source of rising demand declined with the shrinkage of international markets.[56] Consequently it was fortunate that some of the slack in output (and income) growth was taken up by agricultural activities producing for the domestic market. The trend rate of output growth in the domestic agricultural sector doubled, as it rose from 1.4 percent per annum in the 1920s to 2.9 percent in the 1930s.[57] Partly because of this rise in production for the domestic market, the pace of output growth in the agricultural sector as a whole was maintained at the same rate as in the twenties. Increasing income and demand from the domestic agricultural sector was especially important for Brazilian manufacturing because of the absence of industrial exports. In addition, the industrial sector was itself too small to propel forward aggregate output and the domestic demand for manufactures. As late as 1939, the industrial sector accounted for only 22 percent of Brazilian GDP.

One reason why the domestic agricultural sector could play a more effective supporting role in the 1930s was the expansion which had occurred in Brazil's highway network. Partly as a result of the road construction programs implemented in the 1920s, the country had 121,800 kilometers of roads in 1930.[58] This was approximately 3.8 times the size of the country's railway trackage at the time.[59] Further, expansion of the road network proceeded rapidly in Brazil during the thirties. By 1939, the network had more than doubled, reaching 258,400 kilometers. The availability of lower-cost transportation within Brazil's interior increased proportionately, if not indeed in a non-linear manner.

This enlargement of the country's road system hardly ended Brazil's transportation problems. Nevertheless, the increase from 14.3 kilometers of road per 1000 squared kilometers of Brazilian territory in 1930 to a figure of 30.4 kilometers per 1000 squared kilometers in 1939 had important consequences in this context. First, lower transportation costs had favorable effects on the prices received within the domestic agricultural sector. Improved ex-farm prices, in turn, promoted the rapid acceleration in the sector's output which we noted above. And the ensuing growth of income in the domestic agricultural sector enlarged the demand for industrial products within the country. Further, the fall in freight charges also led to lower prices for delivered industrial products than would otherwise have prevailed. This price effect facilitated distribution of manufactures and – independently of the income effect – expansion of the market within Brazil.

The extension of the road network seems also to have facilitated a downward shift on the supply side in the domestic agricultural sector. This supply shift is suggested by a comparison of the price and output configurations as between the 1920s and the 1930s. As noted earlier, the pace of output expansion in the domestic agricultural sector doubled in the later decade. Despite the sharply higher rate of output growth, the rate of price increase in the domestic agricultural sector actually fell, from 4.4 percent to 3.3 percent on an annual trend basis.[60] The mechanism for the downward supply shift may have been falling transport costs. These permitted a rise in the prices actually received by farmers, and in the size of the relevant market for producers in the domestic agricultural sector. They responded, as we have seen, with increased output. This was important not only for the reason emphasized earlier – to provide higher income and demand for industrial goods – but because the greater availability of food supplies from the domestic agricultural sector helped Brazilian industrialization indirectly, through its impact on the country's rate of price inflation.

An important determinant of any country's inflation rate is the pace of monetary expansion. Brazil's nominal money supply rose at a trend rate of 8.4 percent per annum between 1920 and 1929.[61] This compared with a 9.7 percent annual growth rate for the money supply in current prices between 1930 and 1939. Notwithstanding the similarity in the pace of monetary expansion as between the two decades, however, the rates of price inflation were very different. In the 1920s, Brazil's overall rate of inflation was 5.1 percent per annum.[62] In the 1930s, however, the rate of inflation fell to 2.7 percent per annum. The decline in the rate of inflation of almost 50 percent poses an obvious surprise in the face of the similar rates of monetary expansion in the two decades. The increased elasticity of food supply which we have noted for Brazil's domestic agricultural sector helps explain this phenomenon.

Some developments which raised the demand for cash balances in the Brazilian economy in the 1930s are also relevant here. First, aggregate real output grew at a higher rate during the later decade, and thus raised the transactions demand for cash balances. The 12 per cent increase in the pace of real output growth, however, is not sufficient to account for much of the disparity in rates of inflation. More importantly, the income elasticity of demand for cash balances in Brazil also shifted upward, in reflection of the economy's increasing financial development.[63] This shift, in turn, may well have been related to the extension of the road network. This is because falling transportation costs furthered the spread of markets, monetization of the economy, and use of the banking system. All of these changes would increase the demand for money, and thus reduce the inflationary impact of a given rate of monetary expansion.

The changed inflationary conditions of the 1930s helped Brazil's industrial sector in numerous ways. Nominal monetary expansion was increasingly transformed into real liquidity growth, and a stimulus for industrial development. Despite the similarity in rates of nominal monetary increase in the two decades, the country's *real* money supply grew at a much higher rate in the 1930s. Real liquidity in Brazil rose at an annual trend rate of 7.0 percent between 1930 and 1939, as contrasted with only 3.4 percent per annum from 1920 to 1929.[64] Further, the growth in the real money supply during the 1930s was also much less erratic than in the earlier decade.[65] This increased stability meant diminished risk and uncertainty for investors and producers in the 1930s.[66] Finally, the doubling in the pace of real liquidity growth helped offset the impact on domestic industrial output growth of the relatively poor conditions of import supply which Brazil experienced during the Great Depression.[67]

The conditions which we have just discussed – changes in the monetary sector, transport expansion, and growth in domestic agriculture – have not always been noted in accounts of Brazil's intensified industrialization of the 1930s. That is, some accounts have interpreted the acceleration in industrial development mainly in terms of shifting terms of trade between export agriculture and domestic industry, heightened import protection, and inflationary aggregate demand conditions.[68] As we have seen, however, Brazil's experience in the 1930s involved much more than this. Changes in sectors other than manufacturing and shifts in domestic supply conditions were also involved. These also helped make the 1930s a decade in which, as compared with the 1920s, aggregate output growth rose in Brazil, while at the same time the pace of general price inflation fell sharply.

One other feature of the decade sheds additional light on Brazilian industrialization. As noted earlier, the 1930s saw considerable change in the composition of output within Brazil's industrial sector, while the trend rate of output growth also rose sharply. Nevertheless, the annual rate of price increase in the industrial sector was not much higher in the 1930s than in the 1920s – 4.6 percent as compared with 4.3 percent in the earlier decade.[69] Brazilian industry was thus able to respond to a formidable intensification in demand pressures largely with an increase in real output rather than with a higher rate of price inflation. This experience supports our earlier emphasis on the elastic supply of factors in Brazil's industrialization process.

Why Did Brazil not Become an Industrial Exporter Early in the Industrialization Process?

Why did Brazil not become an exporter of manufactured products early in the twentieth century, after its industrialization had proceeded for a number of decades?[70] Because Brazilian industrial development was so heavily dependent on the internal market, this question may appear historically irrelevant. The purpose of the discussion which follows, however, is to clarify *why* the country's manufacturing output depended almost entirely on domestic demand, and why the question of early industrial exporting for Brazil therefore appears so unreal.

Before beginning the analysis, it is worth noting some of the benefits that Brazil would have gained had it, like Japan, begun to export manufactured goods relatively early in the industrialization process. Export sales would have enabled Brazil's industrial development to overcome the demand limitations imposed by the size of the internal market for manufactures. Thus income and employment in the industrial sector could have grown at higher rates. Also, to the extent that the covariance between export sales and fluctuations in the domestic market was less than perfect, exporting would have reduced the risks facing Brazil's industrialists.[71] Lower risk, in turn, would likely have promoted higher rates of capital accumulation in the sector. Finally, exporting manufactured products would also have permitted Brazilian producers to obtain the productivity gains due to larger productions runs and increased intra-industry specialization.

The problem does not seem to have been the limited horizons of Brazil's entrepreneurs. When Brazilian producers were able to compete internationally and the returns to industrial exporting rose, Brazil did in fact export manufactures. This occurred, for example, with the curtailment of normal overseas supply to other Latin American countries during and after the First World War. Furthermore, low productivity levels and high costs in Brazil are also not a sufficient explanation. For, in principle, the exchange rate which translated local costs into international prices could have adjusted to Brazil's low productivity levels. And with a sufficiently high *mil-réis*/dollar parity, Brazilian producers could have competed in overseas markets despite high costs in domestic currency.

The contrast with Japan is illuminating here. A key difference seems to have existed in the relative level of the exchange rates which prevailed in the two countries at the onset of their industrialization. Japan began its modern industrial development without abundant natural resources to serve as the basis for the country's exports. Consequently, the exchange rate which was established at the start of modern Japanese development reflected the high domestic resources cost per dollar which were required to export labor-intensive goods such as spun silk. With an initially high yen–dollar exchange rate, however, Japan could proceed to export other products, such as modern industrial goods, which also involved high domestic resources costs per unit of foreign exchange.[72] Such a flow of new manufactured exports was possible in Japan without a large and discontinuous depreciation in the country's real exchange rate.

By contrast, the exchange rate established in Brazil during the nineteenth century reflected a very different situation. There, the initial conversion ratio mirrored Brazil's favorable natural-resource endowment, and the ensuing low domestic resource cost per unit of foreign exchange. In reflection of this pattern of comparative advantage, however, exportation of manufactures would have required a much higher *mil-réis*/dollar parity than, say, exportation of coffee. Thus Brazil's initial exchange rate was relatively low, a gift of nature. But export of manufactured products would have required traversing what was, in effect, a large kink in the supply of foreign exchange in terms of domestic resources. In order to make this quantum jump, Brazil would have needed a multiple exchange-rate system (or an equivalent system of export taxes), under which a much higher *mil-réis*/dollar parity would have been accorded to manufactured exports.[73]

Brazil's policy-makers did not perceive this possibility. Instead, they attempted to deal with the country's balance-of-payments problems via periodic restrictions on the pace of monetary expansion and through higher import restrictions. And in the 1930s, when the value of traditional exports fell, international markets for manufactures were too restricted for a potential new industrial exporter like Brazil to contemplate seriously. Finally, Brazilian policy-makers interpreted the experience of the Depression in such a manner that after the Second World War, they implemented a set of policies which was to discourage manufactured exports for the next two decades.[74]

Thus the discontinuity, which we have discussed, in Brazil's marginal comparative advantage may have prevented Brazil from becoming an industrial exporter earlier in its industrialization. And after 1930, other impeding factors intervened. Consequently, Brazil was to follow a development pattern in which until the mid-1960s, the country relied heavily on import substitution rather than export expansion in an effort to achieve balance-of-payments equilibrium in the growth process. In addition to the macroeconomic and intersectoral effects, there were also serious consequences for the industrial sector itself. The limitations imposed by the relatively small size of the domestic market constricted the volume of output and employment in the industrial sector. And because of the effects on the country's overall balance-of-payments and foreign-exchange situation, the failure to export manufactures earlier in the industrialization process probably also affected adversely the levels of productivity and costs within Brazil's manufacturing sector.

Conclusions

The data presented in this chapter show that Brazil has been experiencing sustained economic growth in per capita income since approximately the beginning of the twentieth century. Industrial production has grown at especially high rates. However, agricultural output, including the production of food for the domestic market, has been expanding as well. Thus although Brazil was still a poor country with an underdeveloped economy in 1947, it had long since emerged from a state of economic stagnation.

Industrialization had been proceeding at a rapid pace in Brazil for decades before the First World War. The extent and structure of this early industrial development, however, were constrained by Brazil's internal demand conditions. The size of the market for manufactures was limited by the country's low income levels. These also determined a pattern of demand which was oriented mainly to food products and textiles. Nevertheless, Brazil's early industrial development was important, both for its immediate effects and for providing a basis for the intensified industrialization of the 1930s and subsequent decades.

The conditions under which Brazil's industrial development proceeded are also of interest. Because Brazil's industrialization was based almost wholly on the internal market, import substitution and the growth of domestic income were crucial in determining the pace of industrial development. The agricultural sector played a powerful supporting role in this context, both in providing an elastic source of domestic food supply and in enlarging the domestic market for manufactures. More generally, increasing domestic demand was facilitated by the country's high rates of aggregate output growth and expansionary macroeconomic policies. Import replacement was stimulated by high tariffs and other measures which shifted relative prices to the advantage of local producers. But as Brazil's experience in the intensified industrial development of the 1930s indicates, favorable monetary conditions and increases in the supply of transportation and of food were also helpful in providing propitious demand conditions. Finally, with favorable conditions in the product market for industrial goods, problems involving the supply of factors – for example, entrepreneurship, skilled labor, and capital – to the industrial sector were overcome. As a result, Brazil could achieve the sustained industrial expansion which we have observed.

One may wonder, however, how this development process was affected by Brazil's relations with the international economic and political system. This question raises a series of issues concerning the country's political and economic dependency in the first decades of the twentieth century. We consider those issues in the next chapter.

Notes

1   On the slow pace of per capita income growth in Brazil between 1822 and 1900, see pp. 33–7 in Chapter 3, above. Information on rates of growth of Real Output per capita following 1900 is presented in pp. 165–6, below. The conditions which led to the acceleration of economic growth in Brazil toward the end of the nineteenth century are discussed in Chapter 7, pp. 146–53.

2   In computing the pre-1947 growth rates shown in Table 8.1, I have utilized the time series prepared by Claudio Haddad in his *Growth of Brazilian Real Output, 1900–1947* (PhD dissertation, University of Chicago, 1974) rather than the estimates presented in Annibal Villela and Wilson Suzigan, *Política do Governo e Crescimento da Economia Brasileira, 1889–1945* (Rio de Janeiro: IPEA, 1973). This is because Haddad's estimates are based on much more comprehensive primary data, particularly for the agricultural sector. Also, unlike Villela and Suzigan, Haddad included estimates for the Commerce, Transport and Communications and Government Sectors in his series for Real Output. Haddad's methodology and data sources are presented in pp. 43–195 and Tables 13–77 of his dissertation. Villela and Suzigan state their methodology in pp. 241–8 of their book. Albert Fishlow has also prepared estimates of Brazilian GDP and of sectoral output in the years 1920–47. See his 'Origins and Consequences of Import Substitution in Brazil,' in Luis Eugenio di Marco (ed.), *International Economics and Development* (New York: Academic Press, 1972), pp. 356–9. Haddad's index is more suitable for our purposes since it was computed as a Divisia index with weights changing each year in accordance with the value shares of the products in the previous year. That procedure takes account of the rapid change in the composition of output which occurred during these years. By contrast, Fishlow's index is a Laspeyres quantity index with fixed (1939) weights. Further, since Haddad's series are available from 1900 and Fishlow's begin in 1920, use of Haddad's estimates enables us to cover a longer period with series which are internally consistent. Haddad has also presented an econometric test which enhances the credibility of his estimates relative to others available for the period 1920–47. See his paper 'Testing Income Series: An Application of Principal Components,' *Journal of Econometrics*, vol. 4 (December 1976). Note, finally, that the techniques which underly these estimates do *not* generate economic growth as an artifact of the government's growing ability to collect statistics.

3   See the data presented in Simon Kuznets, *Economic Growth of Nations* (Cambridge, Mass.: Harvard University Press, 1971), pp. 11–19.

4   This is computed from data in the 1920 Demographic Census, as cited in Directoria Geral de Estatística, *Recenseamento do Brazil Realizado em 1 de Setembro de 1920*, vol. 5, pp. lxix–lxx.

5   Data presented in John W. Mellor, *The Economics of Agricultural Development* (Ithaca, NY: Cornell University Press, 1966), p. 66, suggest that at the income levels which prevailed in Brazil during the 1920s and 1930s, the income elasticity of demand for the cereals and starch roots which predominated in Brazil's staple foods was probably in the range of 0.2–0.3 percent.

6   One may wonder how Brazil's population survived (and grew) at the low absolute levels per capita caloric intake which are shown in Table 8.3. Two factors are relevant in explaining this situation: underreporting, and distributional conditions. Per capita measures are of course computed under the implicit assumption that total consumption is shared equally among all members of the population. That assumption is clearly not valid for Brazil. As late as the 1960s, an estimated 44

percent of Brazil's population was found to suffer from insufficient intake of calories. (See Fundação Getúlio Vargas, *Food Consumption in Brazil* [Rio de Janeiro, 1970].) Similarly a 1975 study placed the undernourished fraction of the population at between 30 and 40 percent. (See F. D. McCarthy, *Planejamento Nutricional para O Brasil* [Brasília: Ministério da Agricultura, 1975].) Thus it is clear even after the major per capita income growth achieved in the post-Second World War period, a large fraction of Brazil's population did not receive adequate intake of calories. Nevertheless, the data of Table 8.3 do indicate that during the period under consideration, the availability of calories increased much more than did the country's population. Hence, the size of the undernourished fraction of the population (and, *a fortiori*, the absolute number of people receiving insufficient nutrition) must have declined during this period. Underreporting of caloric availability probably also plays a role in lowering all of the absolute figures in Table 8.3. The direction of the bias which underreporting imparts appears straightforward. Domestic agricultural production increased its share in total Brazilian food supply during the first half of the twentieth century; and underreporting was probably greater for domestic agricultural production than for food imports. Underreporting would thus bias downward all of the level figures shown in Table 8.3. However, the shift to a greater share for domestic food supply would lead to a proportionately greater understatement in the rate of growth of total caloric intake and in its absolute level at the end of the period.

7   *Conjuntura Econômica*, vol. 22 (October 1969).

8   See, for example, André Gunder Frank, *Capitalism and Underdevelopment in Latin America* (New York: Monthly Review Press, 1967), p. 170.

9   The *encilhamento* began in 1890, with an executive decree which put into effect an 1888 law facilitating a drastic expansion of credit. Information on the economic and political context of the *encilhamento* is presented in Maria Barbara Levy, *História de Bolsa de Valores de Rio de Janeiro* (Rio de Janeiro: IMBEC, 1977) pp. 141–81. Further data and analysis which negate any special importance for the *encilhamento* in launching the growth either of production or of the capital formation in Brazil's early industrialization are presented in Flávio Versiani and Maria Teresa Versiani, 'A Industrialização Brasileira antes de 1930,' *Estudos Econômicos*, vol. 5 (January 1975). Moreover, if we take a comprehensive perspective, the credit contraction which followed the *encilhamento*'s inflationary upsurge and limited Brazil's economic growth for almost a decade after the *encilhamento* should also be viewed as an integral part of the espisode.

10   Levy, *História da Bolsa*, p. 176.

11   Flávio Versiani, 'Industrial Investment in an "Export" Economy: the Brazilian Experience before 1914,' *Journal of Development Economics* (December 1980).

12   The data underlying these statements and Table 8.6 in the text are from Stanley J. Stein's *The Brazilian Cotton Manufacture* (Cambridge, Mass.: Harvard University Press, 1957), p. 191. Stein notes that his data for the years 1866, 1885, and 1910 are based on 'incomplete statistics'. Neither the degree nor the direction which this reporting bias imparts is known. If, as is likely, output in the early years was under-enumerated to an extent greater than in the later years, this would mean that the growth rates presented in the text are overstated. It would also mean that the absolute size of the Brazilian cotton textile industry was larger in earlier years than indicated by the figures which Stein presents.

13   This is computed from data in Stein, *Brazilian Cotton Manufacture*. op. cit., p. 191, and figures on the 1907 industry survey which are presented in George Wythe, 'Brazil: Trends in Industrial Development,' p. 70, in Simon Kuznets *et al.* (eds), *Economic Growth: Brazil, India, Japan*, (Durham, NC: Duke University Press, 1955).

14   Fishlow, 'Origins and Consequences', op. cit., p. 323.

15   Werner Baer and Anníbal Villela, 'Industrial Growth and Industrialization:

Revisions in The Stages of Brazil's Economic Development,' *The Journal of The Developing Areas*, vol. 7 (January 1973), p. 227.

16 Villela and Suzigan, *Política do Governo*, op. cit., p. 83. Later (pp. 128–30), they refer to the pre-First World War period as having had two spurts, one in the 1890s and another from 1903 to 1913. (The hiatus reflected Brazil's effort at monetary stabilization between 1899 and 1905.) Note also Villela and Suzigan's omission of the industrial development which we have observed for the period before 1889.

17 See, for example, Fishlow, 'Origins and Consequences,' op. cit., pp. 323–6; Baer and Villela, 'Industrial Growth,' op. cit., p. 227.

18 These figures are from Fishlow, 'Origins and Consequences,' op. cit., p. 323, Table III. The underlying data are from the 1920 Industrial Census. The reasons for this concern with the composition of industrial output may not be obvious to some readers. Thus it may not be clear why a dollar of value-added in capital goods should be considered worth more than a dollar of value-added in, say, food products. Viewed sympathetically, however, this concern seems to reflect a 'wealth' concept of national income. Following this approach, diversification and the capacity to sustain income flows against future risks are valued as a separate element, apart from their contribution to current income.

19 Brazil's 1920 Industrial Census focused on 'industrial establishments', and did not survey the industrial workers who were employed in government workshops and in transportation companies such as the railroads. This limitation in coverage led to significant underenumeration of the workers engaged in certain investment-good activities. Thus the 1920 *Demographic* Census lists 96,100 metallurgical workers and 10,800 workers engaged in the construction of transportation apparatus. These numbers contrast with the figures of 6,200 and 16,000 workers, respectively, which the Industrial Census recorded. This discrepancy (84,700 workers) is large relative to the size of the total labor force enumerated in the Industrial Census (331,000 workers, including those in sugar refining), which is the source of the value-added figures cited in the text. The extent of the bias cannot be measured, however, because the number of Demographic Census 'metallurgical workers' who were engaged in craft or service activities is not known. On these points, see *Recenseamento do Brazil*, op. cit., p. LXXI, Table 52, and the accompanying discussion there.

20 See Hollis B. Chenery and Lance Taylor, 'Development Patterns: Among Countries and Over Time,' *The Review of Economics and Statistics*, vol. 50 (November 1968), pp. 409–13. Industrial exporting would have enabled Brazil to transcend the pattern of demand imposed by domestic per capita income. Brazil's failure to develop as an early exporter of manufactures is discussed later in this chapter.

21 See Fishlow, 'Origins and Consequences,' op. cit., pp. 330–5; and Nathaniel H. Leff, *The Brazilian Capital Goods Industry* (Cambridge, Mass.: Harvard University Press, 1968), Chapter 2.

22 A valuable source here is Warren Dean's *The Industrialization of São Paulo, 1880–1945* (Austin: University of Texas Press, 1969), pp. 62–3, 104–17.

23 Nícia Villela Luz, *A Luta pela Industrialização do Brasil* (São Paulo, 1961), pp. 149–50. By 1920 the value of industrial output in São Paulo had reached the value of coffee exports. See Octávio Gouveia de Bulhões, 'Agriculture and Economic Development,' in W. W. Rostow (ed.), *The Economics of Take-Off into Sustained Growth* (London: Macmillan, 1963), p. 230.

24 The figure is approximate. It includes the 313,000 workers enumerated in the Industrial Census; the 18,200 workers reported in sugar refining (*Recenseamento do Brazil*, op. cit., p. lxxx,); and as a rough correction for the omissions of the Industrial Census, half (42,400) of the metallurgical and transportation-apparatus workers enumerated in the Demographic Census but missed by the Industrial Census (see n. 19 above). The Demographic Census records a total of 1,189,000

'industrial workers' in 1920, but many of these were in craft or service-type activities.

25 This figure was computed using data from Directoria Geral de Estatística, *Recenseamento de 1920.* op. cit., pp. lxix–lxxi, 112–22; and from an estimate for Brazilian GDP which was kindly supplied (in a letter dated 12 October 1976) by Dr Claudio Haddad of the Fundação Getúlio Vargas.

26 This figure is from Fishlow, 'Origins and Consequences,' op. cit., pp. 324–5. It compares the industrial value-added by local producers with the total of industrial value-added supplied by imports and by local industry. Fishlow's approach to computing the extent of industrial import substitution differs from conventional measures. It involves subtracting from both the value-added supplied by imports and by local industry the value-added due to inputs from the primary sector, at home and abroad. If we use the conventional measure of import substitution, (the ratio of gross domestic supply of manufactures to gross supply from imports and local producers), we observe a much higher figure in 1919, 75 percent (ibid. p. 323).

27 In the production of shoes, for example, 'The modern factory system, the piecework system, and the home industry are all competitors'. However, only 37 percent of the total work force engaged in shoe production was employed in modern factories. This information is from Arthur H. Redfield, *Brazil: A Study of Economic Conditions since 1913* (Washington: GPO, 1920), pp. 63–4. More generally, industrial dualism may also account for part of the large difference (see n. 24) between the size of industrial labor force enumerated in the 1920 Industrial and Demographic Censuses. The latter included craft and home producers.

28 These unincorporated firms accounted for 69 percent of the total number of establishments surveyed, but only 18 percent of total industrial production. The individual proprietorships had an average of seven workers per firm, as compared with an average of twenty-seven workers in the incorporated firms. Information on these and other points in this paragraph and the succeeding one is from Directoria Geral de Estatística, *Recenseamento do Brazil*, op. cit., pp. 5–6, 48–9, 60–1, and 72–3.

29 Thomas Merrick and Douglas Graham have noted that new definitions used in the 1920 census tended to exclude many women from the enumerated labor force in that year. See their book *Population and Economic Development in Brazil, 1800 to the Present* (Baltimore: Johns Hopkins University Press, 1979), pp. 102–3. This 'methodological' comment has important substantive significance which amplifies the point in the text above. Such a definitional shift reflects changing perceptions of work and of women's status which occurred in the industrialization process.

30 For a description of early Brazilian tariff rates as being only of negligible magnitudes, see, for example, Werner Baer, *Industrialization and Economic Development in Brazil* (Homewood, Ill.: R. D. Irwin, 1965), p. 13. In the next chapter we will discuss the reasons for the frequent misperception of Brazil's early tariff. It is also common to distinguish between the supposed intent of tariff policy (government revenue) and its actual effects (protection to industry). For present purposes the latter will suffice; but see the discussion on pp. 212–3, below.

31 This paragraph draws on materials presented in Luz, *A Luta pela Industrialização do Brasil*, especially pp. 18, 36, 49, 118, 129; Stanley J. Stein, *The Brazilian Cotton Manufacture: Textile Enterprise in an Underdeveloped Area, 1850–1950* (Cambridge, Mass., 1957), pp. 80–5; and D. C. M. Platt, *Latin America and British Trade, 1806–1914* (New York: Harper and Row, 1973), pp. 81–3. Concerning the magnitude of import duties in Brazil during the nineteenth century, see also pp. 73–4 in Nathaniel H. Leff, *Underdevelopment and Development in Brazil, Vol. II. Reassessing the Obstacles to Economic Development* (Allen & Unwin, London, 1982), Chapter 4.

32 This statement and the one which follows are based on detailed calculations which are presented in Versiani, 'Industrial Investment,' op. cit., esp. Appendix B.

33 This is from data cited in Villela and Suzigan, *Política do Governo*, op. cit., p. 348.

34 Thus Warren Dean cites as a routine occurrence the case of a Brazilian bathtub manufacturer who successfully intervened in 1911 to have the tariff on competing imports raised from 300 to 500 percent ad valorem. See Dean, *The Industrialization of São Paulo*, op. cit., p. 72.

35 In 1890, the 'Law of Similars' was passed; this prohibited tariff exemptions for goods which were produced locally. Exemptions continued in some cases, however, and the law was tightened in 1911.

36 These figures are from Table 4.1 in Leff, *Reassessing the Obstacles*, op. cit., Chapter 4.

37 Thus the decline in the tariff percentage during the First World War (see Table 8.8) partly reflects a shift in the composition of Brazilian imports toward capital goods, many of which were exempt from duties.

38 This pattern partly reflected the Brazilian government's desire to maintain the real value of its custom revenues. See Mircea Buescu, *Evolucão Econômica do Brasil* (Rio de Janeiro: APEC, 1974), p. 135; and Versiani, 'A Industrialização Brasileira, op. cit.

39 See Luz, *A Luta*, op. cit., p. 126.

40 W. M. Corden, *The Theory of Protection* (Oxford, 1971).

41 Thus in 1920, Redfield (*Brazil*, op. cit., p. 59) described the cotton textile industry in the following terms: 'One of the results of this increase in manufacture has been that the cost of the domestic product is now lower than the imported one . . . This is due in part to the competition among the native mills, a condition which prevents all of them getting the full protection to the native industry as granted to them by the import duties.'

42 Estimates for the post-Second World War period show that transportation costs often provide as much protection as do import duties. See J. M. Finger and A. J. Yeats, 'Effective Protection by Transportation Costs and Tariffs: A Comparison of Magnitudes,' *Quarterly Journal of Economics*, vol. 90 (February 1976). Given the relatively rapid growth of productivity in ocean shipping during the post-Second World War period, transportation costs probably afforded even more protection in earlier decades. During the nineteenth century, Brazil experienced chronic inflation and long-term depreciation in its (nominal) exchange rate. Some writers have suggested that the declining exchange rate also shifted relative prices to favor import-competing producers such as Brazil's manufacturers. See, however, n. 6 in Leff, *Reassessing the Obstacles*, op. cit., Chapter 4.

43 For reasons discussed on pp. 184–5, below, Brazil did not export manufactured products until relatively late in the country's development process. Hence, the country's industrial expansion depended heavily on internally generated demand.

44 The measure which is used here for large-scale industrialization is the share of industrial output in GNP. This measure and other points in this paragraph are discussed in pp. 87–9 in Leff, *Reassessing the Obstacles*, op. cit., Chapter 4.

45 See Dean, *The Industrialization of São Paulo*, op. cit., Chapters 3 and 4; Stein, *The Brazilian Cotton Manufacture*, op. cit., Chapters 2 and 3. The 1920 Industrial Census provides information on the birthplace of the proprietors of the industrial sector's non-incorporated firms. (These enterprises accounted for 69 percent of the establishments surveyed by the census and 18 percent of total industrial output.) Some 44 percent of these proprietors had been born in countries other than in Brazil, mainly in Italy and Portugal. These data are from *Recenseamento do Brazil*, op. cit., p. 5.

46 *Recenseamento do Brazil*, op. cit., Table 49. This tabulation includes data only for the industrial firms founded between 1890 and 1920.

47 Ragnar Frisch and Frederick Waugh, 'Partial Time Regressions as Compared with Individual Trends,' *Econometrica*, vol. 1 (1933), pp. 387–402.

48 Data for this regression equation are from the following sources: industrial output

and a general price deflator, Haddad, *The Growth of Real Output in Brazil*, op. cit., pp. 10–11, 191; a Laspeyres index of the import quantum, Villela and Suzigan, *Política do Governo*, op. cit., p. 441; the money supply, Paulo Neuhaus, *História Monetária do Brasil, 1900–45* (Rio de Janeiro: IMBEC, 1975), pp. 157–8.

49   The close connection between the expansion and the growth of resources for railroad construction is discussed in Leff, *Reassessing the Obstacles*, op. cit., Chapters 4 and 5. The railroads, in turn, aided Brazilian industrialization both by lowering distribution costs and thus enlarging the internal market for manufactures.

50   This complementarity may seem obvious. See, however, Andre Gunder Frank, 'The Capitalist Development of Underdevelopment in Brazil,' pp. 149, 170. We will discuss broader aspects of this topic in Chapter 9, which considers external dependency in Brazilian development.

51   See, for example, Fishlow, 'Origins and Consequences,' op. cit., pp. 330–9.

52   These growth rates were computed by trend regression from data in Haddad, *The Growth of Real Output*, op. cit., pp. 10–11. Fishlow's series ('Origins and Consequences,' op. cit., p. 357) show an even greater acceleration in the pace of industrial expansion, from an annual trend rate of 3.8 in the 1920s to an annual trend rate of 8.3 percent in the 1930s. The reason for this disparity with Haddad's series seems to be primarily a matter of statistical construction. Unlike Haddad's Divisia index, Fishlow's Laspeyres index gives a higher weight to the industrial products whose domestic production began in the 1930s, and a lower weight to the products that were the mainstay of the industrial sector in the 1920s but whose relative importance declined thereafter.

53   The process which provided the elastic supply of protection is discussed in Chapter 9. That chapter also considers other aspects of governmental policy which were associated with Brazil's accelerated development in the 1930s.

54   The price series which were used to compute these relative-price trends are presented in Haddad, *The Growth of Real Output*, op. cit., pp. 191–2. The agricultural price index which is used refers to the agricultural sector as a whole, including export products.

55   See pp. 146–51 in Chapter 7, above.

56   It has sometimes been suggested that Brazil's coffee retention programs maintained rising income in the coffee sector through the 1930s. However, in their *História Monetária do Brasil* (Rio de Janeiro: IPEA, 1976), Carlos Manuel Peláez and Wilson Suzigan present data which dispute this interpretation. They note (pp. 250–2) that after its recovery in 1934, income in the coffee sector remained on a plateau during the 1930s, and did not regain its 1929 level. Consequently, it is hard to see how income in the coffee sector acted as a stimulus to the vigorous expansion of Brazilian manufacturing during the 1930s. The failure of the coffee sector's income to grow after 1934 holds even without deducting from its income the taxes that were levied to finance the coffee retention program. Other aspects of Brazil's economic recovery are discussed in Chapter 9, below.

57   These figures were computed utilizing data which are presented in Villela and Suzigan, *Política do Governo*, op. cit., p. 426, the series labeled 'crops for the internal market'. The underlying figures for these Laspeyres series come from the Brazilian Institute of Geography and Statistics (IBGE).

58   Ibid, p. 406.

59   Computed from data in Villela and Suzigan, *Política do Governo*, op. cit., p. 393. Note that railway construction in Brazil had been virtually stagnant during the previous decade and a half. Between 1914 and 1928, Brazil added to its railway network with an average increase of only 414 kilometers per year. (These data are from Villela and Suzigan, *Política do Governo*, op. cit., p. 393.) The pace of railway expansion slackened even further in the 1930s. In 1938, the country had only 34,200 kilometers of track.

60   Computed from data in Villela and Suzigan, *Política do Governo*, op. cit., p. 426.

61 This figure was computed by trend regression. The underlying data are in Neuhaus, *História Monetária*, op. cit., p. 180.

62 Computed from Haddad's General Price Index, which is presented on pp. 191–2 of his *Growth of Real Output*.

63 Data presented in Neuhaus, *História Monetária*, op. cit., p. 180, indicate a decline in velocity during the 1930s. Specification and estimation of the country's demand-for-money function, including such pertinent conditions as the spread of the banking network and the responsiveness to changing expectations of inflation, would take us too far afield here.

64 These figures were computed with data from Neuhaus, *História Monetária*, op. cit., p. 180; and Haddad, *Growth of Real Output*, op. cit., pp. 191–2.

65 The R^2 of the regression for the growth of the real money supply was .88 for the years 1930–39, as contrasted with an R^2 of only .23 for the years 1920–29.

66 During the 1930s, industrial prices rose at a steady pace, with much less fluctuation around trend than the agricultural price index displayed. Trend equations estimated using Haddad's data show an R^2 of .97 for the industrial price index, as compared with an R^2 of .41 for agricultural prices. Again, the industrial sector seems to have benefited from diminished uncertainty in the 1930s.

67 If we take the quantum of imports in 1929 as 100, imports declined to a level of 44 in 1932, rose to an index of 56 in 1933, and reached a level of 68 in 1938. (See the data in Villela and Suzigan, *Política do Governo*, op. cit., p. 441.) Note that changes in the capital account of Brazil's balance of payments (including rescheduling of the country's foreign debt) permitted the country's import supply to grow more than the value of exports increased during the 1930s.

68 See also n. 56, above.

69 Computed from data in Haddad, *Growth of Real Output*, op. cit., pp. 191–2.

70 This question was first posed to me by W. Arthur Lewis. In view of the shrinkage of international markets and the rise of barriers to trade during the 1930s, the question is relevant mainly to the three preceding decades.

71 S. Hirsch and B. Lev, 'Sales Stabilization Through Export Diversification,' *The Review of Economics and Statistics*, vol. 53 (August 1971).

72 On use of the concept of the domestic resource cost of foreign exchange for evaluating a country's marginal comparative advantage, see, for example, Michael Bruno, 'Domestic Resource Costs and Effective Protection,' *Journal of Political Economy*, vol. 80 (January 1972).

73 A multiple exchange-rate system (or export taxes) would have been necessary in order to avoid lowering world coffee prices. David Felix has pointed out to me that the discussion in the text ignores the possibility of different conditions on the demand side in the determination of the exchange rate in Brazil and in Japan. He suggests that the Japanese middle and upper classes remained attached to traditional consumption symbols during the industrialization process; and that this condition lowered the income elasticity of demand for foreign exchange (and pressure on the exchange rate) in Japan as compared with Brazil. Further research on the import content of aggregate demand in Brazil and in Japan (and the influence of relative prices as opposed to pure taste differentials) would be helpful in this context. Note further that the United States, like Brazil, a large primary-product exporter with a favorable natural resource endowment, did not have a large discontinuity in its marginal comparative advantage in different activities. By the last quarter of the nineteenth century, the United States had become a large exporter of manufactures. The key difference with Brazil seems to have been the United States's large stock of human capital, which was embodied in its industrial exports.

74 Nathaniel H. Leff, *Economic Policy-Making and Development in Brazil, 1947–1964* (New York: Wiley, 1968), Chapter 4.

9
Pre-1947 Brazil as a Dependent Economy

To what extent was pre-1947 Brazil a dependent economy, one in which the pace and character of economic development were determined essentially in passive response to economic and political pressures from the metropolitan, economically advanced powers? This chapter examines the historical relevance of that interpretation of Brazil's development in the half-century before 1947. Questions of both economic structure and government policy are involved, and we will consider these in sequence.

The External Sector and Brazilian Development

As we saw in Chapter 8, expanding foreign trade and domestic industrialization were mutually supporting rather than antithetical patterns of economic development in Brazil.[1] The country's industrial sector emerged in the nineteenth century, in response to the stimulus of a growing domestic market and protective tariffs. Brazil's industrial development had no need for 'external shocks' such as the disruption of normal trading relations during the First World War. Rather, expanding exports helped provide a growing market for domestic manufactured goods. This occurred directly, as income derived from exports increased the demand for industrial products. In addition, because of the effects on government revenues and investment in infrastructure, expanding foreign trade stimulated the growth of income and demand for manufactures in the domestic sector of the economy. Further, growing foreign trade helped generate the supply of imported inputs that was necessary for the industrialization process. The data presented in our earlier discussion point clearly to the positive linkages between the external sector and domestic industrial development in Brazil. Nevertheless, the contrary interpretation, which posits a competitive relation between these two sectors, has sometimes been proposed. Let us, therefore, examine the assumptions (and the applicability to Brazil) of a model in which growing international trade retards domestic industrialization in a less-developed country which exports primary products like coffee.

The view that favorable foreign trade conditions and domestic industrialization are antithetical appears to be based on two key assumptions. These were not reflected in Brazil's actual experience, however, from the last half of the nineteenth century. First, on the supply side, the model assumes that high returns in the export activity will attract resources there. Hence, the model assumes that without a deterioration in foreign trade conditions – for example, a depression or a world war (which disrupts normal trading relations) – relative rates of return will not be favorable enough to attract resources into an import-competing activity like domestic manufacturing. By imposing tariffs, however, Brazil could shift the *internal* relative-price ratio to favor industry without a collapse in international trade conditions. In addition, under conditions of highly imperfect markets for capital and entrepreneurship, such as existed in Brazil, the export sector and the industrial sector draw upon different sources of factor supply. Consequently, expansion of one sector does not limit expansion of the other.

The notion that expanding primary-product exports hinder internal industrial development also exaggerates the competitive effects on the demand side. Favorable export conditions do indeed lead to favorable import conditions. It does not follow, however, that under the conditions that prevailed in Brazil, the entire expansion in domestic demand for manufactured products resulting from increasing exports was supplied by the higher imports which they made possible. First, the share of manufactures in Brazilian aggregate demand was probably below the share of imports in aggregate supply during the last half of the nineteenth century.[2] Further, rising exports are likely to stimulate an increase in the domestic demand for manufactures which is larger than the concurrent growth in domestic import capacity. Quite apart from multiplier effects, with growing income and an income elasticity of demand for manufactured goods greater than unity, the demand for industrial products which stems from expanding exports will increase more rapidly than supply from abroad.[3] Hence, even with unobstructed import supply, rising exports create a potential market for domestic industrial output. With tariffs imposed on manufactured goods, as in Brazil, export growth leads even more directly to domestic industrial development as long as necessary inputs to the industrialization process are available. As we saw in Chapter 8, the latter condition was in fact satisfied in Brazil.

It is important to recognize that international trade had powerful supporting effects on Brazil's economic development even though the country was not characterized by some typical forms of export dependence. Thus, in 1911–1913, the share of exports in Brazil's gross domestic product averaged some 16 percent.[4] Brazil's export coefficient was thus well below the ratio in extreme 'export economies'.[5] And since exports in the nineteenth century had probably grown at least as much as output in the rest of the Brazilian economy, it is unlikely that the country's export ratio had been higher in earlier decades.[6] Further, Brazil generally maintained a balance-of-trade surplus, which reflected foreign-capital payments and immigrants' remittances. Consequently, the country's *import* ratio was usually below the export share. As these relatively low export and import coefficients indicate, the external sector did not account for a large share of aggregate demand and supply in the Brazilian economy. And in another manifestation of economic non-dependence, by 1919 Brazil had already achieved substantial import substitution in its supply of manufactured goods.[7]

In 1917, foreign banks held approximately 41 percent of the deposits in the Brazilian banking system.[8] Moreover, international loans to Brazil's federal and state governments provided key resources for the construction of economic infrastructure. Presumably these loans reflected Brazilian preferences concerning desired levels of saving, investment, taxation, and government expenditure. Whether the foreign financial presence in the country also constrained Brazil's ability to implement autonomous economic policies is another question, which we will discuss below. First, however, let us consider another form of external dependence: monetary dependence. That is, to what extent did conditions in the country's external sector – for example, exports or foreign-capital flows – affect the determination of Brazil's money supply? Operating through that channel, the external sector could influence the economy as a whole. The impact here would include effects on the level of aggregate domestic output, and on investment and prices.[9]

External Dependence and Domestic Monetary Conditions

In order to test the hypothesis that conditions in Brazil's external sector exerted a major influence on the determination of the country's money supply, the data requirements are straightforward. We require the basic monetary series, and a price deflator with which to compute real (constant-price) series. Paulo Neuhaus has compiled the pertinent monetary data for the period 1900–45; and Claudio Haddad has prepared a price deflator for the years beginning in 1908.[10] Most of the changes in Brazil's money supply between 1908 and 1945 depended on variations in the real monetary base, RMB.[11] We will therefore focus on the determinants of that variable in the years 1908–1945.

Brazil's population and output were expanding steadily during these years. Consequently, a regression of RMB against a trend variable would 'explain' much of the annual variation in Brazil's real monetary base between 1908 and 1945. However, the relevant question in the present context is the impact of additional variables which reflect conditions in Brazil's external sector. Two such variables are exports *(X)* and foreign-capital movements. Since data on foreign-capital flows are not available for these years, we specify as a proxy a closely related variable, the country's annual trade balance *(TB)*. Because a trend variable is also specified, this equation is equivalent to regressing the annual deviations of the real monetary base from its trend rate of growth against the annual deviations of exports and the trade balance from their trend values. In addition, it is important to examine the impact on the real monetary base of variables (other than trend) which were determined within Brazil rather than dictated by external conditions. Accordingly, we also specify the Brazilian government's annual budget deficit *(D)* as an explanatory variable in our regression equation.

Preliminary estimates indicated that *RMB* was more closely correlated with exports and the trade balance lagged one year than with current values of those variables. Accordingly X_{-1} and TB_{-1} were specified; because of this lag, we lose one annual observation. The equation was estimated in double-logarithmic form in order to permit ready interpretation of the regression coefficients as elasticities.[12] With absolute values of the *t*-ratios in parentheses, the estimated equation is:

$$\log RMB = 4.539 + .040 \text{ trend} - .015 \log TB_{-1}$$
$$(8.23) \quad (1.32) \qquad (0.31)$$

$$- .284 \log X_{-1} + .220 \log D \qquad (1)$$
$$(1.85) \qquad (1.69)$$

$$R^2 = .90 \qquad D.W. = .70$$

The low *t*-ratio on the $\log TB_{-1}$ term in equation (1) indicates a coefficient insignificantly different from zero.[13] Thus deviations in the growth of Brazil's monetary base from trend were not related to changes in the country's trade balance. The parameter estimate for the export term does seem to be significantly different from zero. But, far from indicating monetary dependence in Brazil, the export variable has a *negative* sign. This suggests that when exports declined from their normal rate of expansion, the Brazilian authorities responded with an above-average increase in the country's real monetary base.

Finally, the government deficit term, which reflects public-finance conditions within Brazil, is also statistically significant and has the expected positive sign. The positive coefficient on the *D* term provides a further hint concerning Brazil's economic independence. Taxes on foreign trade constituted a significant fraction of the Brazilian government's revenues during this period. Consequently, a decline in exports and imports meant a decline in government tax receipts. Equation (1) suggests, however, that when its tax receipts failed to grow at normal rates, the Brazilian government generally refused to reduce its expenditures accordingly. Instead it ran a budget deficit, accepting the monetary and inflationary consequences.

One further observation on Brazil's monetary autonomy is pertinent. It may be suggested that the parameter estimates of equation (1) are essentially a reflection of conditions after 1929, when the Brazilian authorities were relatively explicit in their pursuit of 'inward-looking' economic policies. In principle, however, strict monetary dependence may have prevailed in earlier decades. To consider this possibility, regression equations were estimated separately for the years 1909–29 and 1930–45. The results for these sub-periods are presented in equations (1a) and (1b), respectively:

$$\ln RMB = 4.171 + .030 \text{ trend} - .105 \ln TB_{-1}$$
$$(7.352) \quad (4.51) \qquad (0.83)$$

$$-.263 \ln X_{-1} + .234 \ln D \qquad\qquad\qquad\text{(1a)}$$
$$(1.53) \qquad (1.74)$$

$$R^2 = .76 \qquad D.W. = 1.60$$

$$\ln RMB = 4.514 + .068 \text{ trend} + .037 \ln TB_{-1}$$
$$(7.07) \quad (7.84) \qquad (1.20)$$

$$-.171 \ln X_{-1} + .226 \ln D \qquad\qquad\qquad\text{(1b)}$$
$$(1.01) \qquad (1.32)$$

$$R^2 = .95 \qquad D.W. = 1.28$$

These equations for the periods before and after 1929 show an important difference in the parameter estimates of the trend terms. The trend rate of growth in Brazil's real monetary base increased from 3 percent per annum in the period 1909–29 to 6.8 percent per annum between 1930 and 1945. This sharp rise may have been related, if only indirectly, to the upward shift in the demand-for-money function which occurred during the 1930s.[14] With greater demand for cash balances, the Brazilian authorities may have felt freer to expand the country's money supply at a higher rate. Of central relevance in the present context, however, are the parameter estimates for the X and the TB terms. Equations (1a) and (1b) show that the general pattern of non-significant or heterodox coefficients for the export and trade-balance terms prevailed in both periods. Hence, even before 1929, the

Brazilian authorities appear to have followed a general practice of increasing the monetary base in response to domestic pressures rather than let the country's money supply be determined by foreign-trade and capital movements.

These domestic pressures involved more than simply the government's frequent budget deficits (see below). The trend terms and the other parameter estimates of these equations, too, reflect internal political pressures to increase the country's money supply. Ultimately, these pressures stemmed from the imbalance between Brazil's propensity to save and propensity to invest, and the ensuing urgency of domestic credit expansion.

Brazilian Economic Policy, Gold-Standard Orthodoxy, and Laissez-Faire

It has sometimes been suggested that before 1945, Brazil's economic policy was oriented toward 'balanced budgets, monetary stability and exchange-rate stability'.[15] Such an orientation, in deference to foreign (or domestic) colonialist pressures, or in accordance with 'imported' economic ideology such as gold-standard orthodoxy, would constitute another form of external dependence. In fact, however, Brazilian fiscal policy was rarely constrained by a concern for a balanced budget. The extent of fiscal unorthodoxy is demonstrated in Table 9.1. The table shows the frequency and magnitude of budget deficits as a percentage of federal revenues between 1889 (the year of a major shift in constitutional structure and regime) and 1947. As Table 9.1 shows, the deficit was greater than 15 percent of government revenues in thirty-one of these fifty-eight years. Moreover, the deficit was not a small magnitude relative to the size of the Brazilian economy. Estimates of Brazilian GDP are available for the years 1911–13.[16] The government deficit in those particular years was not unusually large in terms of Brazilian norms. Nevertheless, the deficit averaged 2.0 percent of the country's GDP in the years 1911–13.

Table 9.1 *Frequency and Magnitude of Central Government Budget Deficits in Brazil, 1889–1947*

Number of Years	Government Deficits, D, as a Percentage of Government Revenues	Number of Years	Government Deficits, D, as a Percentage of Government Revenues
6	$-15\% \leqslant D < -5\%$	8	$15\% \leqslant D < 20\%$
5	$-5\% \leqslant D < 0$	18	$20\% \leqslant D < 50\%$
8	$0 \leqslant D < 5\%$	4	$50\% \leqslant D < 100\%$
8	$5\% \leqslant D < 15\%$	1	$D > 100\%$

Source: Computed from data in Anníbal Villela and Wilson Suzigan, *Política do Governo e Crescimento da Economia Brasileira, 1889–1945* (Rio de Janeiro, IPEA 1973), pp. 56–7; and Oliver Onody, *A Inflação Brasileira* (Rio de Janeiro, 1960), p. 199.

The government's deficits during the twentieth century cannot be attributed to a situation in which, perhaps because of the state's political impotence (or because of domestic doctrinal constraints), tax receipts were absurdly small relative to the size of the economy. In the years 1911–13, the federal government's revenues averaged some 9.2 percent of Brazilian GDP. Moreover, Brazil's state and local governments added appreciably to the size of the total public sector in the twentieth century. The data available for Brazil's state and local governments in the 1920s indicate that in that decade, expenditures by these governmental units amounted to some 70 percent of the federal government's total.[17] Further, government expenditures increased more rapidly than *pari passu* with Brazilian output. From 1920 to 1929, the elasticity of public-sector expenditure with respect to Real Output was approximately 1.4; and from 1929 to 1938, 1.6.[18] These prewar figures compare favorably with the public-sector expenditure elasticities in the 1947–55 and 1955–63 periods, 1.2 and 1.3, respectively. In reflection both of a high expenditure elasticity and of the country's rapid long-term economic growth, real expenditures of Brazil's federal government grew at an annual rate of approximately 5.2 percent between 1900 and 1930.[19]

This buoyancy in public sector expenditure reflects the capacity of the Brazilian state to safeguard its fiscal interests during the twentieth century. For example, during the First World War interruptions in foreign trade reduced the government's revenues from import duties. Thereupon, an important new tax was instituted, which was based on domestic sales. Customs receipts recovered after the war, but the new tax, which was levied on an internal rather than an externally-oriented base, was maintained and subsequently increased.[20] The government's fiscal expansion is reflected in the relatively high elasticities cited above. As the vigorous growth indicates, even before 1929 the Brazilian state was not a puny entity modeled along minimalist political theories. Another indicator of the Brazilian state's activism involves the relation between expenditures and revenues. As the government obtained additional tax revenues, it did not eliminate the chronic budget deficits. With additional revenues, the state's expenditures also shifted to higher levels.

Brazil's expansionary fiscal and monetary policies were in fact often pursued to the point of price inflation. Haddad's general price index, available from 1908, shows prices rising by 5 percent or more in twenty-two of the years between 1909 and 1947.[21] Prices rose by 15 percent or more in nine of these years. An essential concomitant of these inward-looking macroeconomic policies was an autonomous exchange-rate policy. Thus the Brazilian authorities generally permitted the country's exchange rate to depreciate when internal conditions dictated rates of price inflation that were high relative to those of Brazil's major trading partners. Between 1889 and 1920, when the sterling value of Brazil's exports was growing at an annual rate of 4 percent, the *mil-réis* depreciated 80 percent. Between 1920 and 1939, the exchange rate fell from an index of 100 to 23.

Efforts were occasionally made to maintain a fixed exchange rate along gold-standard lines. In deference to Brazil's export interests, however, the parity chosen was usually undervalued. The ensuing expansionary pressures led to further devaluation. Further testimony to the predominance of internal conditions are the circumstances in which Brazil launched its occasional efforts at monetary stabilization. A strong motive here seems to have been periodic concern to reduce excessively high rates of internal inflation.[22] Thus, following the unusually high inflation of the 1890s, the government in 1900–05 balanced its budget and reduced the country's money supply despite rising exports and a large trade surplus. Similarly, in 1928–29, a president who was determined to end Brazil's chronic inflation implemented restrictive macroeconomic policies despite the country's favorable foreign-trade situation. Notwithstanding these episodes, however, the general pattern which resulted from Brazil's autonomous economic policies was exchange-rate depreciation with a strong statistical trend.

The pace of long-term exchange depreciation was indeed so great that it often exceeded the rate of relative-price inflation as between Brazil and its major trading partner during the twentieth century, the United States. Brazil thus experienced long-term depreciation in its *real* exchange rate. This phenomenon can be clarified with the following notation. Let us denote the annual percentage change in the nominal *mil-réis*/dollar exchange rate as $\dot{e}r$; the annual percentage change in US prices as $\dot{p}_\$$; and the annual percentage rate of change in Brazilian prices as $\dot{p}_{mil\text{-}réis}$. Brazil would experience real exchange-rate depreciation, $\dot{d}$, if the following relation prevailed:

$$\dot{d} = \dot{e}r + \dot{p}_\$ - \dot{p}_{mil\text{-}réis} > 0 \qquad (2)$$

Such a situation reflects conditions in which domestic income and monetary growth were maintained autonomously at such expansionary rates that the demand for foreign exchange outpaced its supply. As a result, the cost of foreign exchange in constant *mil-réis* prices rose over time.

If we consider the data for $\dot{e}r$, $\dot{p}_\$$, and $\dot{p}_{mil\text{-}réis}$ in the years before 1947, we find that Brazil did in fact experience significant long-term depreciation in its real exchange rate. Table 9.2 presents estimates of the rate of real exchange depreciation in Brazil and of its components. These estimates were calculated on the basis of logarithmic trend regressions of the variables in equation (2). Haddad's general price index was used to compute $\dot{p}_{mil\text{-}réis}$ and the US wholesale price index for

Table 9.2   *Annual Trend Rates of Real Exchange-Rate Depreciation in Brazil, 1908–47* (in percent)

		$\dot{d}=\dot{e}r+\dot{p}_\$ -\dot{p}_{mil\text{-}réis}$		
	(1)	(2)	(3)	(4)
	$\dot{d}$	$\dot{e}r$	$\dot{p}_\$$	$\dot{p}_{mil\text{-}réis}$
Period				
1908–47	2.3	5.8*	0.6*	4.1*
		(23.06)	(1.92)	(13.74)
1908–20	6.2	3.0*	7.5*	4.3*
		(4.95)	(6.30)	(4.23)
1920–29	−4.7	3.1*	−2.7*	5.1*
		(1.50)	(1.90)	(3.34)
1930–39	3.2	5.9*	1.0**	2.7*
		(4.51)	(0.88)	(4.01)

Note: $\dot{e}r$ denotes the annual percentage trend in the *mil-réis*/dollar exchange rate; $\dot{p}_\$$ denotes the annual percentage trend in the US wholesale price index; $\dot{p}_{mil\text{-}réis}$ denotes the annual percentage trend in Brazilian prices. The absolute value of the *t*-ratio for each trend coefficient is presented in parentheses. An asterisk indicates a trend coefficient whose value exceeds its standard error. Two asterisks indicate a trend coefficient whose value does not exceed its standard error and which is therefore treated as insignificantly different from zero.

$\dot{p}_\$.$[23] The table shows the pertinent data for both the longer-term period 1908–47 and individual sub-periods.

Table 9.2 shows that between 1908 and 1947, Brazil's real exchange rate depreciated at an annual trend rate of 2.3 percent. Column (1) also indicates significant variations in the pace of real depreciation in different sub-periods. From 1908 to 1920 Brazil's real parity declined at a trend of some 6.2 percent per annum; and in the 1930s, at 3.2 percent per annum. By contrast, during the 1920s, when exports grew relatively rapidly, the real parity actually appreciated. Real exchange appreciation occurred in those years despite the 3.1 percent annual trend rate of depreciation in the nominal *mil-réis*/dollar exchange rate, and despite the 5.1 percent annual trend rate of domestic inflation during the 1920s. The general picture conveyed by Table 9.2, however, is of an economy pressing long-term internal expansion with scant regard for nominal or real exchange-rate stability.[24]

Not only did the government often depart from gold-standard orthodoxy in its exchange-rate, monetary, and fiscal policies, but Brazilian economic policy-making was also unconstrained by undue obeisance to imported ideologies such as *laissez-faire*. Within the framework of the policy instruments and resources at its disposal, the government intervened in the economy both with ad hoc subsidies and with public ownership. For example, in 1917, 53 percent of Brazil's railway trackage was owned by the government.[25] Similarly, the high import tariffs which we discussed in the previous chapter do not suggest either a passive orientation or a doctrinaire adherence to *laissez-faire*.[26] More generally, the government intervened directly in the economy and regulated banking, transportation, public utilities, and food prices.[27] Finally, the coffee valorization programs initiated in 1906 provide another example of the Brazilian elite's heterodox and activist orientation. The wisdom (short-term or long-term) of those programs is not the issue here. What is relevant is the fact that the Brazilians undertook purposeful manipulation of their economic environment.[28] In this instance, Brazil was perhaps the only primary-producing country that intervened in the market in an effort to better its terms of trade and transfer income from foreign consumers to domestic producers.

Dependence and Autonomy in the Great Depression and in the First World War

The Brazilian economy's performance during the Great Depression is perhaps the most striking demonstration of Brazil's independence from external economic conditions. The international Depression, which began in the United States in 1929, had a profound impact on dependent economies throughout the world. Consequently, an analysis of the course of events in Brazil during that period can provide further insight on both of our present concerns: the extent of external dependence in Brazil's economic structure, and the degree of autonomy in Brazilian economic policy-making. Table 9.3 presents data on the decline of GNP in the United States and of Real Output in Brazil in the first years of the Depression. The table also provides information on the course of industrial output in both countries following the onset of the international economic crisis.

Table 9.3   *The Depth of the Great Depression in the United States and in Brazil, 1930–33*

| | | Annual Percentage Change in: | | |
Year	US Real GNP	Brazilian Real Output	US Industrial Output	Brazilian Industrial Output
1930	−8.9	−2.1	−14.4	−6.7
1931	−6.0	−3.3	−15.9	+1.2
1932	−14.6	+4.3	−25.3	+1.4
1933	−2.9	+8.9	+16.7	+11.7

Note: Real Output is an index comprising output in agriculture, industry, commerce, transport and communications, and government.

Source: The annual percentage rates of change for the United States were computed from the series of the National Bureau of Economic Research, available in US Department of Commerce, *Long-Term Economic Growth, 1860–1965* (Washington, 1966), pp. 167–9. The Brazilian figures were computed from data in Claudio Haddad, *Growth of Real Output in Brazil, 1900–1947* (PhD dissertation, University of Chicago), 1974, pp. 17, 60.

As Table 9.3 shows, production in Brazil fell by much less than in the United States. Thus, taking 1929 as a base of 100, we observe that by 1933 Brazil's real industrial output and real GDP had attained levels of 108 and 107, respectively. The corresponding 1933 indices for the United States were 63 and 71. Further, not only was the extent of the initial decline considerably smaller in Brazil, but the economy recovered from the Depression much sooner than the United States. The rate of industrial output growth turned positive in Brazil by 1931, and showed continuing increases thereafter. Similarly, Brazil's Real Output recovered in 1932, two years earlier than in the United States (see Table 9.3).[29] Beginning in 1932 and continuing through the 1930s, both manufacturing and aggregate production in Brazil rose steadily, impervious to the sharp recession which struck the United States in 1938.

In neither the magnitude nor the duration of the Depression, then, was Brazil's experience a passive reflex to events in the world economy. One element in Brazil's superior economic performance during the 1930s was the country's autonomy in implementing expansionary monetary and fiscal policies. In order to promote an increase in real output, however, the expansion in internal demand required an elastic domestic supply response. This too was forthcoming, a reflection of structural conditions within Brazilian agriculture and industry. Indeed, as we saw in Chapter 8, internal supply was sufficiently responsive that the pace of price inflation in Brazil during the 1930s was much below that of the 1920s. Under these conditions, the autonomous increase in domestic demand (see below) enabled Brazil to expand output rapidly despite the international crisis. Consequently, after the first impact of the Depression, Brazil maintained a vigorous rate of economic growth through the 1930s.

Note, moreover, that the Brazilian economy's initial reaction to the international crisis was exacerbated by fortuitous conditions within Brazil: the Depression struck Brazil in the midst of an internally-initiated deflation.[30] In 1928, the dollar value of Brazil's exports rose 10 percent; and the country's international reserves, 24 percent.[31] The price level within Brazil, however, increased by 12 percent. This price increase jeopardized the goal of President Washington Luiz, who sought to lead the country to price stability. Accordingly, the president intensified a series of domestic deflationary measures. After the first quarter of 1928, monetary policy was tightened, and the country's stock of base money was held virtually constant (in nominal terms!) through the end of 1929.[32] In 1928 and 1929, the government reversed its chronic tendency toward deficit finance, and for the first time since 1907 ran budget surpluses. The real money supply declined by 2.1 percent in 1929, while prices fell 3.6 percent. As a result of this stabilization program, the growth of Real Output in Brazil declined

Table 9.4   *Consumption of Cotton Textiles in Brazil, 1927–34*

Year	Domestic Consumption (millions of square meters)	Change from Previous Year (%)	Year	Domestic Consumption (millions of square meters)	Change from Previous Year (%)
1927	638	9.4	1931	635	31.2
1928	632	−1.0	1932	633	−0.4
1929	508	−19.6	1933	643	1.6
1930	484	−9.9	1934	716	11.4

Note: Domestic consumption was calculated as domestic production, plus imports, minus exports.

Source: Anníbal Villela and Wilson Suzigan, *Política do Governo e Crescimento da Economia Brasileira 1889–1945* (Rio de Janeiro: !PEA, 1973), p. 438.

sharply to 1.1 percent in 1929. Industrial output fared even worse, falling 2.2 percent from the level of the previous year. These deflationary changes occurred in Brazil well before the Wall Street crash of October 1929. Table 9.4 shows the impact of the internal contraction on Brazilian consumption of a staple industrial product, cotton textiles.

As the data of Table 9.4 indicate, consumption of cotton textiles in Brazil reached its peak for the 1920s in 1927. Further, demand for this basic industrial product within Brazil was falling *before* the onset of the Depression in the metropolitan countries of the world economy. Unfortunately, the international economic crisis struck Brazil just when the country was in the midst of this internally determined deflation. Excess demand and liquidity had already been squeezed out of the economy before the contraction of international lending and commodity markets. Had it not been for the unfortunate timing with which the world Depression came to Brazil, the initial impact on the country would probably have been even less severe than is shown in Table 9.3.

A quick Brazilian policy response to the Depression was also hampered by domestic political conditions. The president, whose term of office was to continue through 1930, stubbornly refused to change his deflationary macroeconomic policies. In addition, coffee export policy was so mismanaged that world coffee prices fell 45 percent between September 1929 and December 1930, a period in which the US wholesale price index fell only 8 percent.[33] Effective policy response was also inhibited because the country was in the midst of the deep internal political crisis that culminated in the Vargas revolution of October 1930. Vargas's political control, in turn, was initially too tenuous for purposeful action in economic policy.

Beginning in 1932, however, government expenditure increased significantly, both in nominal and in real terms, to provide an important stimulus to domestic economic expansion.[34] Table 9.5 presents data on the growth of federal expenditure in constant prices.

Table 9.5 The Growth of Real Expenditure by the Federal Government in Brazil, 1932–1939

Year	Federal Expenditure (millions of 1939 mil-réis)	Change from Previous Year (%)	Year	Federal Expenditure (millions of 1939 mil-réis)	Change from Previous Year (%)
1932	3,653	38	1936	3,717	11
1933	3,119	−15	1937	4,362	17
1934	3,742	20	1938	4,832	11
1935	3,363	−11	1939	4,850	0.4

Source: Computed from data in Paulo Neuhaus, História Monetária do Brasil, 1900–45 (Rio de Janeiro: IMBEC, 1975), p. 191; and from Claudio Haddad, Growth of Real Output in Brazil, 1900–1947, op. cit., p. 191.

Between 1932 and 1939, federal expenditure in real terms increased at an average annual rate of 7.5 percent. Similarly, internal expansionary policies, coming together with a rise in the domestic demand for cash balances, led to a doubling (!) of the country's real money supply during the 1930s.[35] These domestic measures helped provide the economy with adequate aggregate demand and liquidity, necessary conditions for successful reflation. Aided by government macroeconomic policy, then, the Brazilian economy possessed sufficient structural autonomy to generate rapid growth through the 1930s, independently of conditions in the United States and the rest of the world economy.

It may be suggested that the Brazilian economy's relative autonomy from external conditions dates only from the 1930s, but that Brazil was essentially a dependent economy in earlier decades. Such a contention, however, is not borne out by Brazil's experience during the First World War. In that episode, too, the country's external trade contracted sharply, as access to foreign markets was limited. Nevertheless, after the initial impact the Brazilian economy was able to adjust and maintain high rates of output growth, especially in manufacturing. Data on the Brazilian economy's experience between 1914 and 1918 are presented in Table 9.6.

The war curtailed Brazil's access to overseas markets and led to a steep drop in the country's foreign trade. Industrial output recovered by 1915, however; and despite a further decline in export receipts (see Table 9.6), aggregate output turned sharply upward by 1916. The war did stimulate expansion in Brazilian manufacturing, as special efforts were made to produce locally goods which had previously been imported. But Brazil did not need the war either to launch industrialization, or to assure its subsequent progress. On the contrary, industrial development had been proceeding at a high rate in Brazil for decades before the First World War.[36] More generally and most

Table 9.6   *The External Sector and Domestic Output Growth in Brazil,*
1914–18

		Annual Percentage Change in:		
	Real	Volume		
	Export	of	Real	Industrial
Year	Receipts	Imports	Output	Output
1914	−21	−45	1	−9
1915	7	−24	−1	13
1916	−14	9	4	11
1917	−19	−20	5	9
1918	−18	1	2	−1

Note: Real Output is a Divisia index which comprises output in agriculture, industry, transport and communications, and government.

Source: Computed from data in Anníbal Villela and Wilson Suzigan, *Política do Governo e Crescimento da Economia Brasileira, 1889–1945* (Rio de Janeiro: IPEA, 1973), p. 441; Paulo Neuhaus, *História Monetária do Brasil, 1900–1945* (Rio de Janeiro: IMBEC, 1975), p. 190; and Claudio Haddad, *Growth of Brazilian Real Output, 1900–1947* (PhD dissertation, University of Chicago, 1974), pp. 10–11, 191.

importantly in the present context, Brazil's experience during the war demonstrated that long before the 1930s, the country's economic development could be sustained despite a severe contraction in the external sector.

An Assessment of Brazilian Economic Policy in the Half-Century before 1947

The dependency interpretation also raises important questions concerning the degree to which a less-developed country like Brazil could affect the course of its development in a meaningful manner. That issue leads us to consider the impact of government policy on Brazil's economic development.

Clearly, much of the country's economic development during the first half of the twentieth century was the result of straightforward market conditions. Thus the stimulus given by a domestic demand for manufactures which exceeded the import sector's supply capacity was a basic feature of Brazil's modern industrial development.[37] And with rapid growth of aggregate output in the first decades of the century and an income-elastic demand for manufactures, the country's modern industrial expansion was very much powered by market forces. Nevertheless, government policies also affected the pace and thrust of this development process.

The road construction whose strategic role we noted earlier was, of course, supplied via the public sector.[38] Further, as we have seen, both monetary and fiscal policy were usually expansionary. Consequently, apart from the sporadic episodes of monetary stabilization, Brazil's development during this period was rarely constrained by insufficient aggregate demand. Moreover, the output growth which was evoked by buoyant demand conditions led to more than a simple scalar expansion of the economy. Rather, in accordance with differential income elasticities of demand and inter-industry relations, economic expansion involved diversification and entry into new activities. This pattern of growth cum structural change was reinforced by a 'side-effect' of the country's expansionary macroeconomic policies: the long-term depreciation of the real exchange rate which we noted in Table 9.2. That secular shift in relative prices also favored local industrial producers and encouraged investment and production in new import-replacing activities.

Brazil's coffee valorization policies also had promotional effects. The valorization programs involved export taxation, interventionist inventory policy, and (at times) controls on coffee production. By raising international coffee prices, these measures increased Brazilian income and enlarged the size of the market for domestic manufacturers. Moreover, by improving the country's terms of trade, coffee valorization reduced the cost of imported inputs which were complementary to the development process. These effects of coffee policy on Brazilian industrialization were no less important for being second-order consequences which may not have been anticipated by the authors of the valorization programs. At the same time, the tariffs and other import limitations which we discussed in Chapter 8 shifted relative prices against competitive imports, to help promote domestic industrialization.

Brazilian tariff policy has sometimes been charged with being insufficiently 'dynamic' in according protection to new infant-industry activities, and thus to diversify industrial output.[39] This fault, in turn, has been attributed to the nature of the protection-granting process. Tariff changes were often made in an 'unsystematic' manner, and were subject to the pressures of individual firms who intervened in the political and administrative system. This kind of process for granting import protection may be unattractive in many respects. However, it does seem to have been well suited to provide protection for new activities along lines of dynamic comparative advantage. Thus as the market and potential returns for new products grew, so too did the returns to private-sector action aimed at eliciting import limitations in those activities.[40] Hence, as the economic prospects for potential infant industries became increasingly viable, the net private gains to applying pressure on governmental institutions also rose. Such dynamic effects apparently did operate, and helped generate significant changes over time in the structure of Brazil's import protection. Because the country's industrialization was based largely on the domestic market, continuation of rapid industrial expansion necessarily required successive entry into new product lines. And in historical fact, output in Brazil's industrial sector did become increasingly diversified.

Brazil's industrialization policies also included some subsidies to industry.[41] Thus in 1892 the government made available special loans, at negative real interest rates, to industrial firms caught in a liquidity squeeze. Direct subsidies were used in the twentieth century to promote domestic production of key products which, because of capital-market imperfections, might have been beyond the unaided reach of Brazil's industrialists. For example, in the 1920s, this approach was used to develop domestic production of steel and of cement. That experience is especially noteworthy, for some perceptions of Brazilian history have viewed the 1920s as a decade of thoroughgoing *laissez-faire*. Similarly, direct subsidy policies were used in the 1930s to promote paper and aluminum production. Coming together with the growth of the domestic market and factor supplies, these policies helped change the structure and composition of Brazilian industrial output. The development of domestic supply in industrial materials made it easier to maintain manufacturing expansion despite the import difficulties of the 1930s and, subsequently, of the Second World War.[42]

The foregoing discussion of government policy is not to suggest that Brazil's economic development in the half-century before 1947 was oriented by pervasive government planning. Any such expectation would be ahistorical for the period under consideration. And as emphasized earlier, much of the country's industrial expansion was clearly the result of market forces. It would also be anachronistic to expect that Brazil's governments allocated their expenditures according to optimizing developmental criteria. This was an age in which the promotional role for interventionist governments was envisaged largely in terms of providing economic infrastructure, protective tariffs, and *ad hoc* subsidies. Brazilian governments in the decades before 1947 did just that. They also added the extra stimulus of the coffee valorization programs and of expansionary monetary and fiscal policies. If government did little directly to promote domestic agricultural modernization, that too accorded with contemporary conceptions of economic development, which focused on export growth and industrial development.

Governments in pre-1947 Brazil may not have acted with complete purposefulness or awareness of the full economic implications of their policies. We have already noted that some of the effects of coffee policy on Brazilian industrialization were probably unanticipated. Similarly, Brazil's credit expansionists may not have been aware of the consequences of excessive monetary growth for the country's real exchange rate and subsequent import substitution. In other cases, such as tariff and subsidy policy, Brazil's policy-makers clearly did attempt to promote the country's economic development (as they perceived it). Further, it is one thing to note that certain government policies may have had greater stimulating effects than Brazil's policy-makers expected, but a *non sequitur* to conclude that the policy-makers were not concerned to promote the country's economic development. We can make generous allowance for the extent to which random elements rather than purposeful action helped determine Brazil's economic policy-making. Nevertheless, two features remain fairly persistent fixtures in the overall picture: buoyant aggregate demand, and a shift in internal relative prices which favored industrialization. This is too consistent a pattern to attribute to chance.

Our analysis thus far has considered the impact of government policy on economic growth and structural change in Brazil during the first half of the twentieth century. We have not discussed the effects on the distribution of income. This is because evaluative judgments concerning income-distribution effects necessarily reflect subjective preferences. Thus later observers (and some contemporaries) may wish that Brazil's economic expansion had proceeded in a more egalitarian manner. But Brazil's policy-makers apparently did not share those preferences.[43] Hence it is not surprising that the country did not follow such a path. Indeed, Brazil's ability to avoid a more egalitarian expansion path can be taken as further evidence of the phenomenon we have been discussing: the capacity of Brazil's elites to control events and act as subjects rather than as objects of history.

Before concluding our discussion of Brazilian economic policy-making during this period, we should consider other criticisms which have often been made. One charge is that government intervention in the economy was 'haphazard and unplanned'.[44] One can readily appreciate the desire for consistency and prior planning. However, we must take into account the economic doctrines and systematic programs that were historically available to Brazil in the first half of the twentieth century. It is also not evident that the pattern of economic policy-making that Brazil actually experienced was inferior to what would have been achieved using available intellectual and administrative resources for a more *a priori* and rigid approach. The behavior of Brazilian policy-makers can be labeled as pragmatic or opportunistic, depending on the observer's perspective. The main point in the present context is that intellectual rigidities usually did not impede an effective policy response to economic needs and opportunities as these arose.

Similarly, later observers have suggested that government interventionism during this period was 'neither nationalistic nor opposed to the interests of capitalists', and that public policy benefited both the private and the public sectors.[45] Again, it is helpful to view these phenomena within their historical context. Using the norms of the post-Second World War period to judge the degree of nationalist self-assertion in Brazil during the prewar decades would be an anachronism. And the capacity to devise policies which aided more than one set of political participants may reflect political skill (or necessity) rather than behavior to be deplored. Finally, if policy measures benefited one group in Brazil it does not necessarily follow that it was at the expense of others. In the context of a rapidly growing economy, one party can gain without another party losing. Social scientists need not impose the assumptions of a zero-sum game on Brazil's development process during this period.[46]

The Attractiveness of the Dependency Interpretation

Our earlier discussion led to an important conclusion: in terms of its economic structure and actual performance during the first half of the twentieth century, Brazil had considerable scope to pursue its economic development independently of external conditions. Our consideration of the country's import tariffs, and its fiscal, monetary, and exchange-rate policies suggests a similar conclusion. In implementing these measures, Brazil's policy-makers demonstrated their capacity to act autonomously, with a large degree of independence from foreign political pressures and ideologies. One implication of this discussion is that, for this period at least, the dependency interpretation of Brazil's economic history is largely a myth.

The prevalence of this myth is itself an important phenomenon. Moreover, this phenomenon is apparently not confined to Brazil. In other less-developed countries, too, foreign and domestic observers have sometimes disregarded historical reality and denied the presence of economic or political autonomy. For example, Carlos Diaz-Alejandro's study of the pre-1929 Argentine economy noted a similar case.[47] Although many observers have deplored the absence of protective tariffs in that economy, Diaz-Alejandro notes that the country did in fact have high, protective import duties. A study of colonial Ghana records a similar denial phenomenon, in an unwillingness to perceive the indigenous capacity for technical progress and structural change.[48] Those developments in Ghana have often been attributed mainly to the efforts of the colonial authorities. In fact, the initiative of indigenous peasants played a very major role. Note further that both sides of the ideological spectrum have on occasion shown this unwillingness to accept the possibility of autonomous action on the part of people from underdeveloped countries. In the Ghanaian case cited, it was colonialist administrators who exhibited the denial phenomenon; in the Argentina case, it was nationalist intellectuals.

In the context of Brazilian economic historiography, this

phenomenon appears most clearly in connection with the tariff. As we saw in Chapter 8, Brazil's import duties on many manufactured imports were high, and were maintained at levels sufficient to be a key condition in the country's industrialization. Notwithstanding the indisputable evidence on the existence of high import duties and the fact that Brazil's industrial sector expanded rapidly in their wake, some observers have been reluctant to admit the existence and importance of Brazil's protective tariffs. [49]

One possible explanation for this reluctance has been a focus on the motivation rather than on the effects of government policy. The Brazilian authorities often stated that their principal motive in raising import duties was to obtain tariff revenues for the government; and this apparently was the reason for the Brazilian Finance Ministry's support for tariffs. Presenting the tariff issue in such terms may have helped neutralize the opposition of the country's export interests to high import duties. However, the promotional effects of Brazil's tariffs on the country's industrialization were also clear to many contemporary observers. These effects were in fact cited by proponents of Brazilian industrialization. [50] Nevertheless, the tariffs were maintained persistently after the 1840s; indeed, the level of Brazil's import duties rose over the long term. Consequently, it is difficult to claim that the protective effects of the tariffs for industry occurred inadvertently, and without the awareness of Brazil's policy-makers.

Another explanation for the unwillingness to admit the facts of Brazil's tariff policy may lie in the use of an overly simplistic political model, which would suggest that purposeful governmental action on behalf of Brazilian industrialization should have been impossible in the decades before 1929. The industrial bourgeoisie was clearly not the dominant political group in Brazil during this earlier period. By contrast, the coffee-exporting interests, who in principle opposed Brazilian industrialization, certainly did have considerable prominence. Hence, it may appear inconceivable that the government could have instituted protective tariffs on imported manufactured goods. Such an interpretation, however, neglects an important alternative possibility. The state may in some cases act independently of the existing configuration of the material forces in society, and may promote economic modernization for ideological reasons and a desire for enhanced national self-esteem. If such autonomous government action were not a real possibility, it would be hard to explain how many of the 'latecomer' countries which followed Great Britain ever industrialized. In the standard historical pattern, the state accorded import protection to industry in advance of industrialization.

Finally, another explanation involves the presumed importance of imperialist control over Brazilian economic policy-making. If Brazil was in effect a colony of the international hegemonic powers, as is sometimes assumed, it may seem farfetched that the country could implement tariffs which promoted Brazil's industrialization. That interpretation, however, substantially overstates the degree of imperialist control over Brazilian policy-making during this period. From the second half of the nineteenth century, Brazil's elites were able to pursue a course that was characterized by considerable autonomy, both in tariff policy and in other areas as well.[51]

To recognize the existence of protective tariffs, however, would imply an admission that Brazilian policy-makers had more autonomy from imperialist control than has sometimes been granted. Similarly, to note the Brazilian economy's structural autonomy and capacity to determine key macroeconomic variables internally would clash with *a priori* beliefs concerning the country's economic dependence. Given the popularity of the explanation of Brazil's economic history in terms of external control, the resistance to accepting the reality of autonomous action in Brazil is understandable. Another question, however, remains unanswered. Why has the dependency model so often been used for interpreting Brazil's economic experience during this period even though, as we have seen, the model's historical relevance is very limited? Important insights may be provided here by the sociology of knowledge.[52] Regardless of their source, however, the incongruities between the dependency interpretation and Brazilian reality in the first half of the twentieth century are noteworthy.

Some Welfare Effects of the Acceleration of Economic Development in Brazil

The sustained economic growth and structural change which we have discussed in these two chapters appear to have led to higher levels of general welfare in Brazil. Real Output per capita rose at an annual trend rate of 2.3 percent between 1900 and 1947. In addition, the availability of certain goods which may be taken as physical indicators of popular living standards also showed a notable increase.

As we saw in Chapter 8, domestic consumption of staple food products rose perceptibly in Brazil during the first half of the century.[53] Another indicator of general welfare is life expectancy at birth.[54] This index too, rose substantially. As late as 1900, life expectancy at birth in Brazil was approximately 19.4 years. The figure rose to 32.0 years in 1920; 36.7 years in 1940; and 43.0 years in 1950. This slow increase amounted to a 46 percent rise over the half-century.[55]

Similarly, enrollments in Brazil's primary schools, an index of the availability of basic education and literacy to the broader population, also showed a notable increase between 1900 and 1950. Table 9.7 presents data on this phenomenon. As the figures of column (4) indicate, during the first half of the twentieth century the percentage of

Table 9.7   Growth of Enrollments in Brazil's Primary Schools 1889–1950

(1) Year	(2) Primary School Enrollments (thousands)	(3) Annual Rate of Growth since Previous Observation (%)	(4) Enrollments Relative to Total Population (%)	(5) Enrollments Relative to Population aged 7–11 (%)
1889	233	—	2	14
1907	547	4.9	3	20
1920	1,126	5.7	4	29
1930	1,877	5.3	6	43
1940	2,550	3.1	6	46
1950	3,710	3.8	7	55

Source: Computed from data in Robert J. Havighurst and J. Robert Moreira, *Society and Education in Brazil* (Pittsburgh: University of Pittsburgh Press, 1965), p. 85.

primary school enrollments relative to the country's population more than doubled. The increase relative to the pertinent age cohort was even greater (see column (5)). This progress is especially noteworthy because the country's population was itself growing at a high rate (2.1 percent per annum) during this period.

As in the case of life expectancy and nutrition, Brazil began the twentieth century with enrollment ratios that were low in absolute terms (see Table 9.7). These poor initial conditions had an important effect on the country's subsequent development levels. Thus, despite considerable progress, Brazil's enrollments were so small relative to the relevant age cohort that, in 1950, the country could still be classified as underdeveloped. Nevertheless, the rapid rates of enroll-ment growth, which distributed some of the fruits of development beyond the country's socioeconomic elite, are also impressive.

During the first half of the twentieth century, then, Brazil achieved noteworthy gains not only in per capita Real Product, but also in life expectancy, nutrition, and primary school enrollments. Nevertheless, despite sustained economic development in the preceding half-century, Brazil was still very much an economically-poor country at the beginning of the post-Second World War period. In 1947, Brazil's per capita GDP in current prices was only 196 dollars.[56] And not only was the absolute level of per capita GDP low, but Brazil was also far behind in terms of international comparisons with the economically-advanced countries.[57] Thus, in contrast with the figure of $196 just cited for Brazil, per capita GDP of the United States in 1947 was $1622 (current prices), 8.3 times larger than the level in Brazil.[58] This initial disparity has been a major factor in the continuing large difference between Brazil's per capita income levels and those of the economically more developed countries during the postwar period.

Two conditions are immediately relevant in explaining the large size of the international income gap which Brazil faced in 1947. Brazil began its modern economic growth, toward the end of the nineteenth century, from a low level of development. The country's poor initial conditions are apparent in the figures which we noted earlier for life expectancy, nutrition, and primary school enrollments at the end of the nineteenth century. Similarly, the country's urbanization ratio, another indirect index of development levels, was also low.[59] In 1890, only 11 percent of Brazil's population resided in cities of 10,000 or more inhabitants.[60] Thus, because of the low development levels which prevailed in Brazil when sustained economic development began, the subsequent high rates of growth did not lead to large absolute increments in income and development.

Another reason for Brazil's postwar income gap is not so obvious, and has not previously been noted. We discussed earlier the long-term depreciation of Brazil's real exchange rate (see Table 9.2, above). This phenomenon had an important side-effect in terms of the measurement of economic growth in Brazil during this period. Because of real depreciation, the rate of growth of Brazilian per capita income measured in constant dollar prices was much lower than the rate of growth of Brazilian per capita income measured in constant *mil-réis* prices.

The importance of this measurement effect can readily be appreciated. Between 1908 and 1947, Real Output per capita in Brazil rose at an annual trend rate of 2.2 percent, leading to a cumulative rise from a base of 100 to an index of 233.[61] For purposes of evaluating increases in domestic productivity and welfare, this more than doubling of per capita output in constant local-currency prices is the measure which is conceptually appropriate.[62] International income comparisons, however, are conventionally made in US dollars. And during this same period, Brazil's real exchange rate depreciated at an annual trend rate of 2.3 percent. Hence the magnitude of real depreciation was so large that it completely eroded the impact of domestic income growth on the dollar level of Brazilian per capita income in 1947. Thus the decline in the country's real exchange rate had an additional effect which is relevant in the present context. Because of real depreciation, Brazil's impressive economic achievements during the first half of the twentieth century were not reflected in a partial closing of the country's international income gap as expressed in dollars.[63] This experience also has another, more general implication. The measurement problems we have noted are sufficient to raise serious questions concerning the relevance of an externally-oriented index like changes in the international income gap as an indicator of an underdeveloped country's economic achievement.[64]

Conclusions

The data and analysis in this chapter suggest that the Brazilian economy was much less dependent on the external sector and on international conditions than might have been expected on the basis of some earlier interpretations. As we have seen, economic under-development need not be accompanied by external dependency. One may speculate about the reasons for this dissociation in Brazil. The country's size and economic resources, and the character of its socio-economic elite may clearly be relevant. But comparative studies of different countries are necessary if we are to proceed beyond the realm of conjecture in explaining this pattern in Brazil.

More generally, this chapter and the preceding one underline the obvious need to distinguish between different types of underdeveloped countries. A country may be poor; its economy may be stagnant; and its economy may be highly dependent on economic and political pressures which emanate from the economically-advanced powers. Brazil's experience indicates that these categories may not necessarily overlap. In the half-century before 1947 Brazil was clearly a poor country, with low levels of per capita income and socioeconomic welfare. But as we saw in Chapter 8, the economy was not stagnant: Brazil had been experiencing sustained economic growth and structural change for approximately half a century before 1947. And as the present chapter indicates, Brazil's economic structure and policy-making were sufficiently autonomous of external pressures that the country could pursue a development pattern very different from that of a dependent economy.

Brazil's economic independence was demonstrated in the relatively small magnitude and duration of the output declines occasioned by the impact of the Great Depression. Moreover, even these first responses were exacerbated by fortuitous domestic conditions – the fact that the Depression struck in the midst of a severe deflation which Brazil had initiated internally. Brazil's economic autonomy was subsequently shown in the economy's capacity to develop rapidly during the 1930s, regardless of the depressed conditions in the world economy. This autonomy may have become more pronounced (or more self-aware) after 1929. But Brazil had earlier demonstrated a similar independence with its pre-1929 economic policies. Similarly, the economy had shown its ability to sustain development despite the contraction of its inter-national trade during the First World War.

In addition to the structural economic features we have noted, Brazil's economic autonomy was reinforced by the fact that internal rather than external conditions usually determined the growth of the country's real monetary base. Likewise, the country's fiscal and exchange-rate policies generally reflected an unwillingness to be inhibited by the rules of gold-standard orthodoxy. Brazil's inward-looking orientation in economic policy-making was so marked that even before the 1930s, the country experienced substantial long-term depreciation in its exchange rate. Indeed, autonomous macro-economic policies were carried to the point that Brazil's *real* parity also depreciated over the long term. Similarly, Brazil's coffee valorization programs and protective import tariffs indicate both the policy-makers' activist orientation, and their willingness to depart from *laissez-faire*. Brazil's policy-makers may not always have acted with complete wisdom or economic sophistication in promoting the country's economic development. But it was rare that in practice the country's economic policies reflected an excessive deference to orthodox doctrines originating in the metropolitan countries. And although foreign capital played a non-trivial role in Brazil's economic growth before 1947, the political and economic linkages which this involved did not constrain the country from its autonomous tariff and macroeconomic policies.

The contrast between Brazil's policies in all the areas just mentioned and those of countries subject to formal or informal colonial dependency is clear.[65] In fact during the first half century of the twentieth century, Brazil fits the model which Bent Hansen proposed to define a country which, although a primary-product exporter, is pursuing an independent development strategy.[66] The essence of that strategy is the use of export taxes and import duties to approximate a dynamic optimum tariff policy, while the government increases its expenditure to stimulate aggregate demand and provide economic infrastructure. In practice, Brazil followed a course along these lines. These policies in the first half of the twentieth century came in conjunction with the favorable economic changes which had earlier launched Brazil on a more general development path. As a result, the country was able to achieve sustained economic growth and structural change. These five decades were also characterized by persistent political tensions in Brazil. In addition, throughout the period many Brazilian intellectuals viewed their society as beset by profound structural crisis. A similar atmosphere has carried over to subsequent decades, to a point where it is difficult to suggest that anything good happened in the country during this period. Nevertheless, our analysis indicated that per capita output as well as some key indicators of general welfare rose perceptibly in Brazil during the first half of the twentieth century.

Notes

1   See pp. 176–80 in Chapter 8, above. The present chapter must perforce repeat some material which was also directly pertinent in that analytical context. However, we focus here on aspects of the dependency question during the first decades of the

twentieth century which are not discussed elsewhere in this study. For an interpretation of Brazil as a dependent economy, see, for example, André Gunder Frank, 'The Capitalist Development of Underdevelopment in Brazil,' pp. 143–218 in his *Capitalism and Underdevelopment in Latin America: Historical Studies of Chile and Brazil* (New York: Monthly Review Press, 1967). Nathaniel H. Leff, in *Development in Brazil: Vol. II, Reassessing the Obstacles to Economic Development* (Allen & Unwin, London, 1982), Chapter 4, examines the relevance of that interpretation to Brazil during the nineteenth century.

2 The size of the domestic market for manufactured products is approximately equal to aggregate demand minus the demand for food and services. At low per capita income levels such as prevailed in nineteenth-century Brazil this market may have amounted to some 20–25 percent of gross domestic product. See the data in Simon Kuznets, *Modern Economic Growth* (New Haven: Yale University Press, 1966), pp. 234–41, 265–9. On the share of imports in Brazilian GDP, see the discussion below.

3 In formal terms, consider an economy in which income grows as a function of export growth, and foreign supply of manufactured products is determined by the rate of export growth. Let D_t denote the demand for manufactured goods; S_t ($=M_t$), the supply from importation; X_t ($=M_t$), annual export receipts; Y_t, national income; and r, the rate of growth of exports, income, and import supply: (1) $Y_t = Y_o e^{rt}$; (2) $D_t = D_o e^{\lambda rt}$; (3) $X_t = X_o e^{rt}$; and (4) $S_t = M_o e^{rt}$. We assume $\lambda > 1$, reflecting an income elasticity of demand for manufactures greater than unity. If D (t), the size of the market for manufactured products, is greater than the share of imports in GDP, a market for domestically-manufactured products exists initially; and will grow more than proportionately with the increase in income resulting from expanding exports. This seems to have been the case in Brazil, where imports constituted a small proportion of national product. In other cases of a relatively large foreign-trade sector, imports may initially exceed the share of manufactured products in final demand. However, as income grows because of expanding exports, with an income elasticity of demand for manufactured products greater than unity, D (t) will eventually exceed M (t). With a foreign-trade multiplier greater than unity ($r_y > r_x$), income growth based on expanding exports will create a greater market for domestic industrial producers. Similarly, if the rate of growth of imports is less than the rate of growth of exports ($r_x > r_m$) because of growing foreign-capital payments, the domestic market for manufactures will expand more rapidly than supply from imports. Finally, growth of industrial production for the internal market will create another source of income growth and demand for industrial products which does not generate its own import supply; industrialization therefore becomes a continuing process.

4 This ratio was computed from figures which were graciously supplied by Dr Claudo Haddad of the Fundação Getulio Vargas. These estimates are presented in n. 35 of Chapter 2, above. Note further that if Brazilian GDP, like exports, were valued at world-market prices rather than at local prices, the value of Brazilian GDP in 1911–13 would be larger, and the magnitude of the export–GDP ratio even lower than the figure presented in the text. The reasons for this measurement bias are discussed in Dan Usher, *The Price Mechanism and The Meaning of National Income Statistics* (London: Oxford University Press, 1968).

5 For classic analyses of the structural features and dynamics of 'export economies', see Henry C. Wallich, *Monetary Problems of an Export Economy: The Cuban Experience, 1914–1947* (Cambridge, Mass.: Harvard University Press, 1950); and Jonathan V. Levin, *The Export Economies* (Cambridge, Mass.: Harvard University Press, 1960).

6 The expansion of output in Brazil's export sector during the nineteenth century is discussed in Chapter 5, above. With its relatively low export coefficient, Brazil resembles other countries of large population and area, for example, the United

States, Russia, China, and India. For the underlying causes, see the discussion in Charles P. Kindleberger, *Foreign Trade and The National Economy* (New Haven: Yale University Press, 1962), pp. 32 ff.

7 See p. 173 in Chapter 8, above, and the accompanying note there.

8 This figure was computed from data in Arthur Redfield, *Brazil: A Study of Economic Conditions since 1913* (Washington: US Department of Commerce, GPO, 1920), p. 97.

9 For a study of such monetary effects in a dependent economy, see Wallich, *Monetary Problems*, op. cit., esp. Chapters 1–4.

10 The price deflator used is the general price deflator presented in Claudio Haddad, *The Growth of Real Output in Brazil, 1900–1947*, (PhD Dissertation, University of Chicago, 1974), p. 191, Table 76. The monetary series used Paulo Neuhaus, *História Monetária do Brasil, 1900–45* (Rio de Janeiro: IMBEC, 1975), pp. 157–8. After the econometric work reported below was completed, another source of Brazilian monetary data became available. This is Carlos Manuel Peláez and Wilson Suzigan, *História Monetária do Brasil* (Rio de Janeiro: IPEA, 1976).

11 Neuhaus, *História Monetária*, op. cit., p. 176.

12 In order to permit the use of logarithms, even though D and TB sometimes take negative values, those variables were specified in ratio form: government expenditures divided by revenues, and annual exports divided by imports, respectively.

13 The Durbin–Watson statistic for equation (1) is significant at the .01 level, indicating that the estimates are inefficient and the t-ratios are overstated. This is not especially troublesome in the present context. Our main concern here is to avoid accepting as valid estimates which are not in fact statistically significant. The discussion in the text concentrates on the non-significance of the external-sector variables in support of a dependency hypothesis. That interpretation is unaffected by inefficiency in estimation. The general conclusions presented here are also supported by the more efficient estimates reported below.

14 See pp. 182–3 in Chapter 8, above.

15 Anníbal Villela and Wilson Suzigan, *Política do Governo a Crescimento da Economia Brasileira, 1889–1945* (Rio de Janeiro: IPEA, 1973), p. 55.

16 The estimates of Brazilian GDP which were used to calculate this figure are those of Dr Claudio Haddad, see n. 4, above. The data on the government deficit are from Oliver Ónody, *A Inflação Brasileira* (Rio de Janeiro, 1960), p. 197. Ónody and Haddad are also the sources for the underlying data for the ratios, presented in the next paragraph, on the share of government tax revenue in GDP.

17 Dennis J. Mahar and Fernando A. Rezende, 'The Growth and Pattern of Public Expenditure in Brazil, 1920–1969,' *Public Finance Quarterly,* vol. 3 (October 1975), Table 4.

18 Ibid, p. 385. The 'public sector' comprises the federal government, federal autarquias, state, and local governments. The emphasis here is not on the exact magnitude of the elasticities (they were computed using the Villela-Suzigan rather than the Haddad estimates of Real Product). Rather, the point is that the public-sector expenditure elasticities are well above unity. That conclusion would probably be unaltered using the Haddad series.

19 This figure is from Steven Topkin, 'State Intervention in a Liberal Regime: Brazil, 1898–1930,' *Hispanic American Historical Review*, vol. 60 (November 1980) p. 596. Topkin also states (ibid.) that real federal expenditure grew at an annual rate of only 1.5 percent between 1930 and 1945. This difference constitutes another challenge to some previous views. These have tended to see the 1930s as interventionist and in sharp contrast with the allegedly *laissez-faire* approach of Brazilian governments in earlier decades.

20 Data on the magnitude of federal government receipts from import taxes and from the '*imposto de consumo*' are presented in Villela and Suzigan, *Política do Governo*, op. cit., pp. 418–19.

21   These data are from Haddad, *Growth of Real Output*, op. cit. p. 191, Table 76.
22   On these episodes, see the discussion and data in Villela and Suzigan, *Política do Governo*, op. cit., pp. 39–41, 44–6, 56, 439–41; and in Neuhaus, *História Monetária*, op. cit., pp. 15–29, 84–95, 157, 180.
23   Annual observations of the Bureau of Labor Statistics' wholesale price index were taken from US Department of Commerce, *Long-Term Economic Growth* (Washington: GPO 1966), p. 203. Annual observations of the *mil-réis*/dollar exchange rate are from Neuhaus, *História Monetária*, op. cit., p. 184.
24   Although the two phenomena are related, real exchange depreciation cannot be identified with, or ascribed exclusively to exogenously deteriorating international terms of trade. Not only did domestic economic conditions and policies affect the demand for foreign exchange, but on the supply side, Brazil's tariff and allocation policies influenced the rate of export growth. Most important in the present context is the fact that the Brazilian authorities generally pressed forward with internal expansion despite the consequences for the nominal and real exchange rate. For a fuller discussion of the conditions leading to real exchange-rate depreciation, see Nathaniel H. Leff, 'Modificaciones do los Tipos de Cámbio Reales como Instrumento de Política en la Posguerra,' *El Trimestre Económico* (April 1973).
25   Computed from data in Redfield, *Brazil*, op. cit., p. 12.
26   See pp. 174–6 in Chapter 8, above.
27   Topkin, 'State Interventionism,' op. cit., p. 601.
28   For discussion of the first coffee valorization programs, which involved both export taxation and supply limitations, see Antônio Delfim Netto, *O Problema do Café no Brasil* (São Paulo: Faculadade de Ciências Econômicas e Administrativas, Universidade de São Paulo, 1959). Parts of that study have been translated and published in Carlos Manuel Peláez (ed.), *Essays on Coffee and Economic Development* (Rio de Janeiro: Instituto Brasileiro do Café, 1973), pp. 39–150.
29   Albert Fishlow's estimates of Brazilian industrial output and real GDP indicates a picture similar to that of Table 9.3 with respect both to the magnitude and the duration of the Great Depression in Brazil. His figures give the following annual percentage change for Brazilian GDP: 1930, −1.5 percent; 1931, −1.5 percent; 1932, +4.6 percent; and 1933, +8.8 percent. For industrial output, the figures are, respectively: −7.1 percent, +5.8 percent, +1.8 percent; +8.9 percent. These numbers were computed from the data in Albert Fishlow, 'Origins and Consequences of Import Substitution in Brazil,' in Luis Eugenio di Marco (ed.), *International Economics and Development* (New York: Academic Press, 1972), p. 357.
30   I first discussed this phenomenon in a paper entitled 'Long Term Brazilian Economic Development,' *The Journal of Economic History*, vol. 29 (September 1969), p. 485, n. 38.
31   The country's gold reserves rose 48 percent in 1928. This figure and many of the data cited later in the paragraph were computed from series presented in Neuhaus, *História Monetária*, op. cit., pp. 185, 181, and 192–4.
32   The following data (computed from Neuhaus, *História Monetária*, op. cit., p. 158) indicate the deceleration in the growth of Brazil's base money supply. The figures are quarterly percentage changes. They begin in the last quarter of 1927 and end in the last quarter of 1929: +12.2 percent; +8.8 percent; −1.2 percent; +0.9 percent; 1.3 percent; 1.1 percent; 0; 0; −0.8 percent.
33   For a detailed discussion of this episode, see Antônio Delfim Netto, *O Problema do Café*, op. cit., pp. 129–36.
34   For further information on the conditions which promoted Brazil's economic expansion during the thirties, see pp. 180–3 in Chapter 8, above. Considerable discussion has focused on the sources of expansionary government spending in Brazil during the 1930s. Celso Furtado, (*Formação Ecônomica do Brasil* [Rio de Janeiro: Fundo de Cultura, 1963], Chapter 31) emphasized the pump-priming

effects of government expenditures for coffee retention. Carlos M. Peláez, however, correctly noted that much of the expenditure on coffee retention was financed by taxes which constituted a leakage from the domestic expenditure stream. See his articles 'A Balança Commercial, A Grande Depressão, e A Industrialização Brasileira,' *Revista Brasileira de Economia*, vol. 22 (January 1968); and 'Acerca da Política Governmental, da Grande Depressão, e Industrialização no Brasil,' *Revista Brasileria de Economia* vol. 23 (July 1969). See also Fishlow, 'Origins and Consequences,' op. cit., pp. 327–30 for further discussion. Peláez has stressed instead the importance of government spending in 1932 for the São Paulo rebellion and for drought relief in the Northeast. In the present context, the essential point is that government was willing and able to increase its expenditures (for whatever purposes), and thus to expand aggregate demand in the Depression. A complete analysis of the economic consequences of government spending must of course take into account balanced-budget multiplier effects. These render invalid a simple use of the government budget deficit as an indicator of fiscal stimulus.

35 See the data in Neuhaus, *História Monetária*, op. cit., p. 180. For information on Brazil's autonomous policy orientation during the 1930s in areas other than macro-economic policy, see Stanley E. Hilton, 'Vargas and Brazilian Economic Development, 1930–1945: A Reappraisal of His Attitude Toward Industrialization and Planning,' *Journal of Economic History*, vol. 35 (December 1975).

36 See Chapter 8, Tables 8.1 and 8.6; and the discussion on pp. 166–71. Note further that, between 1914 and 1918, industrial output rose at an average annual rate of 4.6 percent, not an especially high figure for long-term industrial growth in Brazil during the 1860s.

37 See n. 3, above.

38 See pp. 181–2 in Chapter 8, above.

39 See, for example, the discussion in Villela and Suzigan, *Política do Governo*, op. cit., pp. 345–8.

40 Jonathan J. Pincus, 'Pressure Groups and The Pattern of Tariffs,' *Journal of Political Economy*, vol. 83 (August 1975); Nathaniel H. Leff 'Bureaucratic Corruption and Economic Development,' *American Behavioral Scientist*, vol. 8 (November 1964).

41 Villela and Suzigan, *Política do Governo*, op. cit., pp. 348–53.

42 Information on Brazil's industrial development during the years 1939–47 is presented in Mircea Buescu, 'A Segunda Guerra Mundiale e A Industrialização do Brasil,' pp. 165–76 in Carlos Manuel Peláez and Mircea Buescu (eds), *A Moderna História Econômica* (Rio de Janeiro: APEC, 1976).

43 See also pp. 99–100 in Leff, *Reassessing the Obstacles*, op. cit., Chapter 5.

44 See, for example, Steven Topkin, 'The Evolution of the Economic Role of the Brazilian State, 1889–1930,' *Journal of Latin American Studies*, vol. 11 (March 1979), p. 340.

45 Topkin, 'The Evolution,' op. cit., p. 340. See also the discussion on pp. 341–2 there.

46 See the data on general welfare effects, pp. 213–5, below. For another example of an implicit zero-sum game conceptualization, see p. 58 and n. 48 in Chapter 4, above.

47 On this case, see the discussion and data presented in Carlos F. Diaz-Alejandro, *Essays on The Economic History of The Argentine Republic* (New Haven: Yale University Press, 1970), Chapter 5.

48 R. H. Green and Steven Hymer, 'Cocoa in the Gold Coast,' *Journal of Economic History*, vol. 26 (September 1966).

49 See p. 171–6 in Chapter 8, above, Of course, foreign and domestic interests attempted to have Brazil's import duties reduced, and they sometimes met with limited success. The point is that *despite* those pressures, Brazil's tariffs were maintained at the high level and with the effects which we have noted.

50 See the extracts from the Brazilian Congressional debates which are cited by Nícia

Villela Luz, *A Luta pela Industrialização do Brasil* (São Paulo: Difusão Europeía do Livro, 1961). This point has also been noted by Flávio Versiani and Maria Teresa Versiani in their paper 'A Industrialização Brasileira antes do 1930: Uma Contribuição,' *Estudos Econômicos* (January 1975).

51 Leff, *Reassessing the Obstacles*, op. cit., Chapter 4.

52 A neglected study which is relevant in this context is O. Manoni's *Prospero and Caliban*, trans. by Pamela Powesland (New York: Praeger, 1964).

53 See pp. 166–7 in Chapter 8, above.

54 Norman Hicks and Paul Streeten, 'Indicators of Development: The Search for a Basic Needs Yardstick,' *World Development*, vol. 7 (May 1979).

55 The estimates presented here are from Eduardo E. Arriaga, *New Life Tables for Latin American Populations in the Nineteenth and Twentieth Centuries* (Berkeley: Institute of International Studies, 1968), p. 42. Using techniques different from Arriaga's, Giorgio Mortara estimated that life expectancy at birth in Brazil was 33.9 years in the period 1870–90, and rose to 43.7 years in 1940–50. See his paper, 'Estudos sobre a Utilização do Censo Demografico para a Reconstrução das Estatísticas do Movimento da População do Brasil,' *Revista Brasileira de Estatística* (January 1941). These figures, too, show a significant increase in Brazilian life expectancy over the period. Moreover, Mortara's estimates, may well under-estimate the rise. Apart from the technical difficulties noted by Arriaga, the rise which Mortara's estimates indicate over several decades seems small in view of the major public-health and economic progress achieved in Brazil between 1870–90 and 1950.

56 This figure was computed using the local currency estimate for Brazilian GDP in 1949, and adjusting backward to 1947 by means of the figures for GDP growth and increase in the GDP implicit price deflator between 1947 and 1949. The data utilized are from the Centro de Contas Nacionais of the Fundação Getúlio Vargas. The year 1949 was used as a basis because it is a benchmark year for which the Fundação in 1976 revised its earlier GDP estimate. The conversion from cruzeiros to a dollar figure was made using the 1947 official exchange rate of .0185 cruzeiros per dollar. That exchange rate is generally believed to have been overvalued. Hence the 196 dollar figure cited in the text may overstate the level of Brazilian per capita GDP in 1947.

57 The meaning and usefulness of such international income comparisons are beside the point here. Indeed, as suggested below, it might be much more sensible to compare the level of 1947 per capita income in Brazil with the levels which prevailed in the country at earlier points in time. However, measurements of a country's international income gap are in fact often made; and are taken as an indicator of the country's economic position.

58 The figure for the United States was computed from data in US Department of Commerce, *Long-Term Economic Growth*, op. cit., pp. 168, 200.

59 On the use of the urbanization ratio as an index of economic development levels, see Simon Kuznets, *Economic Growth of Nations* (Cambridge, Mass.: Harvard University Press, 1971), p. 21, n.

60 Nicholas Sanchez-Albornoz, *The Population of Latin America: A History* translated by W. A. R. Richardson (Berkeley and Los Angeles: University of California Press, 1974), pp. 178–9.

61 This was computed by trend regression from data in Haddad, *The Growth of Real Output*, op. cit., p. 17, Table 3.

62 J. Bhagwati and B. Hansen, 'Should Growth Rates be Evaluated at International Prices?' in J. Bhagwati and R. S. Eckaus (eds) *Planning and Development* (Cambridge, Mass.: MIT Press, 1973), Chapter 3.

63 One cannot conclude that if Brazil's real exchange rate had remained constant in the thirty-nine years between 1908 and 1947, domestic income growth in constant *mil-réis* prices would have raised Brazilian per capita income to a dollar level 2.3

times higher than the one actually observed in 1947. That would be a counterfactual which is internally inconsistent; for real exchange depreciation is more than a statistical quirk. Brazil's high rate of real depreciation reflected relative-price changes which were a central feature in the country's import-substituting pattern of development.

64 The phenomenon discussed in the text is also of wider relevance, both for Brazil and for some other developing countries, in later years. During the postwar period, Brazil (and other countries with an import-substituting development pattern) experienced real exchange-rate depreciation in magnitudes which were large relative to the growth of per capita income in constant local currency prices. Hence domestic income growth failed to narrow the international income gap. Data are presented in Leff, 'Modificaciones en los Tipos de Cambio Reales,' op. cit., pp. 494–5.

65 See, for example, Thomas B. Birnberg and Stephen A. Resnick, *Colonial Development: An Econometric Study* (New Haven: Yale University Press, 1975), pp. 48–50, 215–33.

66 As Hansen expressed it:

> How, then, can we distinguish colonial (exploitative) from noncolonial development? . . . The distinction must rest upon the economic policies pursued . . . an independent country could conceivably have pursued a dynamic optimum tariff policy, combining export taxation with public expenditure policy so as to make the best of a situation with a sloping foreign demand curve that was continuously moving rightwards under the impact of development in the metropolitan countries. A colonial power might, at the other extreme, force upon the country a tariff and public expenditure policy that maximized the gains for the power itself without regard to the consequences for the colony . . . The real test of whether development was colonial or not would then be . . . actual tariff and public expenditure policies . . .

These statements are from Hansen's 'Review' of Birnberg and Resnick's *Colonial Development* in *The Journal of Economic Literature*, vol. 14 (December 1976), pp. 1300–01.

10

Conclusions

A Review

This study has attempted to reconstruct and analyze the major features of the Brazilian economy and its development between 1822 and 1947. These 125 years span the interval from Brazil's declaration of formal political independence to the country's noted economic expansion of the post-Second World War period.

Brazil has achieved rapid economic development since approximately the beginning of the twentieth century. During the nineteenth century, however, the country experienced only a modest increase in per capita income. Part of Brazil's poor growth experience can be attributed to the special conditions of the large Northeast region. Still, our estimates suggest that even excluding the Northeast, Brazil achieved only a relatively small increase in per capita income during the nineteenth century. This long period of meager economic progress occurred at a time when the United States and the countries of Western Europe were experiencing rapid economic development. Consequently, the nineteenth century can be considered a period of economic retardation for Brazil.

The slow growth of per capita income in nineteenth-century Brazil stemmed from several related sources. Until the last decades of the century, the rate of capital accumulation was low. In principle, this may have reflected Brazil's cultural heritage – for example, social values that were heavily biased toward immediate consumption. In practice, the problem seems to have been low marginal productivity of capital. Further, the pace of technical progress in nineteenth-century Brazil was apparently also slow. Productivity growth was held down by the country's small stock of human capital, which raised the costs of developing and diffusing improved techniques. In addition, low incremental returns to capital reduced cash flow within individual enterprises, in conjunction with capital-market imperfections, lowered investment in embodied technological advance. Under these conditions, the growth of the country's labor force was high relative to the rate of capital formation and technical progress. Consequently, the increase of per capita output and of wages was small.

The planters' practice of importing unskilled labor from overseas –

first with slaves from Africa and later with subsidized immigration from Southern Europe – was also of central importance for the slow growth of wages. Direct importation of labor from abroad meant that Brazil's capitalists could in effect shift downward the supply curve of labor in response to their own growing demands for workers. This mechanism made the supply of labor endogenous to the economy's expansion path, and mitigated upward pressure on real wages. It reflected the planters' political influence in nineteenth-century Brazil, and the correlative measures which the government implemented in order to maintain an elastic supply of labor.[1]

Brazil's planters were understandably concerned to minimize their labor costs in a land-rich economy. Hence, it is not surprising that they adopted a monopsonistic approach which led to a lower level of wages than would otherwise have prevailed. The consequences of this class approach for the country as a whole, however, were unfortunate: both capital deepening and labor-saving technical progress were adversely affected. Most importantly, the elastic supply of low-cost labor from overseas permitted Brazil's advanced sector to expand its output and employment during the nineteenth century without large-scale absorption of labor from the country's domestic agricultural sector. Such a process would have entailed a higher initial level of wages and, eventually, an upward movement of real wages, both in the advanced and in the backward sectors of the economy. Because of political intervention, however, that sequence was not permitted to unfold. Instead, the Brazilian economy expanded under conditions which resembled 'unlimited supplies of labor', a feature which had important consequences both for the level and the trend of wages, as well as for the country's distribution of income.

Transportation costs were another key element in Brazil's economic retardation during the nineteenth century. Because of the country's geographical and topographical features, the costs of shipping commodities within the interior were relatively high. And it was a long time before human efforts did much to transform the unfavorable conditions which nature had provided. Unfortunately, transportation costs were of special importance for Brazil's economic development. With natural resources distributed unevenly across the country, economic distances within Brazil were large. Also, the country's factor endowment made for land-extensive cultivation and a high degree of disaggregation across space.

In this context, the absence of low-cost transportation facilities hampered Brazil's economic progress in a number of ways. First, high transportation costs lowered the elasticity with which incremental output was supplied in response to expanding demand. And as we saw in our discussion of Brazil's nineteenth-century inflation, price inelastic supply was especially important for domestically-produced foodstuffs. Inelastic supply of wage-goods, in turn, lowered marginal returns to capital, and hence the rate of investment and expansion in the advanced sector. Further, high-cost transportation was a problem of special severity for development in Brazil's domestic agricultural sector. The goods produced in this large sector generally had a low ratio of value to weight. Consequently, heavy freight charges had a disproportionately large impact in lowering the net prices which producers of these goods received for their output. With upward-sloping supply curves, lower prices led to reduced output levels in the sector. And the adverse relative prices which producers faced diminished their incentives for greater participation in Brazil's market economy. Thus income in the domestic agricultural sector suffered both because of quantity effects and because of price effects.

Partly because of these conditions which impeded development in the domestic agricultural sector, exports were the principal avenue to a higher value of per capita output in Brazil during the nineteenth century. The international economy offered growing markets and favorable terms of trade for many commodities which could be produced with Brazil's factor endowment. The country's producers responded to these opportunities both by expanding output of traditional export commodities and by initiating production of new ones. In aggregate terms, the country's exports increased notably in the nineteenth century. Growing exports also promoted other changes of far-reaching importance, for example, the provision of social overhead capital. Nevertheless, export growth did not serve as an engine for generalized economic development in nineteenth-century Brazil.

First, the elastic supply of low-cost labor from abroad dampened the stimulus from expanding exports to domestic development. Further, Brazil's export sector was too small during most of the century to exert much leverage on growth in the economy as a whole.[2] Moreover, the rate of aggregate export growth was itself smaller than might have been imagined. Between 1822 and 1913, the value of Brazil's exports in constant sterling prices rose at an annual trend rate of 4 percent. In per capita terms however, the rate was only 2.2 percent. This was hardly a sufficient stimulus for trade to serve as an engine for generalized development. There were also major disparities in the pace of export growth by commodity and by region; and these, too, precluded a country-wide pattern of export-based development. In particular, exports of sugar and of cotton, which were grown mainly in the Northeast, did poorly as compared with coffee, which was produced in the Southeast. Because of the Northeast's large share in Brazil's total population during the nineteenth century, the region's unhappy experience with respect to exports lowered the pace of the country's overall economic development.

By contrast, the Southeast of Brazil, which had more buoyant export growth, also experienced a greater degree of economic development during the nineteenth century. As noted, the expansion of international trade facilitated the supply of economic infrastructure in the region. In addition, the growth in income based on exports helped provide a domestic market for industrial development. After 1850, a textile industry emerged in Brazil whose output grew at high long-term rates in the fifty years before 1913. There is also evidence of similar growth in some other industries during this period. This early industrial development was concentrated in Brazil's Southeast.

A major problem for large-scale industrialization in nineteenth-century Brazil, however, was the small size of the domestic market for manufactures relative to total expenditure within the economy. Per capita incomes were low, and the market was further limited by the country's high internal transportation costs. Under these conditions, the government's policy of granting local manufacturers tariff protection could enhance the domestic industry's competitive position *vis-à-vis* imports. But protection *per se* could do little to increase the total volume of purchasing power spent on industrial products in an economy where most income was spent on food and services. And by raising still further the relative price of manufactures, tariffs did not bring these products closer to the reach of a predominantly poor and rural population.

Most discussions of Brazil's economy in the nineteenth century have focused on delayed industrialization, and/or on the possible deficiencies of international trade as a source of economic development. But as we have seen, the main reason for Brazil's slow overall economic development in the nineteenth century lay elsewhere: in the country's domestic agricultural sector.[3] A large portion of the country's labor force was engaged in this sector. Low income and inelastic supply in this sector also constrained the pace of development in the rest of the economy. As noted earlier, the growth of output (and income) in Brazil's domestic agricultural sector were seriously hampered by deficient natural transportation facilities. Moreover, even in the more densely settled parts of the country, investment in waterway development or in road construction was not adequate to make low-cost transportation widely available. Under these conditions of poor internal communications, the timing and the scope of railroad construction were of special significance for Brazil's economic development. This is because the alternative transportation modes which affected the net social savings due to railroads were shipments by mule over primitive roads, or in small boats over underdeveloped and non-connecting waterways.

Despite its crucial importance for the country's development, large-scale railway construction lagged seriously in nineteenth-century Brazil. Private returns did not reflect the external economies which the railways provided for the country's broader economic development. And the capacity of Brazil's government to augment private returns through a broad subsidy program (or to implement a large public-investment effort) was very limited. The problem here was mainly in Brazil's public finances. Through most of the period, the state's fiscal resources were insufficient to sustain a large development effort.[4]

The government's principal tax and borrowing base was the external sector. But throughout most of the nineteenth century, this sector was too small to provide abundant revenues. In addition, the central government's allocation patterns reflected the budget priorities and constitutional structure of a regime that was concerned to avoid political and territorial fragmentation. Thus spending for integrative purposes took precedence over expenditure for economic infrastructure. And the tax revenues of the total public sector – comprising the provincial and local governments as well as the central government – were limited by a fiscal system which was highly centralized. It was not until the end of the century that the growth of the external sector and shifts within Brazil's political system led to a large increase in the scale of government spending for social-overhead capital. Foreign investment for railroad construction in Brazil also accelerated at this time. As a result of these changes, the country's railway trackage increased sharply. This shift came, however, only in the last decades of the nineteenth century.

With the advent of lower-cost transportation, a more generalized pattern of economic development began, at least in the Southeast. The railroads were built piecemeal, and largely to satisfy existing markets. Nevertheless, they had profound consequences for the country's economic development. Piecemeal expansion cumulated to large-scale effects in terms of total trackage and the total geographical area which the railroads served. And consistent with our earlier discussion concerning the economic advantages which attended a reduction in freight costs, new and unexpected sources of internal trade emerged. Thus railways which had been built with the primary objective of transporting export staples to the ports came to carry large volumes of goods produced in the domestic sector of the economy.

Producers in the domestic agricultural sector responded to the new markets and to the favorable movement in relative prices which low-cost transportation made possible. Because of this sector's large weight within the Brazilian economy, even a small rise in its rate of output growth had a large impact on the pace of aggregate income expansion. Extension of the railways also had far-reaching effects on the structure of the economy and its development possibilities. Rising income in agriculture enlarged the market for industrial products. At the same time, the fall in internal transportation costs led to import substitution in food. These developments amplified the domestic linkage effects of export and industrial expansion. Thus increased availability of low-cost transportation had multiple consequences for the country's development: greater income in Brazilian agriculture, higher domestic supply elasticities, and intensified intersectoral linkages between domestic agriculture, export production, and manufacturing. All of these effects followed from the drop in internal freight costs. Toward the turn of the nineteenth century, the Brazilian economy shifted to a markedly higher rate of long-term growth. The extension of the railroads seems to have been a key factor in that shift.

Following the onset of a more general pattern of economic development, output per capita in Brazil rose steadily. Furthermore, the pace of per capita output growth in Brazil during the first half of the twentieth century seems to have been relatively high in terms of international comparisons. Sustained economic expansion at a rapid pace from the first decade of the century also brought important structural changes to the Brazilian economy. In particular, industrial output rose at especially high rates; and as a result, manufacturing industry became a major sector within the Brazilian economy. This change, however, was necessarily built upon a long period of earlier industrial development.

Brazil's early industrialization was generally supported by government protection against imports. The supply of factors for industrial development seems to have been relatively elastic; and the pace of industrialization was governed mainly by the growth of the internal market. The latter depended on two conditions: the expansion of aggregate demand and domestic import substitution. Local industry had achieved considerable replacement of overseas supply as early as 1919. Nevertheless, import substitution was to continue as an important source of demand in subsequent decades, particularly in new product lines. Aggregate demand usually rose at a rapid pace, a consequence of Brazil's expansionary monetary policies. And in the first half of the twentieth century, Brazilian agricultural supply was relatively elastic. Hence, expanding aggregate demand was not simply dissipated in food price inflation. As a result of buoyant demand and elastic domestic supply conditions, output in Brazilian industry rose at a trend rate of approximately 5.9 percent per annum between 1900 and 1947.

Brazil's development during this period also took place within a context of substantial national independence, both in economic policy-making and in economic structure. Industrial development had been proceeding rapidly prior both to the Depression and to the First World War. Neither for its inception nor for its subsequent progress did Brazilian industrialization require a separation from the world economy. Brazil's economy also displayed its autonomy in its capacity to maintain development despite such 'external shocks'. This capacity reflected features which have not always been noted. For example, the accelerated industrialization of the 1930s stemmed in part from such internal developments as a large expansion in the country's road network, major changes in the financial sector, and a decadal doubling in the rate of growth of domestic agricultural output. As this experience indicates, the pace of industrial development in Brazil depended on much more than the level of protection and conditions in the country's foreign trade sector.

Brazil's economic policy-making in the half-century before 1947 also showed considerable autonomy from outside pressures. The country's monetary, fiscal, and exchange-rate policies rarely followed the doctrines which emanated from the political (and intellectual) centers of the international economy.[5] The pace of monetary expansion, a key macroeconomic variable, was determined in response to internal rather than external conditions. In fact, Brazil's policy-makers pursued autonomous expansionary policies to the point that the country experienced significant depreciation in its real parity during the first half of the twentieth century. Similarly, Brazil's protective tariffs and the valorization programs which were devised in an effort to raise international coffee prices also show an activist and interventionist approach. As the implementation of these policies indicates, imperialist political and doctrinal pressures did not dominate economic policy-making in Brazil during the pre-Second World War decades. Some similarities are even apparent between the macroeconomic policy measures adopted and the pattern of Brazilian economic policy-making in the period following the Second World War. Indeed, in some respects, the continuities go back to the nineteenth century.[6]

Some General Implications

Brazil's economic history between 1822 and 1947 also has some broader analytical implications. Because studies of long-term economic backwardness and development have been relatively uncommon, the opportunities for feedback from empirical reality to *a priori* theories of economic development have also been rare. In many instances, this case conforms neatly to familiar ideas concerning economic development; in other ways, Brazil's historical experience suggests complementary perspectives.

Brazil's experience clearly provides support for views which stress the importance for economic development of progress in a country's domestic agricultural sector. Slow productivity growth in that sector impeded aggregate income increase in Brazil. Limited domestic purchasing power also constrained the emergence of a large industrial sector. Further, inelastic supply conditions in the domestic agricultural sector helped impart an inflationary bias to the Brazilian economy. And coming in conjunction with more rapid growth in the export activities, poor conditions in the domestic agricultural sector contributed to the persistence of a dualistic economic pattern in Brazil. In a comparative perspective, the Brazilian experience suggests how relatively unimportant was abundant land *per se* – as distinct from low transport costs, favorable institutional conditions, and technical progress – for the economic development of the United States.

Similarly, the inception and progress of industrial development in Brazil fits a pattern suggested by Ragnar Nurkse.[7] As he emphasized, once the size of the domestic market for manufactures expands in a less-developed country and provides effective incentives for production, the supply of capital and of other factors to the industrial sector can be highly elastic. Brazil's experience confirms this stress on the illusory nature of many potential problems on the supply side (e.g. 'vicious circles') as a barrier to industrialization, and thus suggests the possibility of rapid industrial growth in less-developed countries. This historical case also supports some theoretical ideas advanced by Albert Hirschman.[8] The intensification of forward and backward linkages which followed railway expansion in the Southeast seems to have stimulated further decision-taking for development. Not only did the new market opportunities spur individual producers to expand output and investment in their particular activities, but in political terms, government promotional efforts for the Southeast were also facilitated. This is because the benefits of developmental policies now spilled over within the entire block of interdependent activities within the Southeast. These input–output linkages helped mitigate in Brazil the conflict between export, agricultural, and manufacturing interests which have wracked countries like the United States or Argentina in the course of their industrialization.[9]

As just indicated, it is helpful to view the industrialization process within its broader intersectoral relations. In that perspective, Brazil's experience also suggests optimism concerning the possibilities for rapid industrial development. For example, one usually assumes that the expansion of an economy's various sectors necessarily involves tradeoffs, such that higher growth in one sector (e.g. exports) entails lower growth in another (e.g. domestic manufacturing). In technical terms, the economy-wide transformation curve is assumed to be concave to the origin. Our study of Brazil's experience suggests an alternative possibility. As we have seen, one sector may provide external economies to the other. Also, because of factor-market imperfections, the different sectors may draw on different input supplies. Under such conditions, one sector's expansion is not at the expense of the other's. In effect, the transformation curve is convex to the origin in the relevant range. This situation, which has analytical and welfare implications very different from some textbook treatments of industrialization, has not received sufficient attention in the development literature.[10]

Brazil's experience also suggests other ways in which some two-sector models are less than completely helpful for understanding historical cases of economic backwardness and development. First, Brazil's expansion took place in the context of an economy that was open both to factor movements and to trade in commodities.[11] Consequently, the closed-economy models common in the literature are not as useful as one might expect. Also, in Brazil, unimproved land was initially the surplus factor of production. The dynamics of economic change under those conditions have not been a major topic in the theoretical literature.[12]

Paradoxically, the political and economic responses which a land-surplus model generated in the context of an open economy transformed nineteenth-century Brazil into an economy that was characterized by a highly elastic supply of labor. For this reason, one of the mainstays of development theory turns out to be very helpful for understanding Brazil's historical experience. I refer to W. Arthur Lewis's model of 'economic development with unlimited supplies of labor'.[13] Some special conditions, however, affected the operation of the Lewis model in the Brazilian context. As noted, many of the workers who provided the supply of labor to Brazil's advanced sector came from overseas. Supply and demand conditions in the international labor market of the nineteenth century were such that a relatively large number of such imported workers was available to Brazil. These workers added to a labor force which was in any case growing rapidly due to high rates of natural demographic increase. Under these conditions, the overall supply of labor was highly elastic in Brazil throughout the nineteenth century. As a result, the country's advanced sector could expand without a large-scale process of drawing labor from the country's backward sector, eventually creating a situation of rising real wages. Thus in this open dual economy, growth of the modern sector did little to transform the country's large backward sector by altering factor proportions and choice of technique. Indeed, because of Brazil's high rates of natural demographic increase, growth of the advanced sector probably did not reduce the absolute size of the backward sector very much, for the latter was maintained by large incremental flows of populations.

Further, by the time mass importation of workers to Brazil was stopped, the country's rate of natural demographic increase had risen sharply. The pace of labor importation to Brazil slackened in the 1920s and 1930s. But the acceleration of natural increase led to a situation in which the country's overall rate of population and labor-force growth increased. Thus Brazil's population expanded at an annual rate of 2.1

percent per annum between 1920 and 1940 (and 2.4 percent per annum between 1940 and 1950); this compared with the 1.8 percent long-term rate of demographic increase in Brazil during the nineteenth century.[14] Under these conditions, a highly elastic supply of labor continued in Brazil for much longer than might have been expected in the original formulation of the Lewis model. The situation in this empirical instance may be compared with efforts at emptying a basin – the size of the population in the backward sector – which is constantly being replenished. Consequently, between 1822 and 1947 there is no evidence of a Lewis 'turning point', after which labor became scarce, with ensuing shifts in real wages and income distribution. And for the same reason a more generalized pattern of economic development could begin in Brazil only when the value of output per person in the backward sector itself began to rise.

That eventually occurred in Brazil, toward the end of the nineteenth century. The historical process in this instance followed some lines of a development model suggested by an earlier theorist, Adam Smith. Growth in the size of the market opened new sources of demand, as well as the gains from internal specialization.[15] The enlargement of the domestic market was made possible, as we have seen, by railroad construction and the ensuing fall in intraregional transportation costs. However, the long delay before this process acquired significant momentum indicates that rapid economic development did not occur in Brazil through the operation of automatic market forces. As prominent theorists have stressed, the external economies generated by socioeconomic infrastructure can be central to the development process.[16] But under such conditions of a divergence between private and social returns, the market mechanism does not provide a socially optimal allocation of resources. For this reason, optimizing public-finance activity and government intervention were necessary for development to proceed rapidly. In this respect, too, Brazil's experience accords with familiar economic theory.

Looking Back on this Historical Experience

Concluding a study which considers 125 years of Brazilian history, one may wonder about the welfare consequences of the economic processes we have discussed. Brazil's economic expansion during the first half of the twentieth century led to a major long-term increase in per capita income. Further, some of the fruits of this economic growth were distributed to people beyond the country's upper classes. Life expectancy – an index of general health conditions – rose in Brazil during this period. Primary school enrollments also increased significantly, indicating that a much larger portion of the population was gaining access to literacy. There was also important progress in terms of structural change and diversification within the Brazilian economy.

Brazil began its modern economic development, however, from low absolute levels of socioeconomic welfare. Consequently, large percentage increases in indices of socioeconomic development did not translate into large absolute gains. Thus Brazil's initial conditions with respect to productivity and the distribution of income at the onset of more rapid development had important consequences for welfare in the country several decades later. Moreover, substantial economic growth in the first half of the twentieth century had little impact on the level of Brazilian per capita income as measured in dollars. This was because of the special measurement effect involved in real exchange-rate depreciation.[17] Because of this phenomenon, the rate of growth of Brazilian per capita income in constant dollar prices was much lower than the rate as measured in constant local currency prices. And for the same reason, economic growth in Brazil was not reflected in a narrowing of the income gap which separated Brazil from the economically more advanced countries.

Further, it would be naive to expect that continuing economic development in some sense solved Brazil's economic and social problems. The benefits and costs of economic change were not shared equally between persons, classes, or regions within the country. Moreover, economic progress often brought with it new tensions between 'winners' and 'losers' in the development process, both at the individual and at the national levels.[18] In addition, expectations may well have risen as a function of achievements, and thus opened a new aspirations gap.[19] Also, structural economic change created new problems which had to be confronted if the country was to proceed with further economic progress. Finally, as many observers have noted, rapid economic development often acts as a destabilizing force which loosens earlier social and political ties, and engenders new sources of resentment and alienation.[20] The conflict and tensions prevalent in Brazilian society after 1947 indicate that Brazil was no exception to this general pattern. However, if we view development as a process rather than as a completed state, twentieth-century Brazil had clearly begun sustained development. The country's opportunities, problems, and capabilities were different at the end of this period than at its beginning. And to the extent that the new problems were less severe, and/or the capacity to cope with them had grown, then Brazil had also achieved a measure of economic progress in the twentieth century.

If we attempt to assess the welfare effects of the economic changes which took place in Brazil during the nineteenth century, the picture is more somber. In aggregate terms, the Brazilian economy expanded notably between 1822 and 1900. Structural shifts such as enlargement of the monetized economy and the internal market network also took place. In addition, outside of the Northeast, the value of output per capita probably increased somewhat. However, there were large disparities in the way the increases in productivity were distributed. As noted, Brazil had a highly elastic supply of labor, both in the advanced and in the backward sectors of the economy. Under these conditions, the increment in productivity went mainly to the owners of capital and improved land. And for this reason, most of the country's population experienced little improvement in their material welfare over the century.

This assessment must be qualified in some respects. At the beginning of the period, slaves had constituted some 30 percent of the country's population. Then slavery declined, and was ultimately abolished in Brazil during the nineteenth century. Consequently, if only on non-economic grounds, the level of human well-being was undoubtedly higher in Brazil at the end of the period, without slavery and its special inhumanities.[21] Further, the nineteenth century also saw the emergence of new activities and the spread of low-cost transportation in Brazil. Economic diversification and the opening of new opportunities for individual advancement may also be counted as positive gains. Moreover, one must be clear about the situation with which one is comparing the country at the end of the nineteenth century. Even for much of the free population, Brazil in 1822 had been no economic idyll with respect either to the level of per capita income or to equality in its distribution.

Viewed in very narrow terms, however, perhaps the most that can be said for the nineteenth century as a period in Brazil's economic history is that it helped lay the basis for the country's subsequent economic progress. Moreover, in considering this overall experience, it is impressive to note how meager was the progress achieved relative to the time elapsed. This conclusion persists even if we restrict our view to the post-1900 decades, when the pace of economic expansion was much more rapid than it had been in the nineteenth century. It was very long before development led to perceptible economic gains in Brazil, for elapsed time was an important element in the process. Partly for this reason, it would be easy to end this study with a sense of sadness over the missed opportunities in Brazil during the nineteenth century.

An opportunity cannot be missed, however, unless it was in fact attainable. Consequently, we are led to a basic question: *could* Brazil's long-term economic course have been very different from the path that was actually followed? One can readily imagine alternative scenarios which would have led to higher rates of development in nineteenth-century Brazil. One alternative would have involved an expansion pattern based on rising productivity within the domestic sector rather than the orientation toward exports and the international economy.

One can also imagine ways in which nineteenth-century Brazil's development might have been happier even within the framework of export-led growth. For example, if Brazilian governments had invested earlier and on a larger scale in social overhead capital and 'public improvements' (as in the United States), or if Brazil had restricted the inflow of overseas labor (as occurred in Australia), the pattern of the country's economic development might have been very different.

The preceding chapters suggest that these alternative scenarios were not, in fact, historically available for nineteenth-century Brazil. Thus in a country where a central thrust of government policy was to increase the supply of workers from overseas, it is idle fantasy to speculate on a development pattern based on restricting the importation of labor. Similarly, in view of the pattern of returns that were available in the nineteenth century (not least, to the government itself, in terms of tax revenues), it is not surprising that the country's expansion path inclined towards export growth. And in the context of Brazil's economic and political conditions, it would not be realistic to have expected public-investment programs with a scale and timing very different from what in fact occurred.[22] By the same token, with Brazil's low level of social overhead capital and modest rate of technical progress, it seems unlikely that an alternative pattern of development based on the economy's domestic sector would have been feasible.

One objective of historical research is to elucidate the limits of what was possible. Such analysis can clarify the extent to which events followed the course they did not because of accidents and random factors, but rather because of initial conditions and their intrinsic logic over time. As such, the study of history can spare later observers dispiriting reflections which have no basis in possibility. Brazil's economic history during the nineteenth century seems to have been a relatively extreme case in this genre. The pattern of economic change appears to have been very much governed by existing structural parameters, with little scope for an alternative course.

Concluding Comments: A Research Perspective

This study has focused attention on features of Brazil's historical economy concerning which most observers have always been aware. Thus it is no novelty to mention the importance of the railroads, of the domestic agricultural sector, and of the elastic supply of low-cost labor from abroad. Nevertheless, these subjects receive relatively little discussion in most works on Brazil's economic history. By focusing on these features, this book has sought to give a more balanced view of Brazil's underdevelopment and development than is possible in studies which are aware of these features, but fail to appreciate their strategic importance. Also, by devoting more attention to these phenomena, we have been able to discern elements of their causes and consequences which may not always have been well understood.

On some subjects, this study has offered new perspectives on Brazil's economic history. For example, our analysis of the country's income growth in the nineteenth century disclosed a new picture concerning the likely magnitude of the country's economic progress in these decades, and the timing with which Brazil began its modern economic growth. Similarly, the discussion in Chapter 5 suggested a fresh perspective on why international trade failed to promote generalized economic development in Brazil during this period. But although some analytical progress may have been made, much remains to be learned about long-term economic development in Brazil. One by-product of this study, in fact, is a number of suggestions for directions which future research in this area might take. These suggestions relate both to a general perspective in research on Brazilian economic history, and to some questions which follow from the present study.

For example, why did Brazil's governments not provide low-cost transportation facilities within the interior earlier in the century? More generally, to what extent did the political system act to promote (or retard) Brazil's economic development. In a similar vein, what role did sociocultural conditions play in the country's poor economic experience during the nineteenth century? And what effects did international imperialism have in delaying or distorting nineteenth-century Brazil's economic progress? These particular questions are addressed in the companion volume to this study.[23] They involve what are in many ways the most fundamental issues for research on the economic history of Brazil – and indeed for the study of economic underdevelopment in general. But before we could discuss those questions (in this specific historical context), it was necessary to clarify the more immediate conditions of Brazil's economic structure and dynamics between 1822 and 1947. That was the task of the present volume.

In its broader implications, this study suggests the importance of achieving a balanced view on a basic issue in Brazilian economic historiography: the relative significance of the external sector and of the domestic sector in the country's economic past. Both overall perspective and an improved understanding of specific topics are involved here. For example, we have seen that Brazil's long-term inflation in the nineteenth century had its roots in the domestic political economy rather than in pressures which originated in the external sector. Thus the secular rise in Brazilian prices during the period cannot be attributed factually to an adverse trend in the external terms of trade. By contrast, inelastic domestic supply conditions and the growth of the domestic money supply are directly pertinent. Similarly, if we want to understand why Brazil experienced relatively little economic development during most of the nineteenth century, the answers are to be found mainly in the conditions of the domestic sector. The same is true when we seek an explanation of Brazil's transition to sustained development toward the turn of the century. Moreover, to the degree that the external sector did affect the country's economic development in both of these periods, it was in a positive manner.

As this discussion suggests, the time may now have come for an 'inward-looking' strategy in research on Brazil's economic past. Such a strategy would give higher priority to research on topics related to Brazil's domestic sector rather than continuing to emphasize activities related to foreign trade. The need for a helpful analytical perspective is all the greater because, as already mentioned, many topics in Brazil's economic history remain to be elucidated. Moreover, some of the subjects on which least is now known relate to the country's domestic sector.[24] Also, because of its different perspective on some points, this study has itself raised some new questions. If these are questions which are useful for future research, if new insights have been provided, and if some misperceptions have been cleared away, then this study will have helped achieve some progress in understanding both economic development and Brazil's economic history.

Notes

1 See Chapter 4, above.
2 On the points which follow in this paragraph, see pp. 90–1, in Chapter 5.
3 For the material on the railroads, the domestic agricultural sector, and Brazilian economic development which these paragraphs summarize, see pp. 144–53 in Chapter 7, above.
4 On the points which follow, see Chapter 5 of Nathaniel H. Leff, *Underdevelopment and Development in Brazil, Vol. II: Reassessing the Obstacles to Economic Development* (Allen & Unwin, London, 1982).
5 On these points, see Chapter 9, above.
6 Concerning the extent of political and doctrinal autonomy in Brazilian policy-making during the nineteenth century, see Chapter 4 of Leff, *Reassessing the Obstacles,* op. cit.
7 Ragnar Nurkse, 'The Size of the Market and the Inducement to Investment,' in *Problems of Capital Formation in Underdeveloped Countries* (New York: Oxford University Press, 1961), pp. 4–20.
8 Albert O. Hirschman, *The Strategy of Economic Development* (New Haven: Yale University Press, 1958), Chapters 5–8.
9 Other perspectives on this political transition in Brazil are presented in Nathaniel H. Leff, in *Economic Policy-Making and Development in Brazil* (New York: Wiley, 1968), pp. 27–9.
10 See, however, Harry G. Johnson, 'Factor Market Distortions and the Shape of the Transformation Curve,' *Econometrica*, vol. 34 (July 1966).
11 See pp. 88–9 in Chapter 5, above.
12 For some of the rare efforts, see Gerald K. Helleiner, 'Typology in Development Theory: The Land Surplus Economy (Nigeria),' *Food Research Institute Studies*, vol. 6 (1966); Evsey Domar, 'The Causes of Slavery or Serfdom: A Hypothesis,'

Journal of Economic History, vol. 30 (March 1970); Daniel Kazmer, 'The Agricultural Development of Siberia, 1890–1917,' (PhD dissertation, MIT, 1973); and Bent A. Hansen, 'Colonial Economic Development with Unlimited Supply of Land,' *Economic Development and Cultural Change*, vol. 27 (July 1979).

13 W. A. Lewis, 'Economic Development with Unlimited Supplies of Labour,' *The Manchester School*, vol. 22 (May 1954). On the application of this model in the special circumstances of nineteenth-century Brazil, see Chapter 4, above.

14 Ministério de Planejamento, *Demografia* (Rio de Janeiro, 1966), p. 39.

15 Adam Smith, *The Wealth of Nations* (orig. publ. 1776), edited by E. Canaan (New York, 1937), Book I, Chapter 3.

16 Paul N. Rosenstein-Rodan, 'Problems of Industrialisation of East and South-eastern Europe,' *Economic Journal*, vol. 53 (June 1943).

17 See pp. 214–5 in Chapter 9, above.

18 This statement does not imply a simplistic picture of grievance and political action in the development process. One of the most serious armed contests in Brazil during the first half of the twentieth century was initiated by a major 'winner' in the development process. I refer to the 1932 rebellion of São Paulo State in an effort at secession and independence. The state's elite resented the role of (as they perceived it) the 'locomotive' which pulls forward a long train of empty box-cars, the rest of Brazil.

19 For an analysis of a constant (or increasing) frustration gap in the development process, see Richard S. Weckstein, 'Welfare Criteria and Changing Tastes,' *American Economic Review*, vol. 52 (March 1962).

20 See, for example, Mancur Olson, Jr., 'Rapid Growth as a Destabilizing Force,' *Journal of Economic History*, vol. 23 (December 1963), pp. 529–53.

21 See pp. 57–8 in Chapter 4, above.

22 This last conclusion draws on data and analysis which are presented in Leff, *Reassessing the Obstacles*, op. cit., Chapter 5.

23 Leff, *Reassessing the Obstacles*, op. cit.

24 For example, it would be helpful to know much more about such topics as demographic structure and change and about the various sub-sectors within the domestic agricultural sector in nineteenth-century Brazil. Some of this information has already been collected – by anthropologists, geographers, rural sociologists, and other social scientists – but has not yet been adequately utilized by economic historians.

Statistical Appendix

Table 1 *The Population of Brazil, 1822–1913* (in thousands)

Year	Population	Year	Population	Year	Population
1822	4,651	1853	7,570	1884	12,673
1823	4,730	1854	7,686	1885	12,916
1824	4,812	1855	7,803	1886	13,163
1825	4,894	1856	7,923	1887	13,414
1826	4,977	1857	8,044	1888	13,671
1827	5,062	1858	8,167	1889	13,932
1828	5,148	1859	8,291	1890	14,199
1829	5,252	1860	8,418	1891	14,528
1830	5,343	1861	8,547	1892	14,857
1831	5,425	1862	8,678	1893	15,216
1832	5,508	1863	8,810	1894	15,853
1833	5,592	1864	8,945	1895	15,960
1834	5,677	1865	9,082	1896	16,346
1835	5,763	1866	9,221	1897	16,741
1836	5,852	1867	9,362	1898	17,145
1837	5,941	1868	9,505	1899	17,560
1838	6,032	1869	9,650	1900	17,984
1839	6,124	1870	9,797	1901	18,392
1840	6,218	1871	9,947	1902	18,782
1841	6,313	1872	10,099	1903	19,180
1842	6,400	1873	10,289	1904	19,857
1843	6,507	1874	10,486	1905	20,003
1844	6,606	1875	10,687	1906	20,427
1845	6,707	1876	10,891	1907	20,860
1846	6,809	1877	11,099	1908	21,303
1847	6,912	1878	11,311	1909	21,754
1848	7,018	1879	11,528	1910	22,216
1849	7,125	1880	11,748	1911	22,687
1850	7,234	1881	11,973	1912	23,618
1851	7,344	1882	12,202	1913	23,660
1852	7,456	1883	12,435		

Note: National Censuses were taken in 1872, 1890, and 1920. Estimates of Brazil's population in earlier years are available for 1819, 1830, and 1854. These bench mark figures are available in *A Economia Brasileira e Suas Perspectivas* (Rio de Janeiro: APEC, 1962), p. 4. The annual figures were derived by logarithmic interpolation between these benchmark years.

Table 2 The Brazilian Currency Stock, Current Prices, 1822–1913 (in thousands of mil-réis)

Year	Value	Year	Value	Year	Value	Year	Value
1822	10.2	1845	52.0	1868	158.9	1891	474.0
1823	11.0	1846	52.6	1869	193.2	1892	532.0
1824	12.4	1847	51.3	1870	194.6	1893	599.3
1825	12.9	1848	50.3	1871	194.4	1894	661.6
1826	14.4	1849	49.7	1872	186.2	1895	649.0
1827	22.6	1850	49.0	1873	183.5	1896	684.2
1828	22.4	1851	46.6	1874	182.1	1897	734.0
1829	21.5	1852	49.2	1875	178.6	1898	749.0
1830	21.4	1853	51.9	1876	175.8	1899	711.5
1831	26.8	1854	60.8	1877	181.1	1900	681.6
1832	30.7	1855	65.7	1878	201.4	1901	655.0
1833	31.1	1856	77.2	1879	208.7	1902	635.7
1834	31.7	1857	86.4	1880	206.4	1903	631.3
1835	31.7	1858	84.4	1881	206.7	1904	613.3
1836	34.6	1859	85.8	1882	207.2	1905	612.1
1837	37.5	1860	76.3	1883	205.4	1906	681.0
1838	40.5	1861	65.3	1884	203.3	1907	695.9
1839	40.7	1862	67.2	1885	206.3	1908	667.5
1840	41.1	1863	71.3	1886	200.3	1909	781.5
1841	41.5	1864	90.9	1887	201.3	1910	872.7
1842	45.0	1865	109.2	1888	195.7	1911	915.9
1843	47.8	1866	121.3	1889	210.2	1912	958.4
1844	49.6	1867	131.6	1890	323.7	1913	885.4

Note: This series is based almost exclusively on the country's stock of paper currency. The data used are from Carlos Manuel Peláez and Wilson Suzigan, História Monetária do Brasil (São Paulo, 1976), Table A.1. Although some metallic currency had been minted in Brazil before the beginning of the period, gold and silver money had generally left the country to settle international accounts. I have therefore included in the initial currency stock only the small sums of pre-1822 copper and bronze mintings, which are believed to have remained in circulation. This inclusion may explain some of the discrepancy between the currency stock and the monetary series (Table 3, below), which is also from Peláez and Suzigan. Data on copper and bronze coinage were taken from Instituto Brasileira de Geografia e Estatística, Anuário Estatístico, 1939/40 (Rio de Janeiro, 1941), p. 1354. This source is henceforth referred to as Anuário Estatístico.

Table 3 *The Brazilian Money Stock, M₁, Current Prices, 1839–1913 (in thousands of* mil-réis)

Year	Value	Year	Value	Year	Value	Year	Value
1839	39.4	1858	96.7	1877	222.3	1896	820.4
1840	40.0	1859	96.9	1878	249.2	1897	885.1
1841	40.6	1860	90.7	1879	264.1	1898	913.1
1842	44.3	1861	82.0	1880	260.4	1899	869.8
1843	47.0	1862	88.2	1881	258.9	1900	733.7
1844	48.7	1863	93.5	1882	254.2	1901	677.8
1845	51.1	1864	110.8	1883	245.6	1902	686.1
1846	51.1	1865	128.1	1884	257.2	1903	683.8
1847	50.1	1866	136.1	1885	262.4	1904	725.0
1848	51.2	1867	149.7	1886	246.0	1905	726.2
1849	49.0	1868	182.3	1887	247.3	1906	777.7
1850	48.6	1869	218.1	1888	253.2	1907	855.9
1851	45.0	1870	219.5	1889	270.4	1908	863.8
1852	48.3	1871	228.3	1890	538.7	1909	960.5
1853	51.0	1872	226.0	1891	811.4	1910	1092.4
1854	63.1	1873	224.9	1892	720.1	1911	1228.1
1855	72.0	1874	221.5	1893	733.4	1912	1272.8
1856	82.6	1875	207.2	1894	785.3	1913	1150.6
1857	95.3	1876	215.1	1895	801.7		

Source: Carlos Manuel Peláez and Wilson Suzigan, *História Monetária do Brasil* (São Paulo, 1976), Table A.3.

Table 4   *Purchasing-Power-Parity Price Index for Brazil, 1822–1913*
(1842=100)

Year	Value	Year	Value	Year	Value	Year	Value
1822	56.9	1845	103.8	1868	162.0	1891	138.7
1823	56.3	1846	97.3	1869	137.2	1892	164.0
1824	61.0	1847	99.1	1870	119.6	1893	170.8
1825	61.3	1848	96.2	1871	115.0	1894	176.2
1826	58.5	1849	88.0	1872	123.1	1895	175.6
1827	79.6	1850	79.2	1873	116.5	1896	197.3
1828	87.5	1851	74.6	1874	112.0	1897	238.7
1829	106.8	1852	81.7	1875	102.6	1898	260.0
1830	114.7	1853	94.1	1876	109.5	1899	271.0
1831	107.7	1854	108.7	1877	107.8	1900	233.3
1832	74.1	1855	108.7	1878	106.3	1901	183.0
1833	102.9	1856	107.8	1879	110.1	1902	172.0
1834	69.6	1857	114.4	1880	110.9	1903	175.5
1835	68.3	1858	104.7	1881	108.8	1904	162.7
1836	76.4	1859	110.6	1882	114.8	1905	132.3
1837	95.9	1860	111.1	1883	112.2	1906	140.9
1838	102.6	1861	108.5	1884	110.5	1907	154.0
1839	98.5	1862	109.1	1885	112.8	1908	138.1
1840	98.5	1863	106.1	1886	106.4	1909	144.4
1841	95.3	1864	107.2	1887	137.3	1910	144.8
1842	100.0	1865	112.5	1888	164.7	1911	152.2
1843	97.2	1866	118.8	1889	76.4	1912	155.2
1844	102.9	1867	126.9	1890	92.6	1913	177.0

Note: This index was derived using data and procedures which are described in Appendix I of Chapter 6.

Table 5   The P_E Price Index, 1822–1913

Year	Index	Year	Index	Year	Index	Year	Index
1822	95.6	1845	438.8	1868	1,437.2	1891	3,644.0
1823	101.1	1846	540.0	1869	1,820.7	1892	4,957.8
1824	107.0	1847	522.3	1870	1,676.9	1893	5,900.0
1825	104.2	1848	581.0	1871	1,443.8	1894	6,773.4
1826	111.0	1849	461.3	1872	1,557.7	1895	6,164.6
1827	144.1	1850	372.6	1873	1,515.9	1896	8,358.9
1828	177.4	1851	340.9	1874	2,023.6	1897	9,323.8
1829	158.9	1852	394.2	1875	1,713.7	1898	8,990.1
1830	141.0	1853	685.7	1876	1,942.6	1899	8,783.4
1831	142.1	1854	892.4	1877	2,441.2	1900	7,973.9
1832	104.1	1855	883.4	1878	2,785.2	1901	7,277.4
1833	171.6	1856	1,094.5	1879	2,557.1	1902	6,646.9
1834	191.8	1857	1,120.2	1880	2,294.4	1903	6,332.3
1835	138.0	1858	1,096.2	1881	2,346.0	1904	6,656.8
1836	150.2	1859	1,300.2	1882	2,491.6	1905	6,098.0
1837	251.1	1860	1,310.1	1883	2,468.9	1906	6,532.1
1838	349.9	1861	1,065.8	1884	2,383.4	1907	6,843.7
1839	273.6	1862	860.0	1885	2,550.1	1908	6,899.3
1840	290.0	1863	804.4	1886	2,297.9	1909	6,543.5
1841	290.0	1864	906.7	1887	2,315.8	1910	5,956.4
1842	375.8	1865	1,066.0	1888	2,273.3	1911	7,233.2
1843	423.0	1866	1,400.0	1889	3,131.8	1912	7,044.9
1844	423.1	1867	1,326.5	1890	3,215.1	1913	7,219.0

Source: Eulália Lobo et al., 'Evolução dos Preços e do Padrão de Vida no Rio de Janeiro, 1820–1930,' Revista Brasileira de Economia 25 (October 1971), pp. 260–3.

Table 6 *The Brazilian Exchange Rate, 1822–1913 (in* mil-réis *per £)*

Year	Value	Year	Value	Year	Value	Year	Value
1822	4.90	1845	9.44	1868	14.12	1891	16.10
1823	4.72	1846	8.91	1869	12.76	1892	19.95
1824	4.97	1847	8.57	1870	10.88	1893	20.70
1825	4.63	1848	9.60	1871	9.99	1894	23.78
1826	5.00	1849	9.28	1872	9.60	1895	24.15
1827	6.81	1850	8.35	1873	9.20	1896	26.48
1828	7.73	1851	8.24	1874	9.31	1897	31.09
1829	9.75	1852	8.75	1875	8.82	1898	33.39
1830	10.52	1853	8.42	1876	9.47	1899	32.27
1831	9.60	1854	8.69	1877	9.77	1900	25.26
1832	6.30	1855	8.71	1878	10.46	1901	21.10
1833	6.42	1856	8.71	1879	11.23	1902	20.10
1834	6.28	1857	9.01	1880	10.86	1903	20.00
1835	6.12	1858	9.39	1881	10.96	1904	19.70
1836	6.24	1859	9.58	1882	11.34	1905	15.09
1837	8.12	1860	9.30	1883	11.13	1906	14.84
1838	8.56	1861	9.39	1884	11.60	1907	15.67
1839	7.59	1862	9.12	1885	12.91	1908	15.84
1840	7.74	1863	8.80	1886	12.84	1909	15.85
1841	7.92	1864	8.97	1887	10.70	1910	14.81
1842	8.95	1865	9.60	1888	9.51	1911	14.88
1843	9.30	1866	9.90	1889	9.08	1912	14.86
1844	9.53	1867	10.70	1890	10.64	1913	15.04

Source: Oliver Ónody, *A Inflação Brasileira, 1820–1958* (Rio de Janeiro, 1960), pp. 22–3. Ónody cites the *Anuário Estatístico* as his source.

Table 7 *The Sterling Value of Total Brazilian Exports, Current Prices, 1822–1913* (in thousands of £)

Year	Value	Year	Value	Year	Value	Year	Value
1822	4,031	1845	5,333	1868	13,739	1891	27,273
1823	4,376	1846	5,953	1869	15,596	1892	30,994
1824	3,856	1847	6,440	1870	16,779	1893	32,213
1825	4,621	1848	5,949	1871	17,953	1894	30,675
1826	3,320	1849	5,998	1872	21,125	1895	32,751
1827	3,659	1850	7,354	1873	21,989	1896	28,533
1828	4,154	1851	8,157	1874	21,385	1897	26,514
1829	3,427	1852	8,016	1875	22,228	1898	25,229
1830	3,340	1853	8,936	1876	20,019	1899	25,785
1831	3,378	1854	9,640	1877	19,545	1900	33,664
1832	5,050	1855	10,628	1878	18,662	1901	40,798
1833	6,076	1856	11,997	1879	18,985	1902	36,614
1834	5,507	1857	11,695	1880	20,871	1903	37,132
1835	6,081	1858	10,808	1881	20,110	1904	39,410
1836	6,060	1859	11,469	1882	17,940	1905	45,425
1837	4,168	1860	12,695	1883	18,603	1906	53,886
1838	4,387	1861	12,987	1884	19,110	1907	54,939
1839	5,586	1862	13,333	1885	16,314	1908	44,558
1840	5,482	1863	14,414	1886	17,854	1909	64,138
1841	5,098	1864	15,179	1887	24,012	1910	63,431
1842	4,476	1865	15,531	1888	21,704	1911	67,468
1843	4,561	1866	15,828	1889	28,535	1912	75,352
1844	4,767	1867	15,963	1890	26,378	1913	65,277

Source: Oliver Onody, *A Inflação Brasileira, 1820–1958* (Rio de Janeiro, 1960), pp. 279–81. The *mil-réis* data presented there were converted to sterling by the use of the exchange-rate series presented in Table 6.

Index